D0922779

PUNK SLASH! MUSICALS

★ **DAVID
LADERMAN**

PUNK SLASH!
MUSICALS

TRACKING SLIP-SYNC ON FILM

University of Texas Press
AUSTIN

Copyright © 2010 by the University of Texas Press
All rights reserved
Printed in the United States of America
First edition, 2010

Requests for permission to reproduce material from this work should be sent to:
  Permissions
  University of Texas Press
  P.O. Box 7819
  Austin, TX 78713-7819
  www.utexas.edu/utpress/about/bpermission.html

♾ The paper used in this book meets the minimum requirements of ANSI/NISO
z39.48-1992 (R1997) (Permanence of Paper).

LIBRARY OF CONGRESS CATALOGING-IN-PUBLICATION DATA

Laderman, David.
    Punk slash! musicals : tracking slip-sync on film / David Laderman. — 1st ed.
      p.   cm.
    Includes bibliographical references and index.
    ISBN 978-0-292-72170-8 (cloth : alk. paper)
      1. Rock films—Great Britain—History and criticism.   2. Rock films—United
States—History and criticism.   I. Title.
    PN1995.9.M86L353   2010
    791.43'6578—dc22
                                                                2009024363

Portions of this book appeared previously, in slightly different form, as "(S)lip-Sync:
Punk Rock Narrative Film and Postmodern Musical Performance," in *Lowering the
Boom: Critical Studies in Film Sound*, edited by Jay Beck and Tony Grajeda. © 2008
by the Board of Trustees of the University of Illinois. Used with permission of the
University of Illinois Press.

FOR CLAUDIA AND TRISTAN, WHO ROCK MY WORLD
WITH THE ULTIMATE GRACE AND LAUGHTER

You're into the time slip
And nothing can ever be the same

—*The Rocky Horror Picture Show*

★ CONTENTS

★ ACKNOWLEDGMENTS

I AM DEEPLY GRATEFUL to the following people for their crucial input and assistance in the realization of this project: Scott Simmon, Eric Smoodin, Gayatri Gopinath, Bishnu Ghosh, Sergio de la Mora. Thanks likewise to Jay Beck, Tony Grajeda, Kevin Donnelly, David E. James, Joshua Clover, Laura Grindstaff, Liz Constable, and Tony Kashani.

I am also indebted to the intellectual and institutional support of the Cultural Studies Graduate Group at the University of California, Davis (especially Caren Kaplan and Anna Kuhn) and the College of San Mateo. Many thanks to the folks at the University of Texas Press, especially Jim Burr, Nancy Bryan, Sarah Hudgens, Victoria Davis, and Kip Keller. Thanks to Photofest for illustrations. Special thanks to Dave Gresalfi, encyclo(psychotro)pedic fount for all things Underground, who also furnished vital assistance with illustrations.

For their peripheral but equally significant influence, inspiration, and love, let me also thank Gary (brother in every way), Steve and Jeff and Brian (bandmates always), Carol and Pete (first met at a guitar lesson in Los Angeles, circa 1958, soon thereafter to begin composing me), Graham and Miles (future New Wavers), Marcel and Isabelle, and, most of all, for everything and more, Claudia.

CHAPTER 1

LET'S DO THE TIME WARP

WELCOME TO THE PUNK-MUSICAL FILM CYCLE

JORDAN—INTIMATE INSIDER of the early London punk scene, circa 1976; notorious salesclerk at Vivienne Westwood and Malcolm McLaren's seminal punk fashion shop, SEX; comrade of Johnny Rotten and Siouxsie Sioux—is up on a stage in the role of Amyl Nitrate, strutting around in a most shocking costume: plastic British flag wrapped around her torso, high heels, Roman warrior helmet, loads of splotchy makeup. She is auditioning for the media czar of a future British dystopia, one that looks remarkably like 1977 London. She is not singing; she is lip-syncing to the blasting music track, a punk version of "Rule, Britannia." At a certain moment in the performance, military aircraft can be heard flying overhead: is the noise part of the sound track or part of the fiction? Jordan seems distracted, loses her place, slips out of sync. And the gesture seems to work, highlighting her irreverent uninterest in keeping either the seams of spectacle hidden or her body and "voice" together.

This moment from Derek Jarman's *Jubilee* (1978) is symptomatic and symbolic of a range of attitudes characteristic of punk's early days. Indeed, such a performance gesture recurs in several other punk-musical films that emerged over the next few years. Today such playful slippages in synchronization are more commonplace; but in the early 1980s, they reflected punk's critique of new modes of music representation and consumption. I aim to delineate this critique by considering a somewhat neglected cycle of punk narrative films. Lacking the ultrasloppy no-budget look of many punk documentaries, these narrative films achieve their distinctive complexity in how they represent punk music, dealing variously with musicians, fans, clubs, concerts, songs, marketing, and managers. More importantly, they help us appreciate the threshold over which punk traveled into its more diversified afterlife.

Because these films integrate conventions of independent films as well as movie musicals, they form a compelling articulation of punk music. Sometimes inadvertently, they also become a reflection not merely of punk music, but also *on* punk music. Spurned by punk purists as too commercial and passed over by mainstream film histories as too trashy, this punk-musical cycle demonstrates a unique genre manifestation in which the musical gets ripped apart and then reinfused with punk inspiration.

Primarily British and American, the punk-musical film cycle includes *Jubilee* (Derek Jarman, UK, 1978), *Breaking Glass* (Brian Gibson, UK, 1980), *The Great Rock 'n' Roll Swindle* (Julien Temple, UK, 1980), *Times Square* (Alan Moyle, U.S., 1980), *Ladies and Gentlemen, the Fabulous Stains* (Lou Adler, U.S., 1981), *Starstruck* (Gillian Armstrong, Australia, 1982), and *Sid and Nancy* (Alex Cox, UK/U.S., 1986). For context, I will touch on other relevant films that represent the punk music subculture, including *Blank Generation* (Amos Poe and Ivan Kral, U.S., 1976), *Blank Generation* (Ulli Lommel, U.S., 1980), *Rock 'n' Roll High School* (Allan Arkush, U.S., 1979), *Out of the Blue* (Dennis Hopper, U.S., 1980), *Smithereens* (Susan Seidelman, U.S., 1982), *Liquid Sky* (Slava Tsukerman, U.S., 1982), *Repo Man* (Alex Cox, U.S., 1984), and *True Stories* (David Byrne, U.S., 1986).

On the surface, most of these punk films convey a conspicuous subversion of conformity; they are loudly anti. In various ways, they deconstruct the musical genre, translating much of punk's anarchic, anticommercial energy into film narrative. Yet they also illustrate how punk music's "revolution" against dominant music-industry trends depended largely upon a certain ironic embrace of popular culture. Thus, they are interesting precisely because they are not purely punk, since they straddle a variety of borders surrounding punk.

On this note, my use of the term "musical" to characterize this cycle of punk-music narrative films is deliberately revisionist. That is, a punk musical by definition is going to be an antimusical to some degree—a variation on any genre that rejects its rules from within. A rather boisterous irony is the key to this contradictory positioning by which punk occupies but overthrows the contours of the musical genre: not the cool intellectual irony of Stanley Kubrick's or Robert Altman's films, but the noisy irony that laughs during self-destruction—perhaps somewhat akin to the mockery expressed in an episode of *The Simpsons*. In the spirit of such noisy irony, and in reference to this book's title, we can appreciate how punk "slashes" the musical in two ways: slashing the genre with figurative violence, thus vehemently wounding it; but also slashing the genre as a punctuation mark, thus partially embracing it.

Indeed, one primary way these films engage in a radical revision of the musical is by fusing the genre with an independent- and cult-film sensibility. In distinct ways, these punk films force the musical and the indie film to join hands, undoing genre conventions while simultaneously expanding the formal terrain of the genre. I therefore pay particular attention to the sound-image dynamic of these films, both in the representation of performance and as sound track. I also focus on the gender critique they convey through their use of female punk lead performers. Last, I consider how these films reflect critically upon the advent of new electronic music technologies as well as upon the broader culture of the time, which is perhaps best designated by the names Reagan and Thatcher.

"Slip-sync" is the key term that will carry us through our critical survey, the main tool for carving out and digging into the punk-musical film cycle. Deriving specifically from performance sequences like the one described above from *Jubilee*, slip-sync hinges upon the more mainstream performance technique of lip-sync. But in slip-sync, the singer-performer slips out of sync, alienated from yet caught up by the performance spectacle. Rupturing lip-sync from within, slip-sync articulates both resistance (the singer refusing, or unable, to be synchronized) and conformity (the sound track, or the performance spectacle, subsuming the performer). Slip-sync thus conveys punk's anxiety regarding new electronic technologies of simulation as well as music-industry submission to intensified visualization.

At the same time, a visionary audio vision, a new sound-image dialectic, emerges through punk slip-sync, reflecting a significant shift in the cinematic narrative representation of musical performance. It articulates rock-music performance through a peculiar sound-image fissure, one that is sometimes playful and often reflexive. The notion of slip-sync I am proposing as a distinctly punk and cinematic gesture thus falls within Stacy Thompson's incisive explanation of punk economics. Punk's subversive attitude toward the commodity yields an overall aesthetic that privileges "shows over recordings and raw over clean production: punks valorize modes of punk commodities that they take to represent affect rather than professionalization" (*Punk Productions*, 123).

I will argue that in this punk-musical film cycle, the slip-sync textual and narrative operation becomes either a deliberate or an inadvertent commentary upon the tension between "affect" (the spontaneous performing body) and "professionalization" (cinematic and narrative performance spectacle). In a variety of ways, punk slip-sync in these films deconstructs the performing body by representing it as both fusing with and refusing mass-media technology and celebrity-culture commercialism.

My replacing of the term "lip" with "slip" intends to evoke the displacement of sound: slipping as the dislodging of something from its proper place; sound slipping away from its apparent source, especially the singing body (thus "lip" becomes "slip"); slipping as a gesture that involves improvisation, a somewhat accidental or unexpected gesture, one that moves against design. Theorized as a marginal performance terrain inhabited by punk, camp, and cult film, slip-sync displaces and exceeds lip-sync, becoming something "wrong" in the performance, yet something that embraces this wrongness.

The slip-sync moment in these punk films thus engenders a split in the show, a rupture involving what we might call a double excess: the performer exceeds the performance by disengaging, yet the performance spectacle exceeds the performer by continuing, in a sense, without him or her while still carrying along the performer's voice. All the while, the performance spectacle assimilates the authenticity signified by the performer's dissociation. Indeed, punk slip-sync seems like a postmodern riff on Jane Feuer's notion of the "myth of spontaneity" in classical musicals, which usually privilege authentic "bricolage" performances over those that are "prepackaged" ("Self-Reflexive Musical," 443–444).

In the postmodern context of punk performance, slip-sync is more ambivalent and ambiguous; spontaneity and standardized design become effects of each other, become less easy to distinguish. Over and against the classical or pop musical, punk slip-sync should be understood as a gesture that splits open the "privileged kind of space" that, according to Ian Garwood, facilitates a "fit" between the persona of the musical performer and the cinematic staging of his or her performance ("Pop Song in Film," 108–109). Such splitting open of this fit, however, is subtle and slippery.

As a kind of enigmatic almost-sync, punk slip-sync can thus also be usefully contextualized by Steven Connor's notion of ventriloquism as "the curious, ancient and long-lived practice of making voices appear to issue elsewhere from their source" (Dumbstruck, 13–14). As we will see, the sliding separation in these punk musicals between the singer's voice as bodily expression and the singer's voice as mediated effect dramatizes a peculiar convergence of both forms of ventriloquism identified by Connor: active ("the power to speak through others") and passive ("being spoken through by others") (14). In slip-sync scenes throughout these punk musicals, performers appear to become perturbed by, or at least aware of, the ventriloquist ramifications of the performance framework surrounding them. Connor's polyvalent sense of ventriloquism becomes a useful metaphor, illuminating both the visionary, or active, and the institutional, or passive, manipulation of thrown voices.[1]

Slip-sync occurs in certain key films, such as *Jubilee* and *Sid and Nancy*, as a concrete performance gesture. However, some of the punk-musical sequences I will be discussing offer looser or more indirect versions of slip-sync, articulating the latter on a narrative or thematic level, almost as a metaphor. Put differently, each of the films offers distinct variations on slip-sync performance, sometimes as a moment of rupture, at other times as an overall unhinged sound-image design, and at yet other times as a subtextual theme related to artist-industry conflicts. Thus, while my primary aim is to discuss slip-sync as a specific textual operation, I also intend to unpack the notion across various discursive levels, opening it up as an interpretive trope that speaks to narrative and cultural issues beyond specific moments of performance within the films.

Slip-sync therefore designates not only an aesthetic gesture full of performance tension, but also an overall narrative tone or attitude, which should be understood as punk: a resistance to figurative synchronization with performance venue, film genre, the music industry, and the stable institutions of dominant culture more generally. But as we shall see, slip-sync not only operates within each film on numerous levels, but also cuts across the films, becoming likewise the key critical operation of reading them, binding them as a cycle. We are thus rescuing the films from a scattered oblivion, which may be a more truly punk destiny for them. Nevertheless, let us work against such a destiny, elucidating correspondences between them and resonances beyond them. They have slipped between the cracks in the canon long enough.

A few words are in order on my use of the term "punk," which, like my use of the term "musical," can be characterized as loose, casual, open. I respect those who might take issue with this informality as being perhaps too convenient or watered down. I do not deny that there did exist an original, "pure" punk-music scene and subculture or, for that matter, that pure punk-music scenes and subcultures continue to thrive today. But for the present study, "punk" will signify much more than what is delimited by this restrictive definition, which sometimes engenders a certain narrowly applied nostalgia. While a purist sense of punk informs and hovers around my analysis (and I will touch upon this definition below), I use the term "punk" in broader, more diverse, and more diluted ways, partially in order to account for the potency of its influence.

Thus, some of the film imagery and music I discuss may be more accurately described as New Wave rather than punk. On the other hand, parsing the difference between punk and New Wave can seem like splitting hairs, since the two rebellious music styles, which both emerged in the late 1970s, were so crucially and intricately bound up with each other. A fair and commonplace speculation is that New Wave was a more accessible and potentially commercial version of punk. But this distinction, which in many ways is not one, bears exactly on my angle: how punk became absorbed by, or left its mark upon, other cultural productions—for example, what I am calling the punk-musical film cycle. I am not calling it the "New Wave–musical film cycle" because "punk" more accurately captures the historical and aesthetic core sensibility inspiring these films, even if they move some distance away from this core sensibility, sounding and appearing more New Wave.

We will therefore be furnishing a historical context to the sundry ways punk has survived and thrived for thirty years beyond its "end," a moment that might as well be marked by the final Sex Pistols' concert, held in 1978 at the Winterland Ballroom in San Francisco. The last gig of their gloriously disastrous American tour has been mythologized as punk's last hurrah, when a glowering Johnny Rotten snarled at the crowd, "Ever feel like you're being cheated?" (Marcus, *Lipstick Traces*, 88–90) As a film critic for the *New York Times* recently observed: "Like a song by the Ramones or the Sex Pistols, it [punk] was over before you knew what hit you" (Rafferty, "What Are You Staring At?"). But as my quotation marks around "end" intend to convey, the end of punk, in typically punk fashion, was also its opposite, its anti-end: its beginning.

From today's perspective, the "no future" punk motto has become ironically negated and inverted: yes, future. It comes as no surprise, therefore, that the first line of the recent anthology *No Focus: Punk on Film* reads "punk was (and perhaps is) wildly schizophrenic" (Sargeant, 6). Or that the first line of the introduction to a recent coffee-table "encyclopedia" of punk begins: "In writing about punk rock, certain contradictions must be considered" (Cogan, *Encyclopedia of Punk*, viii; see also Rombes, *New Punk Cinema*, 7). In my view, one of the most compelling contradictions around punk is how its paradoxically self-destructive emergence launched a perpetual recycling effect that is, indeed, essentially punk.[2]

Essentially punk. Whatever that may be, let us recall before continuing a few of the more salient features defining the original punk movement.

Punk emerged primarily as a radically underground music scene in New York in the late 1970s. The first New York punk scene is often associated with avant-garde artists, perhaps second-generation hipsters drifting from Andy Warhol's Factory into seedy East Village nightclubs. This scene, which dates from approximately 1974 to 1976, was characterized by underground music committed to rejecting the commercial music industry and erasing "the difference between performer and audience member" (Thompson, *Punk Productions*, 11).

Running from approximately 1976 to 1978 and largely orchestrated by Malcolm McLaren and his "creation" the Sex Pistols, the London punk scene engaged in a more sardonic embrace of commercialism. McLaren apparently borrowed much from the earlier, more authentic New York scene, but injected it with a heavy, though ironic, dose of sensationalism. Replacing the cool collectivity of the New York club scene with a viral antagonism during performances, British punk "attempted to negate the spectacle itself, but its attack upon the spectacle assumed the paradoxical form of hyper-spectacle" (Thompson, *Punk Productions*, 24).

Despite, or perhaps because of, early punk music's often violently rebellious nature and image, it attracted disaffected working-class youth, especially in Britain. Whether of the New York or London variety, late-1970s punk seemed to be an apt, though extreme, reflection of the political cynicism left in the wake of Watergate, the Vietnam War, inflation, and high unemployment.

Disgusted by the pretentious and pompous arena rock popular in the early 1970s, the original punk bands reverted to simple raw energy and amateur musicianship. Instead of conventional concert venues, they preferred dive bars, strip clubs, low-life nightclubs, and scrappy warehouses. While the earliest punk bands often vociferously antagonized their audiences during performances, an equally violent fusion of fan and band permeated the original punk scenes—fans stumbling onto the stage, band members stumbling into the audience, fans forming bands, etc.

This "antirock" club music scene is where the distinctive punk fashion look—safety pins, tight black leather, Doc Marten boots, spiked and dyed hair—originated and still thrives. This is also where the notorious pogo dance was born: audience members jumped violently up and down, pounding the floor as the music furiously pounded them, and thrashed side to side, deliberately ramming anyone within reach, an appropriately stripped-down and visceral form of contact and community.

Perhaps the most important punk concept to emerge out of the original punk music scene was DIY: do it yourself. A 1976 issue of the formative punk zine *Sideburns* furnishes the best core explanation of DIY: next to a crude but accessible diagram of three guitar chords is the exhortation "Now form a band" (Savage, *England's Dreaming*, 280). Anticorporate and celebratory of the amateur, DIY has evolved into a flexible credo for citizens working to engage in creative and productive activities outside the conventional restrictions of commercial, institutional culture. Like, and often intertwined with, grassroots political activism, DIY implies the forging of an alternative network of information flows and object exchanges. Independently produced zines, videos, bootleg recordings, and multifarious other forms of communication constitute a crucial dimension of punk's particular claim to alternative authenticity.

This sense that punk offers something authentically alternative is what has persisted over the years, attracting new generations of participants in new locations and new configurations. From Los Angeles hardcore in the early 1980s to Washington, D.C., straight edge in the mid-1980s to Seattle grunge in the early 1990s; from Goth to industrial to rave; from riot grrrl to lo-fi to trip-hop, punk—or at least punk's legacy—has been resurrected and rearticulated in various stylistic guises. For example, the Nortec music collective in Tijuana, Mexico, applies punk theory to hybrid electronica dance music as cultural activism (see Asensio, "The Nortec Edge"). Likewise, recent scholarship on "new punk cinema" traces the influence of punk's DIY philosophy on a variety of global independent film movements (Rombes, *New Punk Cinema*).[3] A recent issue of *Wired* magazine even compares blogging to the early years of punk: "Punk rock became a beacon for creative people of all walks. We thought that energetic counterculture would last forever, but it didn't. So enjoy the blogs while you can" (Hamsher, "Blogging Is So Punk").

Since its brief moment of "pure" explosion three decades ago, punk has rippled continuously and dynamically throughout popular culture, testifying to, and perhaps outdoing, the power of those original power chords. If, in fact, "punk is an open and constantly morphing movement" that is "best seen as a virus, one that mutates constantly and resists codification—or vaccination," such staying power is one of the main reasons this early cycle of punk-musical films deserves to be analyzed and historicized (Cogan, *Encyclopedia of Punk*, x). These films form one of the first instances of punk's circuitous cultural dissemination.

Another compelling reason this punk-musical cycle demands our critical attention is the recurrence of strong female performances. These films often focus on complex gender politics within the punk subculture, a focus that in turn becomes a potent feminist comment on the larger rock-music culture. This narrative centering of the female breaks the gender hierarchy pattern of both the classical and pop rock musical. A film cycle driven by such strong female leads also presents a glaring contrast to the cinematic landscape of the early 1980s and its embrace of the patriarchal action hero. However, as we will see, such "feminism" is not without its complications.[4] While many of the punk-musical films highlight the patriarchal roadblocks that insidiously persist within the punk subculture, they also incorporate traces of the backlash against feminism that emerged in the neoconservative cultural and political climate of the early 1980s. In any case, I situate this punk-musical cycle alongside more experimental feminist films of the early 1980s that likewise explore sound-image desynchronization, thereby constituting a parallel version of slip-sync. By positing this correspondence, we are suggesting that punk slip-sync has everything to do with these performers' being young women and with the struggle they articulate to perform.

One significant recent echo of the punk-musical cycle's critical representation of gender was the riot grrrl music phenomenon of the early 1990s, perhaps the most potent reincarnation of the spirit of punk (Bayton, *Frock Rock*, 74–80; Nehring, *Popular Music, Gender, and Postmodernism*, 156–165; Thompson, *Punk Productions*, 58–70). Spearheaded by underground bands like Bikini Kill and Bratmobile, the riot grrrl movement was heavily inspired by the DIY, anticorporate punk subculture, but injected it with a politicized feminist perspective. A complement to the alternative grunge-rock scene (itself a revival of the punk spirit), the riot grrrl subculture demonstrated how zine publishing and other forms of media activism could be effectively integrated with a lively lo-fi music genre. Many of the punk musicals of the early 1980s foresee riot grrrl's testy appropriation of punk as well as riot grrrl's own struggles against appropriation by the mainstream media.

At the other end of the pop-culture spectrum from riot grrrl, various pop-music lip-sync scandals dating from the late 1990s were likewise envisioned by punk slip-sync. Milli Vanilli got caught "singing" live to prerecorded tracks of someone else's vocals; at a concert in Madison Square Garden, the R&B hip-hop singer R. Kelly "put down his microphone in the middle of a song and let his recorded vocals keep singing" (Nelson, "Lip-Synching Gets Real," 30); Elton John scolded Madonna for lip-syncing during certain elaborate concert numbers (she denied doing so); during a performance on *Saturday Night Live*, Ashlee Simpson started lip-syncing to the wrong song. All these incidents of slippage in synchronization around lip-syncing were previsioned, although in more dystopian terms, by punk musicals. That is, these films implicitly examine a whole range of issues relating to the problem of maintaining authenticity in the context of a deeply mediated performance mode. If riot grrrl epitomizes slip-sync as a visionary moment of feminist resistance to what Philip Auslander calls "mediatized" performance (*Liveness*, 5), live lip-sync suggests the more demonizing connotations of slip-sync, namely, a brazenly inauthentic commercialism.

Let me next sketch a further preface to the cycle itself by elaborating upon some of the frameworks suggested above. My goal here is to establish various lenses through which we can better situate and appreciate the impact and complexity of these films. This will involve articulating punk in relation to various cinematic and cultural forces and generating a historical and theoretical sense of slip-sync, briefly unearthing some surprising precursors. Our first lens expands upon the issues around live lip-sync just mentioned, by theorizing the slip-sync gesture more fully in relation to its broader companion concept: in/authenticity.

CHAPTER 2

SITUATING SLIP-SYNC

IN/AUTHENTICITY, *SINGIN' IN THE RAIN*, *A HARD DAY'S NIGHT*, *THE ROCKY HORROR PIC-TURE SHOW*, *BLANK GENERATION*, *ILLUSIONS*, *NICE COLOURED GIRLS*, NEOCON 1980S

✳ PUNK, SLIP-SYNC, AND IN/AUTHENTICITY

The key notion that hovers significantly around slip-sync is authenticity—perhaps more as a question than a notion. Of course, the question of authenticity permeates various discourses of postmodern culture, typically couched in terms of loss: is authenticity still possible, or still a relevant concept, in postmodern society? (Hutcheon, *Poetics of Postmodernism*, 6–11; Connor, *Postmodernist Culture*, 7). In the more specific realm of mediatized performance, authenticity likewise needs to be reconceived.

One vital thread of punk theory and practice has always prided itself on reclaiming a radical authenticity for postmodern rock culture. On the one hand, punk trashed conventional rock authenticity: "Punk aimed to pierce through the cloak of 'authenticity' that characterized the progressive, serious, macho, arena-rock of Led Zeppelin, The Eagles and other supergroup bands for whom virtuosity had created a distancing effect between themselves and audiences" (Rombes, *New Punk Cinema*, 6). On the other hand, punk discourse generates an "endless insistence on authenticity," but in the same scream brazenly insists that authenticity can be entirely inauthentic (Hegarty, *Noise/Music*, 95).[1] Greil Marcus puts it this way: "That was punk: a load of old ideas sensationalized into new feelings almost instantly turned into new clichés, but set forth with such momentum that the whole blew up its equations day by day. For every fake novelty, there was a real one. For every third-hand pose, there was a fourth-hand pose that turned into a real motive" (*Lipstick Traces*, 77).

The punk-musical narrative films of 1978–1986 in many ways are about such postmodern revisions of authenticity. This is why I believe it is crucial to approach punk slip-sync, and the punk-musical film cycle generally, as a kind of conceptual signifier of the slippage from cynical late-1970s neomodernism (Orr, *Cinema and Modernity*, 2–4) into the 1980s postmodern culture of simulation and spectacle. Simon Frith and Trevor Horne describe punk accordingly as "the ultimate art school movement" that "tried to keep in play bohemian ideals of authenticity *and* Pop art ideals of artifice" (*Art into Pop*, 124). The failure of this effort, for them, "ushered popular music into postmodernism" (124). Indeed, Dick Hebdige sees punk as the ultimate subculture by virtue of how it fed off of the dominant commercial culture (*Subculture*, 113–116). Slip-sync, as both performance gesture and theme, becomes the lucid expression of punk's schizoid positioning between the neomodern and postmodern: slip-sync as authentic disembodied resistance, and slip-sync as inauthentic mediatized spectacle.

Recent theories of sound, music, and performance shed some light on the issue of authenticity as it bears on punk slip-sync. James Lastra, Steve Wurtzler, and Philip Auslander have all challenged the notion of authentic original presence in sound and music. Lastra deconstructs "the originality effect" in film sound ("Reading, Writing, and Representing Sound," 83–84), while Wurtzler theorizes contemporary popular music as "copies without originals" ("She Sang Live," 92–93). Both critics argue against a facile live/recorded distinction.

Stressing a broader historical dimension, and emphasizing the act of listening, Jonathan Sterne shows how the myth of authentic original sound permeated sound technology throughout the twentieth-century: "The 'original' sound embedded in the recording . . . certainly bears a causal relation with the reproduction, but only because the original is itself an artifact of the process of reproduction. Without the technology of reproduction, the copies do not exist, but, then, neither would the originals" (*Audible Past*, 219). As we will see, the blurring of this border between original and copy, between live and recorded, is central to the impact of punk slip-sync.

Along these lines, we should take note of Jacob Smith's recent history of recorded vocal performance styles in the twentieth-century, *Vocal Tracks: Performance and Sound Media*. Executed in the wake, and the spirit, of deconstructive sound studies by Lastra, Rick Altman, and others, Smith's chronicle offers an in-depth focus on the entertainment industry's mediation of the popular singing voice as well as the insinuation of that voice within such mediation. Underlining the always crucial effect of "authenticity," Smith traces a variety of instances in which the "slippery" and "protean" quality of the human voice seems to break free from, or rupture, different forms of technological reproduction (3). This furnishes an instructive critical framework, one that runs parallel to our analysis of slip-sync. For example, resonating keenly with slip-sync is his notion of "flooding out": a moment in mediated texts "when a performer loses his or her composure and vocally floods out, shattering the performance frame and thereby offering a tantalizing suggestion of authentic and spontaneous expression" (6). Punk slip-sync may be understood as a variation on flooding out, in which such vocalized loss of composure exceeds both the musical performance context within the film narrative, and the cinematic reproduction constituted by the film itself.

The work of Philip Auslander pertains more specifically to the punk-musical film cycle because he addresses recent trends in rock-music live performance, especially the paradox, or "scandal," of live lip-sync, mentioned above. Auslander argues that performance in our highly mediatized culture can no longer be characterized as "live." The more salient term would be "liveness"—a contrived effect of being live, a superseding of the distinction between live and recorded (*Liveness*, 2–7). According to Auslander, scandals of live lip-sync—in which performers pretend to be singing live but in fact are mouthing to a prerecorded voice track—should not be seen as scandals at all. Rather, such instances accurately reflect the contemporary state of music production and performance, which is fully determined by electronic reproduction and simulation. Auslander calls for a radically revised sense of authenticity, one that foregoes nostalgia for romanticized originality; that is, authenticity that embraces liveness.

At the same time, Auslander does not seem to allow for works that escape or problematize his notion of ubiquitous liveness. This is where I would situate punk in relation to liveness, as a movement expressing a more dialectical and resistant form of authenticity, one that both contradicts yet embodies liveness. Punk music as portrayed in these films mocks the new liveness music culture from within; it pushes to ugly caricature the new high-tech and corporate music industry as newly inauthentic. Though celebrating raw, "untalented," and "unproduced" music as a form of authenticity and an antidote to liveness, punk nevertheless also mirrors, and thus on some level becomes, part of the hypercommodified culture through which liveness flourishes.

For a broader historical perspective on rock, film, and authenticity, let us take note of Keir Keightley's discussion of how early rock-and-roll films "manufactured authenticity" by default, that is, by dramatizing what was clearly not authentic. Most often in these films, inauthenticity is clearly localized within the music industry, rather than with musicians or fans ("Manufacturing Authenticity," 166). He argues that this cinematic articulation of rock-music authenticity was formative for future generations of rock-music ideologues. Lawrence Grossberg, the critic who perhaps has most fully explored the notion of authenticity in relation to rock music, elaborates this antipathy toward rock showbiz by conceiving of authenticity more broadly, as an aspect of identity: "Only by making youth belong somewhere could it [rock music] speak to both the identity and the difference of its audience" (*We Gotta Get Out*, 206). Of course, the punk-music subculture fits neatly within this definition of authenticity, especially the notion that rock differs from "mere entertainment." Punk music—and, once removed, the punk-musical film cycle—rearticulates this ideology of authenticity, but from within the inauthentic music industry, turning it inside out and upside down through a distinctive, radical mimicry.

This tension around authenticity and punk comes into sharper focus in Grossberg's notion of "authentic inauthenticity." A kind of parallel concept to Auslander's liveness, authentic inauthenticity posits artifice and an essentially relativized reality as the "truth" of the new media culture. Grossberg, more cynical than Auslander toward liveness and more nostalgic for the live, argues that the entire visual realm of contemporary media contaminates the auditory realm. For him, the postmodern proliferation of visualized rock music (epitomized by MTV) has engendered the omnipresence of authentic inauthenticity, which insinuates "that authenticity is itself a construction, an image, which is no better and no worse than any other" ("Media Economy," 206). Grossberg very clearly privileges sound over image—whether promotional images, as in advertising and publicity, or narrative images, as in film and video. Like Auslander's liveness, Grossberg's authentic inauthenticity comes off as a bit paranoid and all encompassing; it does not lend itself to variation or subtlety, or to the possibility that the image itself can be truthful and authentic (or, conversely, that music might be essentially inauthentic). Focusing on MTV-era youth-culture films of the mid-1980s, he claims that the logic of authentic inauthenticity depends upon "ironic nihilism" and "ironic cynicism" (206). To be sure, these terms relate more vividly to punk music and films; yet, oddly, he does not address any of the punk musicals, perhaps because they are indeed too subversive for the MTV-style film canon he is constructing.

In response to Auslander and Grossberg, and in anticipation of my analysis of the punk musicals, let me propose the term "in/authenticity." This term intimates that authenticity can be a legitimate force and value, but one that is perpetually haunted by the gross inauthenticity permeating 1980s commercial culture.[2] As we have already noted, such a tightly woven tension between authenticity and inauthenticity is a long-standing feature of discourses on punk.[3] My argument is that the slip-sync gesture and theme articulate a rupture from inside inauthenticity, a clash between resistance and commodification. Put differently, these punk-musical films, through slip-sync, dramatize the conflicted transition from live to liveness, from authenticity to in/authenticity.[4]

One way to enter this sense of punk slip-sync as resistance to liveness, or as in/authentic, is through the theories espoused in Jacques Attali's *Noise*. Admittedly, this influential work is rather abstractly conceived and expressed, and any attempt to apply it involves some degree of projection. While many of Attali's central ideas anticipate those of Grossberg and Auslander, they more importantly capture the dissenting position of punk in relation to them. Attali conceives of music as a means of prophecy and power, that is, as part of a dialectic between an avant-garde subversive political critique that calls forth the future, and a stabilizing power structure that contains and encodes passion and inspiration. Noise, for Attali, is the kind of music that breaks the stabilizing code, that leads society into the future, into the new. Noise is a rupture, a split in the seam of the familiar.

Attali's privileged term "noise" readily invokes punk, though we should recall that punk in many ways engaged in both a return to the primal scene of rock as well as a "no future" attitude, both being somewhat contrary to his visionary, avant-garde connotations. Among the historical concepts that Attali uses to characterize different periods of music ("representation," "repetition"), his last concept, "composing," roughly elucidates punk music in general, and slip-sync in particular. Attali sees composing as a kind of pure aesthetic pleasure in making music, an excess beyond the codes and use value of society. Composing eschews exchange value and reproduction, celebrating instead the process of creativity and production. Citing experimental jazz and Jimi Hendrix, he speaks of composing as liberating time itself.

Punk slip-sync, rather than embodying such aesthetic purity as idealized revolution, more accurately marks out a disjunctive moment in which composing struggles to occur within repetition (the latter is his umbrella term for the technology and culture, dating from the early twentieth century, that reproduces music for mass consumption): the singing voice and body separate from that which reproduces them as spectacle. The slip-sync rupture of these punk musicals thus dramatizes a striking overlap of Attali's music of repetition (commodified, simulated spectacle) with the music of composing (a negating gesture of excess), an overlap we also read as the return of authenticity within inauthenticity—thus, as in/authenticity.[5]

Closer to the terrain of our punk-musical film cycle is the work of David James on punk and authenticity. In a series of lucid meditations on the relationship of the punk subculture to consumer society, he contrasts the textual strategies of the experimental no-wave films of late-1970s New York with punk as portrayed on MTV and in more assimilated narrative cinema. Reacting to the commercialization and denigration of punk on early-1980s MTV, the early-1980s hardcore punk videos, like the no-wave films, aimed to reclaim punk as an excess that was both radically authentic and radically political.

James explains that these truly marginal, truly punk works circulated outside and against the controlled flows of capital and therefore possessed little narrative framework. Echoing Attali's notion of composing, James contextualizes the raw music-performance footage of these films and videos as an end in itself, not as a pretext to some other narrative or documentary meaning. Likewise, he shows how hardcore punk visuals did not celebrate or fetishize the "rock star" (*Power Misses*, 225). Such anti-rock-star imagery became the historical seed for the slip-sync disjuncture I will be discussing, in which body and voice become undone.

Most relevant to our concept of slip-sync is the contrapuntal relationship between sound and image that James identifies in these videos, a type of synchronization based on difference, one that is not illusionistic or narratively driven (236). It seems no coincidence that James refers to some post-*Jubilee* music videos by Derek Jarman when postulating the one essential dimension of authentic punk films and videos: their subversion of lip-syncing (247). My aim here is to reconsider the narrative independent films that James expresses suspicion toward and to reexamine their relation to such hardcore subversion. I would in fact describe their articulation of such subversion through slip-sync as being more dialectical than that of the hardcore videos. Slip-sync goes beyond contrapuntal sound-image relations, articulating conflict between artisanal and commercial production forces, as well as other narrative and thematic contradictions. Through the slip-sync performance gesture, the punk-musical film cycle incorporates elements of, and draws inspiration from, no-wave films and hardcore videos, even if such elements and inspiration become diluted through the filters of the musical genre and independent narrative.

✶ PUNK AND THE CLASSICAL MUSICAL

As will become clear, one of the more general but highly significant features of this punk-musical film cycle is its "extreme makeover" of the classical-musical film genre. At first glance, the classical musical seems remote, both chronologically and politically, from the punk sensibility. However, much of the basic critical vocabulary used for appreciating the classical Hollywood musical can be readily imported, with some poetic license, into the world of punk musicals. Rather than to insist that classical musicals directly influenced punk musicals, my aim is to sketch some potential and provocative connections between the two. At the very least, such connections implicitly argue for situating these punk musicals inside the history of film genres.

As a starting point, let us watch for how punk musicals rearticulate the three basic types of musicals laid out in Rick Altman's seminal *The American Film*

Musical: folk, fairy tale, and backstage. The punk musical's garish costuming, but also its experimental performance sequences that play with theatricality, push to postmodern extremes the fairy-tale musical's "over-sumptuous, over-stylized sets" and "winks at the audience" (147–148). The punk musical's treatment of performers or fans who try to succeed in the music industry reiterates the backstage musical's showbiz voyeurism (223). Lastly, the DIY ideals of the punk subculture share some not-too-distant affinities with the folk musical's emphasis on music as part of everyday rituals as well as with its denigration of professionalized music in favor of a more democratic music, open to everyone (287). I am not suggesting that the punk films merely update these classical features; after all, the ubiquitous utopian tone of the classical musical is roughly violated by punk's nihilistic inversions. However, I think the punk musical's basic relation to such classical-musical features intimates how the translation of punk music into film-genre narrative rendered the music more accessible, perhaps more conservative, but also more interesting because of the tension between such ironic negation and narrative accessibility.

Additional compelling correspondences between the classical musical and punk are inadvertently suggested in Jane Feuer's *The Hollywood Musical*. Each of her chapters addresses an array of genre features that anticipate the look and feel of punk musicals: bricolage, the role of the amateur, musicals as articulations of folk art and community, and spectators as participants. For Feuer, the classical musical celebrates community so as to bridge the gap created by the passage of folk art into mass-reproduced art (3). Likewise, punk sought to reconstitute community in rock culture by bringing rock back to its low-end, nightclub (versus concert arena), and working-class roots.

In accomplishing this bridge, the musical celebrates bricolage performance—a tentative, tinkering, makeshift style of performance—over and against engineered performance, which is stiff, technologized, and prepackaged—even though, as Feuer points out, every Hollywood musical's bricolage effect is entirely engineered, thus mystifying the actual manufactured process of production (4–5). Punk too relies upon bricolage aesthetics, not only in its sloppy, bedraggled, cut-and-paste approach to fashion, but more especially in its DIY approach to music and film production. Over and against the music industry's engineered rock-star system, punk opens its arms to anyone willing to sing and play, and loves the raw, unpolished, noisy sound of passionate amateurs. Indeed, the musical's celebration of the amateur, the audience, direct address, and the popular song (versus sophisticated music) all resonate with punk's political drive against rock and pop-music elitism.

Many of the correspondences between punk and the musical that I am reading into Feuer's genre theory get further elaboration in her chapter "A

Postscript for the Nineties," which deals with teen rock-music films of the 1980s. Here, she argues that the modernist reflexive tendencies of the late classical musical through the 1970s (*Cabaret*, *Nashville*, etc.) reach an apex with *Pennies from Heaven* (1981). For her, this film's "excessive intertextuality"— original versions of numerous classic songs "plugged in" for blatantly phony lip-syncing—is "critical" and deconstructive rather than nostalgic (128–129). Interestingly, Altman too concludes his study of the musical with *Pennies from Heaven*, claiming that it signifies the transition from music as something performed to music as a reproduced commodity (*American Film Musical*, 353). The film's appearance in 1981 during the punk-musical cycle should be interpreted as no coincidence. Its conspicuously reflexive use of lip-syncing—at times a female voice comes out of a male body, and vice versa, and many of the overtly optimistic songs are staged with ironic pessimism—becomes a lateral variation on the simultaneous slip-sync strategy of the punk musicals. In comparison, the latter mobilize a more frontal and political critique of the onset of electronic simulation culture.

In other words, I am arguing that the punk-musical cycle forms a kind of antidote to the 1980s MTV-teen musical landscape both Feuer and Altman see, through distinct lenses, as conservative and oppressive. Feuer notes how, after *Pennies from Heaven*, a more conservative reflexivity permeates popular teen musicals like *Dirty Dancing*, *Flashdance*, *Fame*, and *Footloose* (the same fare Grossberg derides, for similar reasons). The pastiche at play in these musicals, for Feuer, is postmodern rather than modernist, and reconstructive rather than deconstructive. Not surprisingly, she cites music videos as "the ultimate postmodern musical" (*Hollywood Musical*, 130–132). Again, Altman agrees, seeing MTV and 1980s teen musicals as completing the displacement of the classical musical by the new electronic culture of rock and television, in which music is rendered "common, secular, manufactured, and mediated" (363) instead of being live and inspiring audiences to make music themselves. My aim is to reconstitute the punk musicals of the time as critical reactions to what might be called the *Flashdance* trend. While punk musicals are not at all nostalgic for the kind of special live performance Altman and Grossberg prefer, they do reject the crass commercialism and banality of the pop-music teen films; as we will see, often this rejection occurs through viciously ironic parody.

Recent counterreadings of the musical, though not directly reflecting a punk perspective, at least further illuminate what happens when punk inhabits the musical. Susan Smith, for example, challenges the traditional view of musicals as overtly patriarchal. She instead shows how the role of the female singer, in both classical and contemporary musicals, often presents a problem for male control within the genre (*The Musical*, 54). She argues that the female singer's voice comes to represent resistance to the patriarchal mentor. Her revised reading of gender in the musical elucidates my analysis of punk music performance, since most of the films feature a female punk lead who very much embodies the kind of subversion Smith describes, but with the added subversion deriving from punk sensibility. These punk divas forcefully and self-consciously articulate rebellion against the patriarchal conformity of the musical genre.

Punk musicals challenge the genre not only in the area of gender, but also through various heavy-handed injections of camp, irony, and parody. In this regard, Steven Cohan's *Incongruous Entertainment* is surprisingly relevant to the punk-musical cycle. What he perceives in the MGM musicals—perhaps the classiest and most classical of the genre—can easily be linked with the overall tone of the punk-musical film cycle.

Cohan interprets the MGM musicals through a camp sensibility in which authenticity shares the stage with artifice, and a queer perspective informs both the production and reception of the films. His interpretation of the "mannered Otherness" and excessive stylization of the MGM shows as camp serves as a crucial bridge to the punk revision of the musical. Compared to their classical antecedents, punk musicals, as we will see, are more overt and disturbing in their irreverent interweaving of artifice and authenticity. Likewise, punk musicals articulate an extreme, and extremely self-conscious, "queerness" (a queerness not necessarily pertaining to sexuality; thus my quotation marks). Cohan's reading of the MGM musicals as camp also dovetails with my discussion below of the independent cult film and its marked camp sensibility, a crucial context for comprehending the punk riff on the musical. Indeed, J. Hoberman and Jonathan Rosenbaum's *Midnight Movies* discusses "camp" and "punk" right next to each other, noting that "both ironically reclaim the dated styles of the recent past, discovering their fashions and fetishes in thrift shops and old movies" (275).

To further focalize a common site for punk and the classical musical, as well as to theorize and situate slip-sync, let us look back to a significant and surprising historical precursor. Much has been written about the various levels of reflexivity in *Singin' in the Rain* (1952), but the reflexive aspect I wish to focus on offers an early intimation of punk slip-sync. We should recall that the film dates from just before the dawn of rock and roll; more importantly, it coincides with the widespread use of lip-sync in film and television. As many will remember, the film wrestles with the problem of voice dubbing throughout. The syncing up of voice with body and with image yields dramatic conflict, but also reflexively opens up a critique of the film industry and the film medium. Within the gleeful mood typical of the musical, the film's central conflict around keeping voice and body together becomes a conflict around technology—in this case, new film-sound technology (in the case of the punk-musical cycle, electronic technologies of reproduction).

In the narrative logic of *Singin' in the Rain*, the new technology of sound permits a more dynamic and fuller spectacle, but also bears within it new forms of incoherence and subversion. In this respect (and with a little imagination), the character of Lina Lamont (Jean Hagen) can be understood as a prototype of the punk diva featured in many of the punk musicals. Demonized throughout, the butt of endless jokes, she refuses synchronization, anticipating what the punk musicals will more ambivalently foreground: the subversion of the show by disassembling the show's own ruse of body-voice coherence.

The first instance of slip-sync occurs during the preview of *The Duelling Cavalier*, the studio's first attempt at a synchronized sound film. Disaster strikes when the sound track goes "out of synchronization," as the assistant to the producer exclaims in terror. Hilarious as the sound already is for other reasons, the unsynced sound track provokes the most comic anxiety, culminating in the bit in which Lina and the villain exchange "no no no" (in the wrong voices, and while his head nods yes) and "yes yes yes" (still in the wrong voices, her head shaking no). The audience breaks into laughter at how poorly the voices are synced up with the moving lips of the actors. Added to this joke, and anticipating future narrative developments, is the hysterical quality of Lina's voice. So two gags intersect around voices not matching bodies: synchronization and voice quality.

The entire scene is coded as a comic failure of the silent-film industry to transition smoothly to sound—something is wrong. We should note that highlighted here is a relevant example of Feuer's sense of reflexive commentary within musicals. For *Singin' in the Rain*, the production of spontaneous and authentic sound is celebrated over artificially produced and overly stylized sound. Sync sound mistakes, along with the lavish, phony initial musical production of *The Duelling Cavalier*, are derided in favor of performances that are more "natural" or spontaneous—or at least appear to be so.

Indeed, perfectly illustrating Feuer's notion that the spontaneity privileged by the musical is very much a myth, the film's solution to various sound problems is to use the right kind of artifice, one that involves another take on slip-sync. Commiserating over the preview debacle, Don (Gene Kelly), Kathy (Debbie Reynolds), and Cosmo (Donald O'Connor) mock the unsynced sound gag, then come upon the "brilliant idea" of dubbing Kathy's voice for Lina's. Cosmo's demonstration of the idea itself suggests slip-sync, as he instructs Kathy to sing behind him while he lip-syncs comically. In fact, part of the comic effect here derives from the bodily dissonance and difference on

2.1. *All eyes on the girl with the right voice: Don (Gene Kelly), Kathy (Debbie Reynolds), and Cosmo (Donald O'Connor) in* Singin' in the Rain *(1952), just before Cosmo's "brilliant idea" to dub Kathy's voice for Lina's. Photo courtesy of Photofest.*

display, since a female voice is matched to male singing lips. The specter of slip-sync looms around the scene, which configures technological innovation as playing around with the gendered synchronization of bodies and voices.

Later, the scenes of Kathy dubbing in the studio expose the process of synchronization and sound-film production in general as contrived and manufactured, subtly suggesting the potential for slippage or miscues that hovers around this process. In yet another intriguing slip-sync twist, apparently Debbie Reynolds's singing voice was dubbed in by other singers throughout the film—including by Jean Hagen (Wollen, *Singin' in the Rain*, 56; Silverman, *Acoustic Mirror*, 45–47). In other words, Kathy's "authentic" voice, both on the audio track and in the narrative, turns out to be in/authentic. Finally, the scene in which Lina's plot is foiled when the curtain is pulled to reveal Kathy as the actual singer likewise exposes voice dubbing and synchronized music as a ruse, a contrivance, a process of production, coded here as a humorous spectacle resolving the narrative.

In conclusion, we might take a cue again from Susan Smith, who emphasizes the film's gender hierarchy. For Smith, Lina embodies the potential for female subversion. Through a kind of slip-sync—by not syncing correctly or properly—she represents a female voice that does not fit the studio's body, that does not fully synchronize for entertainment or consumption (*The Musical*, 72–73). Is it too much of a stretch to interpret Lina's shrill, irritating voice, and her overall excessive, gaudy masquerade presence, as a precursor to punk in general, or to Chloe Webb's Nancy Spungeon in particular? Perhaps. Self-consciously and sardonically, punk musicals carry this gender critique further, focusing on female performers who endow Lina's ostracism with an aggressive political bite.

From within the classical-musical paradigm, especially as filtered through Feuer's myth of spontaneity, *Singin' in the Rain* articulates slip-sync as a comic problem that becomes happily resolved as voice and body become properly stitched together seamlessly, affording the natural and "right" musical performance. Michel Chion's general term for the appearance in film of such a "spontaneous coupling of sound and image" is synchresis (*Audio-Vision*, 63); that is, an instance of image and sound seeming to go together, and belonging together, in a naturalized union (one that covers both diegetic and nondiegetic sound).[6] *Singin' in the Rain* raises the disturbing specter of slipped synchresis in the narrative context of an unsettling performance, here reflecting the nervous transition from silent to sound films. The film toys with voice-body synchronization in a way that anticipates punk slip-sync, though the latter reflects more bitterly on the encroaching transition, not from silent to sound, but from live to liveness.

✳ PUNK AND THE ROCK MUSICAL

Closer to punk than the classical musical is the rock or pop musical, though such closeness should not intimate much affinity. The world of rock and pop music just preceding punk, whether conceived of as big business or big art, was the direct target of punk's rebellion. Indeed, we might recall that *Pink Floyd The Wall* (Alan Parker, 1982, UK), which came out during the punk-musical cycle, perfectly embodies all the lofty pretensions that punk despised. Perhaps not surprisingly, most detailed accounts of rock-music films have not considered the early-1980s cycle of punk musicals.

Rock musicals, in fact, are as old as rock itself, and seem to have crucially accompanied the various historical and stylistic changes in rock music. *Jailhouse Rock* (1957), *A Hard Day's Night* (1964), *Tommy* (1975), *Hair* (1979), *Pink Floyd The Wall* (1982), *This Is Spinal Tap* (1984), *La Bamba* (1987), *The Commitments* (1991), *Velvet Goldmine* (1998), *Hedwig and the Angry Inch* (2000), *Almost Famous* (2000), and, more recently, *Control* and *I'm Not There* (both 2007) are just a handful of titles testifying to the substantial diversity and impact of rock musicals.

From one perspective, the rock musical is seen as a relatively conservative variation on the classical Hollywood musical. Barry Keith Grant argues that the classical conventions inherited by the rock musical circumvent rock's subversive edge, taming its rebellious sexual energy and transforming rock's antisocial attitude into a celebration of the status quo ("Classical Hollywood Musical," 199). Grant tends to reify rock music as intrinsically rebellious, which is only partially true. Couldn't one say that much of rock music always already contained these conformist elements, at least in its widespread function as commercialized entertainment? Punk, in fact, could be said to exaggerate both the visionary and the sensationalizing tendencies of rock music.

Moreover, Grant seems to miss how rock music has transformed the classical musical into a more modernist and postmodern form through a variety of formal and discursive strategies, such as documentary, mockumentary, animation, irony, hallucination, and collage. The punk-musical film cycle needs to be considered a strategy for working through and against this postclassical sense of the rock musical.

In passing, Grant notes punk's rebellious and shocking veneer as a kind of reclamation of rock's supposed intrinsic subversion. Yet the examples he cites are punk documentaries, and though these admittedly challenge rock music's mainstream appropriation by the musical genre, the comparison is inapt, since the musical is a narrative, not a documentary, form (204). The early-1980s cycle of punk musicals, as we shall see, is more appropriate to his discussion, and the individual films are more complex than his argument implies.

Indeed, most discussions of 1980s rock or pop film musicals pay scant attention to punk, focusing instead on the more mainstream synergy characterizing the rock sound track of teen films, and on the influence of music videos, as suggested by Jane Feuer and Rick Altman in their codas to the classical musical. And we know how Lawrence Grossberg sees the 1980s teen films: they abuse rock music by attaching it superficially to superficial narrative films ("Media Economy," 204).

From a different angle, J. P. Telotte sees a more realistic incorporation of song and dance in 1980s pop musicals. He discusses pop musicals like *Saturday Night Fever*, *Footloose*, and *Dirty Dancing* for their "sobering," more cynical attitude toward the "expressive limitations" of song and dance as a solution to problems, as well as their more realistic performance context ("New Hollywood Musical," 48). Yet he also notes how these "new musicals" reinscribe the classical musical's sense of utopian community through the synergistic, multimedia marketing potential they exploit (58–61; see also Reay, *Music and Film*, 95–98). Again, punk musicals offer a compelling alternative to such compensatory "feel good" trends built around marketing, as well as an articulation of sound and vision more complicated than any of the 1980s pop teen fare addressed by Telotte and Grossberg.

One critic who has targeted punk musicals specifically is Kevin J. Donnelly. In "British Punk Musicals: Rebellion into Money, Nihilism into Innovation," he offers a descriptive overview of British punk films from the late 1970s through the early 1980s, focusing on the attraction of "amateur rockumentary" styles. Throughout, he is rather dismissive of the films, suggesting that they were not too good at conveying punk music (echoes of Grossberg), and that they left little imprint on British pop-music film history. We will suggest otherwise. In fact, we will draw inspiration from a later Donnelly reading ("Entertainment and Dystopia: The Punk Anti-Musical"), which details how *The Great Rock 'n' Roll Swindle* inverts and deconstructs the traditional musical. In fact, I will be exploring all the punk musicals in this vein initiated by Donnelly.

For now, let us briefly consider a classic rock musical that pushes further than *Singin' in the Rain* in the direction of punk slip-sync: *A Hard Day's Night*. Along with the Elvis Presley films of the late 1950s, this first and most influential of the Beatles films dynamically transforms the classical musical into a prototype for the pop-rock musical of 1960s youth culture. Indeed, the film still holds considerable sway today, as testified to by a film like *Spice World* (1997). What *A Hard Day's Night* retains from the classical musical is an overall wholesome worldview that idealizes community (Grant, "Classical Hollywood Musical," 202). Yet the film distinguishes itself from the 1950s-era classical and rock musicals through its modernist sensibility, its New Wave style, and its more self-consciously playful reflexivity.

Most distinct from the norms of the classical musical is *A Hard Day's Night*'s approach to its sound track and musical performances. Offering more of an audiovisual collage, *A Hard Day's Night* combines a gritty black-and-white "kitchen sink" look with fantasy-like sequences. Indeed, the film's sound aesthetic follows in the wake of the European art film of the late 1950s. Federico Fellini's sound technique, for example, deliberately exaggerates the postdubbing effect, so the voices seem to have slipped from their proper place inside the moving lips of the actors. A French New Wave film like Jean-Luc Godard's *A Woman Is a Woman* (1961), appearing three years before the Beatles film, similarly plays with sound and synchronization in a reflexive way that highlights the image-sound dialectic. I am thinking especially of the scene early in the film in which Anna Karina performs in a nightclub (during the day!). She puts on a record, begins lip-syncing to it, "performing" for the camera. But each time the song lyric is heard, the music track goes silent, so we hear her voice (not hers but the phonograph's) as dislodged, literally extracted from the

2.2. *Playfully media-ted: the Fab Four in* A Hard Day's Night *(1964). Photo courtesy of Photofest.*

conventional coherent sound design of classical musical performance, the latter being affectionately parodied here.[7]

Whereas slip-sync in *Singin' in the Rain* is more a thematic than a formal dimension, in *A Hard Day's Night* slip-sync becomes more intrinsically bound up with musical performance, a stylistic aspect of the sound design. It also has shed some of the comic "wrongness" that accompanied it in the Hollywood musical. In other words, though *A Hard Day's Night* is clearly full of humor and breezy charm, it incorporates a slip-sync aesthetic as an earnest structural innovation that heralds the modernist gist of future rock musicals.

Such a New Wave approach to sound occurs, for example, early in the film in the sequence on the train. On their way to a television-performance rehearsal, the Fab Four escape to the luggage car, where they break into the song "I Should Have Known Better." After they sit down to play cards, the song begins playing on the sound track, presumably nonsync. However, we see both Ringo and George rocking their heads in time with the music; this playfully blurs the boundary between sync and nonsync sound. Suddenly, as the first vocal begins, an abrupt, hand-held jump cut shows John "singing" the song, with the other members pretending to play their instruments. I say "pretending" not merely because their instruments have magically appeared. George strums an electric guitar, though we hear an acoustic on the sound track; likewise, Ringo pounds his drumsticks on something, but we never actually see the drum kit. Most conspicuously pretending is Paul, who also lip-syncs with John, especially peculiar since the song only has one vocal track (John's). While John's lip-syncing is fairly convincing, Paul's becomes a kind of illogical, though charming, excess: smiling, he's not too concerned about correctly mimicking the lyrics. Such a reflexive departure from traditional synchresis sets the stage for both the celebratory, promotional aesthetic of MTV (fast cuts, playfully self-conscious lip-syncing) and the more unnerving punk slip-sync.

✳ PUNK AND INDEPENDENT CINEMA

While the punk musicals loosely incorporate key features of the classical- and rock-musical genres, they are more coherently and directly inspired by underground, independent, and cult film practices. Our punk-musical cycle thus signifies the important historical juncture at which the independent nongenre film and the musical genre film fuse.

Most recent histories of the New Hollywood agree that a compelling alternative vision to the dominant blockbusters of the 1980s came from the resurgent American independent film movement hailing primarily from New York. The early films of Jim Jarmusch, Jonathan Demme, David Lynch, the Coen brothers, and Spike Lee are quirky and character oriented, with an offbeat style and an ironic, often coolly reflexive sensibility. The punk-musical film cycle just precedes this 1984–1986 group of debut indie features, seeming to furnish the soil out of which they grew. Jon Jost singles out Susan Seidelman's punk first feature, *Smithereens* (1983), for "hitting pay dirt," opening the distribution door to the New York indie movement ("End of the Indies," 54).

Though the punk musicals have a narrow association with punk music scenes, their punk tone and production values get revived and revised in the dark irony pervading films like *Stranger Than Paradise*, *Blood Simple* (both 1984), *Something Wild*, and *Blue Velvet* (both 1986). Lynch's first feature film, *Eraserhead* (1977), a New York cult classic, seems in its bleak, bizarre pessimism to directly reflect the burgeoning New York punk scene surrounding the film's release. Jarmusch attributes the inspiration for his first feature film, *Permanent*

Vacation (1981), to punk, specifically the punk film by Amos Poe, *The Foreigner* (Thompson, "Punk Cinema," 26). In other words, the New York punk scene helped generate not only the punk-musical cycle but also the independent-film spirit that would live on for several decades (Hawkins, "Dark, Disturbing, Intelligent," 89–90).

To fully appreciate the nexus of punk music and independent, underground cinema, let us rewind a bit further, to the very first punk shows. According to Gina Marchetti (who published a timely piece on the topic in 1982), these tiny nightclub gigs on the underground fringes of a bloated rock-music culture almost instantaneously spawned a series of no-budget, radically independent punk documentaries. Employing film aesthetics and production values commensurate with the rough and raw punk music they were capturing, films such as *Blank Generation* (1976), *The Punk Rock Movie* (1978), *Rude Boy* (1980), and *D.O.A.* (1981) have become canonical punk documentaries (Thompson, *Punk Productions*, 159–162). They faithfully reflect the energy and spirit of the original burst of punk-rock music and informed, for example, the "scorch and burn" documentary videos of the early-1980s Los Angeles punk-music scene referred to above (James, *Power Misses*, 224–225).

Equally formative regarding the earliest convergence (not "synergy," too corporate a term) of punk and film are the no-wave no-budget narratives of the New York punk underground. Growing directly out of the intermingling of the punk-music scene with Andy Warhol's Factory, circa 1975–1978, these films combine neo-noir subject matter, a sadomasochistic sensibility, and Super 8 amateur aesthetics (Hoberman and Rosenbaum, *Midnight Movies*, 283). Jack Sargeant links this "cinema of transgression" to the "pre-punk" trash cinema of John Waters, describing the films of Scott B and Beth B, Amos Poe, Vivienne Dick, Richard Kern, and Eric Mitchell as "post-punk/no wave" B movies (*Deathtripping*, 13–14; see also Giles, "As Above, So Below," 46–48). Labeled recently by Joan Hawkins as "downtown cinema" ("Dark, Disturbing, Intelligent," 90), most of these films are set in the East Village and feature marginal appearances by punk musicians. Rightly considered punk in tone and production style, they extend Warhol's ironic critique of Hollywood, but with a sloppy, irreverent return to narrative that equally bashes the institutionalized avant-garde (Dika, *Recycled Culture*, 49–50). In this sense, they are best appreciated as avant-garde revisions of the film noir genre, not the musical. That is, the films reflect the same punk zeitgeist that simultaneously appeared musically in the clubs. However, unlike the soon-to-follow punk-musical cycle, they are not much interested in music.

Other liaisons between punk and independent film should be noted in order to further situate and appreciate the punk-musical film cycle.[8] Independent film's low-budget production context and aesthetic seems jump-started with renewed inspiration by punk's DIY ideology and practice. Likewise, indie film's regionalism and anticorporate subtext can be traced to punk's more extreme emphasis on nightclub performance and local subcultural practices, both of these ritualized against commercial forms. One might also speculate on the link between indie film's ironic genre revisionism and punk's noisier citations of popular culture, or on the link between the ultraviolence of some indie and cult films and punk's devotion to violent shock. Hawkins specifically explores some of the aesthetic and thematic influences of punk film on new American indie cinema. For her, punk "downtown cinema" is the neglected, "repressed" avant-garde of the 1980s and 1990s ("Dark, Disturbing, Intelligent," 91). Beyond the "sense of community or place" that marks both punk and independent cinema, she cites a "clear socio-political agenda" aimed at shocking audiences and an "attempt to lay bare the dark underside of middle-class and middle-American life" (91). What also "crosses over" from the no-budget downtown punk films to the later, more accessible indie films is a rejection of sentimentality and an ironic portrayal of "grim episodes" (91).

The interface between punk and independent cinema is also underscored in the British (as opposed to American) environment. In England, the early London punk-music scene informed the more marginal strains of the 1980s British film renaissance: for example, directors like Derek Jarman and Julien Temple got their first filmmaking training directly inside the birth of London punk music. But we should also note the links between punk and the broader film culture. The latter is best understood through the rise of the heritage film, starting with *Chariots of Fire* (1981), and running through the more challenging, idiosyncratic works of Peter Greenaway, Jarman, Ken Loach, and Mike Leigh, which variously incorporate documentary and experimental elements (Higson, "Re-Presenting the National Past," 109–110). To be sure, punk is associated more with experimental than heritage tendencies, and the early-1980s musicals of my focus emerge within this primarily realistic (Leigh) or surrealistic (Greenaway, Jarman) context. Punk characters are represented in Leigh's *Meantime* (1984), in the more popular Stephen Frears–Hanif Kureishi collaborations *My Beautiful Laundrette* (1985) and *Sammy and Rosie Get Laid* (1987), and in Isaac Julien's *Young Soul Rebels* (1991). Likewise, one could argue that punk indirectly informs the baroque, often shocking excesses of Greenaway's oeuvre.

But even the luscious, upper-class, period-piece veneer of the heritage film can be related to the punk film. Most heritage films bear a "soft" critique of conformity, one that harmonizes with the explicitly anti-Thatcher rage of punk. Indeed, British heritage films are generally considered a crucial component of the American independent-film movement, since many were distributed widely in the United States in the early 1980s, helping the American indies find "alternative" audiences over and against the blockbuster crowd. The coincidence of punk-musical films and heritage films is, to my mind, no coincidence: though in drastically different ways, each deconstructs the British imperial-literary tradition and confronts the more immediate specter of Thatcherite Britain. As we will see in the next chapter, Jarman's *Jubilee* proves a fascinating blend of punk and heritage.

Perhaps the most important notion linking independent film and punk is that of excess, most typically associated with cult, camp, or trash cinema. The punk subculture seems essentially defined by a certain kind of excess; and punk films, whether downtown nightclub documentaries or hardcore videos, carry such excess into the filmic realm. Our punk-musical cycle likewise incorporates excess, in tamer but equally striking ways. Pushing Cohan's point regarding the affinities between camp and the musical, Ian Conrich explores those between the cult film and the musical: both feature "performances of extravagance and exuberance, obvious energy and ability, open emotions, fantasy and sudden explosions of spectacle" ("Musical Performance," 115). The punk-musical cycle occupies one region of this space where cult and musical overlap. Slip-sync becomes usefully contextualized by Conrich's notion that "musical performance in the cult film frequently works as a deliberate and knowing perversion" of utopian performance, offering instead "the depiction of a screen dystopia" (116).[9]

More specific categories of cult film lend themselves to highlighting the contours of the punk-musical cycle. Many punk musicals bear traces of several species of cult film: exploitation film (epitomized by Roger Corman's stamp as both director and producer); "paracinema," explained by Jeffrey Sconce as films that fail miserably yet gloriously at the Hollywood formula, but that also prove anathema to the art cinema prized by the cultural elite ("'Trashing' the Academy," 546–547); and the trash cinema best embodied by the work of John Waters (later, younger trash-film directors like Jon Moritsugu and Gregg Araki more vividly incorporate punk aesthetics and themes).[10] All of these cult-film types go too far in some respect or possess too much of something, all of which resonates lucidly with punk's shocking postures.

Indeed, the category of the cult film seems to best bring punk and cinematic excess together,[11] and the products of this fusion can be broken down into two camps: the classic Hollywood film that lives on for various subcultures through counterreadings of its excesses, and the more deliberately and self-consciously extreme films that emphasize the forbidden—in their subject matter, formal aspects, production, and exhibition (Kawin, "After Midnight," 18). The punk-musical cycle effectively combines bad Hollywood style with the deliberately bad taste that transgresses mainstream sensibilities. One could speculate on how the whole punk-music subculture itself seems to be a living incarnation of such an artistic practice.

Slip-sync, with its double excess around performer and spectacle, can thus be understood as partaking of the "unfamiliar style, frame and imagistic texture" of the cult film (Corrigan, "Culture of the Cult," 26).[12] Yet another related lens that helps us situate and evaluate the punk-musical cycle, especially its slip-sync strategy, is Kay Dickinson's unique and provocative recent study, *Off Key: When Film and Music Won't Work Together*. Her central thesis (not unrelated to Sconce's regarding paracinema, mentioned above) is that certain failures of film and music to work together—in cheesy rock-and-roll movies from the 1950s, in Ken Russell's musician biopics of the 1970s, and in berated films of the 1990s featuring "pop stars who can't act," such as Madonna and Mick Jagger—reflect larger social tensions around leisure and labor as well as the overall post-Fordist move of entertainment culture to synergize distinct media. In her introductory "overture" reading of the "widely damned" Elvis film *Harum Scarum* (1965), she emphasizes the perceived inauthenticity Elvis exudes as a kind of authentic rock star trapped in an inauthentic, bad movie. More importantly for us, she also notes the film's lip-syncing that does not match (10), theorizing the broad and lively critical concept of the "mismatch," which at least indirectly characterizes my idea of slip-sync.

Dickinson distances her study from the deliberate, usually more reflexive mismatches of independent films. Her preferred focus is on "mainstream mismatches," which "are often presumed to dream of consistency and then to jeopardize their chances of attaining it through their supposed lack of dexterity" (20). I think the films of the punk-musical cycle do and do not fit squarely into Dickinson's critical realm. Dickinson's mismatch is produced in a highly professionalized and institutionalized context; punk's frenetic amateurism thus would yield a fundamentally different breed of mismatch. Yet unlike the punk documentaries, most of these punk musicals have one boot in the muddy independent and cult world of such frenetic amateurism, and the other boot in the glossier, more professionalized world of rock-entertainment cinema and the musical genre. While these punk musicals may not "dream of consistency," they do seem to fall short in various ways as they mine the musical genre. We will see how often the slip-sync moment or effect is not so much a deliberate error as a failure of synchronization that becomes meaningful from within a punk perspective.

It is not my intention to force Dickinson's mismatch and my slip-sync into synchronization. Rather, I would contextualize these punk musicals and their slip-sync strategy within a spectrum of works that bring music and film together in ways that, whether by design or default, do not fully or properly come together. Indeed, her insistence on relating various film-music mismatches to the contradictions of the larger social economy is not unrelated to my contention that punk slip-sync speaks much to the onset of Reaganomics and the culture of widespread electronic simulation.

The punk connection to cult film is best embodied in what many consider to be the ultimate cult film, a raucous paradigm of excess as cult musical: *The Rocky Horror Picture Show* (1975). It is worth recalling that *Rocky Horror* appeared during the time and place of punk's emergence: the stage production ran during the mid-1970s in London and New York; the film adaptation was produced by a U.S. studio but shot in Britain, with most of the original British stage cast. Plus, much of the film's "shocking" sensibility clearly has a finger on the pulse of punk, which was still underground at the time. This link is perhaps best crystallized in Frank-N-Furter's black leather S&M-style Victorian corset outfit.

Moreover, a couple of years later some personnel from *Rocky Horror* worked on Jarman's *Jubilee*, the earliest punk film of the cycle (more on this in the next chapter).[13] *Rocky Horror* producer Lou Adler would go on to direct one of our later American punk musicals, *Ladies and Gentlemen, the Fabulous Stains*; *Rocky Horror*'s lead star, Tim Curry, is featured in another, *Times Square*. Beyond these production links, Gaylyn Studlar highlights the theoretical and aesthetic alliances between punk, cult, and trash cinema by bringing together *Rocky Horror*, *Liquid Sky*, and John Waters's *Pink Flamingos* for their representations of femininity as a perversion, an excess ("Midnight S/Excess," 139). Studlar reminds us how such "radical" films can reiterate conservative gender attitudes, an important insight for our critical survey. In any case, the ripple effect of *Rocky Horror* on our cycle is substantial, and worth unpacking a bit further.

First, there is something metaphorically slip-sync about *Rocky Horror*. Jeffrey Weinstock notes the film's "odd temporality": chronology in the narrative does not entirely make sense, and the film is filled with temporally incorrect political references and a hodgepodge of time-period contexts (*Rocky Horror*, 20). One could also interpret the film's cult viewing status of midnight movie as a kind of time warp, a viewing context that is not exactly outside of time but that goes against the grain of traditional temporal conceptions of film viewing and leisure activity generally.

On this note, the various audience reactions to the film may be related to the slip-sync concept. The film's legendary audience participation at midnight screenings, which incorporates mimicry and verbal interaction, can be understood as occurring both inside and outside the film. Itself a lateral precursor to punk's DIY fandom, *Rocky Horror*'s midnight fan ritual synchronizes with the film's narrative, since it depends upon dialogue and music cues; yet it also is ontologically unsynced with the narrative, slipping across the surface of the film's musical performances. In this sense, and in the spirit of slip-sync, musical performance is not fully contained in or by the film, but bleeds over into (slips over into) the audience (32–51). In fact, two American films discussed later in this book—*Times Square* and *Ladies and Gentlemen, the Fabulous Stains*—each dramatize such proactive, participatory punk fandom, alluding to the *Rocky Horror* fan phenomenon but also illustrating its slip-sync connotations.

Moreover, *Rocky Horror*'s zany pastiche and parody of the science fiction, horror, and musical genres likewise foreshadow the punk articulation of slip-sync. Through its contrived camp tone (one that has aged remarkably well), the film appropriates familiar generic markers, unsyncs them, then remixes them into a hybrid concoction that is easily assimilated to the punk cut-up aesthetic. If we listen to Dick Hebdige on the debut of punk, we can read the influence of *Rocky Horror* in between the lines, and not at all far behind: A "new style was being generated combining elements drawn from a whole range of heterogeneous youth styles . . . The whole ensemble, literally safety-pinned together, became the celebrated and highly photogenic phenomenon known as punk which throughout 1977 provided the tabloids with a fund of predictably sensational copy and the quality press with a welcome catalogue of beautifully broken codes. Punk reproduced the entire sartorial history of post-war working-class youth cultures in 'cut up' form" (*Subculture*, 25–26).

Viciously laughing at classic genres while violating their rules, *Rocky Horror* is a film out of time, a film that has slipped, or leapt, out of sync. Weinstock highlights this "meta-cult" aspect of the film for how it queers "the cinematic tradition" and for how it "denaturalises gender" (*Rocky Horror*, 83). In retrospect, the film becomes a crucial lynchpin between the close of the classical-genre era and the onset of the cynical, ironic New Hollywood of the 1970s that just precedes and informs punk.

But *Rocky Horror* offers the most as a precursor to punk musicals specifically in its musical performance style. The song-and-dance numbers in the film are distinctive partially because they do not completely work, or fit. There is always something "wrong" or excessive or improper, something out of place or out of time—all connotations related to my concept of slip-sync. It is not so much that the singer slips out of sync in *Rocky Horror*, though in certain places the lip-sync is rather obvious, not quite matched up. Rather, the breaking into

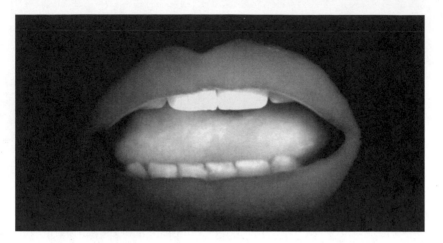

2.3. *Exaggerating the "lip" in slip-sync: oversized, disembodied female lips mismatched with a male singing voice at the start of* The Rocky Horror Picture Show *(1975).*

song is often done clumsily or too melodramatically—an awkwardness that foresees and informs the punk slip-sync gesture and style.[14]

Worth brief consideration in this respect is the film's notorious credit sequence. We hear the elegantly schmaltzy song "Science Fiction Double Feature," which cites titles and scenes from a variety of classic Hollywood movies, an effective overture to the kooky, hybrid pastiche to follow. As the credits appear in gory red lettering, we see the song being sung by a huge lipsticked mouth. Perhaps deliberately evoking a similar, early-1970s Rolling Stones icon, these provocatively androgynous lips fill the screen in tight close-up, prefiguring slip-sync in several ways. First, they are disembodied, lips without a face, floating like some giant sea creature against a black void. More to the point, the singing lips slip out of sync ever so slightly. Weinstock notes the tension between Richard O'Brien's "particularly plaintive" and "thin tenor voice," and Patricia Quinn's "lascivious red lips," which "disguise" this voice (83). In this way, the sequence intimates a gap or separation between voice and body, one that, anticipating punk, problematizes traditional gender as well as traditional performance synchronization in film.

We probably can assume that the ostensible intent of this striking visual is to shock, related to the kind of excess that, as we have seen, characterizes the film itself, the cult-film sensibility, and punk. The shot shows too much of these singing lips, shows them too closely. Yet what transpires, especially for the keen slip-sync viewer, is another, more incidental and reflexive excess: we are forced to observe the slippage that inevitably occurs between histrionically moving lips (mediatized performing body) and the vocal on the sound track (mediatized voice). To wit, the sequence shoves slip-sync in our face, not the more subversive and self-conscious variety we will see in the punk musicals, but the potential slipperiness between sound and vision underlying any mediatized representation.

Having briefly considered historical precursors to punk slip-sync from the classical musical (*Singin' in the Rain*), the pop-rock musical (*A Hard Day's Night*), and the cult film (*Rocky Horror*), let us finally turn to a precursor that is really inside the downtown-cinema punk-underground film movement. Released one year after *Rocky Horror* (thus underlining *Rocky Horror*'s proximity to punk), *Blank Generation* (Amos Poe and Ivan Kral, 1976), eschewing all but the thinnest veneer of organization, is comprised simply of raw footage of various punk bands performing at small clubs like Max's Kansas City and CBGB. Its punk approach to sound foresees slip-sync in crucial ways, but more accurately as a kind of antisync: all the performance footage is presented with the music slightly out of sync, creating a perpetual disconnect between sound and image. Here, there is really no slip (or: there is constant slip), since sound and image from the start are never synchronized: the visuals are always at a different point in the song than what we hear on the sound track.

Indeed, the film's apparent slippage in synchronization is even more pronounced than this small disconnect suggests. Poe, one of the directors, sheds some light on what I am describing as the slip-sync sound design of the film,

2.4. *Seminal, "writerly" precursor of punk's slipped synchronization:* Blank Generation *(1976), featuring New York protopunk musician and sometime film star Richard Hell, playing here with the Heartbreakers.*

explaining that all the music was postdubbed from either poor-quality demos or cassette recordings made during other performances, and that the sloppy or slipped synchronization was a self-conscious attempt to capture the spirit of punk by rejecting more professional sound-recording options (Sargeant, "Downtown Upheaval," 85). So in true punk fashion, the live-music sound track to the film derives from sources other than what we are seeing, thereby challenging conventional sound-image authenticity by articulating in/authenticity. Such radical disjuncture aims, however, for a loose and reflexive impression of synchronization.

While *Blank Generation* is a documentary, unlike the narrative films of the punk-musical cycle, the film nevertheless establishes a fundamental punk sound design that rejects everything about the commercial music industry, including lip-syncing and synchresis, and that, I contend, greatly influenced the later narrative films. Noting in passing the film's "non-synchronous songs," Gina Marchetti links the film's "technically crude" formal approach to punk's preference for intimate performance venues, where "the punk audience is as important and active as the musicians" ("Documenting Punk," 273). Stacy Thompson has recently imported Roland Barthes's term "writerly" to characterize this punk film aesthetic and its "open formal structure" that encourages the audience (of the music or the film) to produce meaning (*Punk Productions*, 162–163). While Thompson champions Don Letts's *The Punk Rock Movie* in this regard, *Blank Generation* to my mind offers a better example of a writerly text because of its uniquely slip-synced sound track. The slip-sync sequences I will be discussing in early-1980s narrative films owe much to this writerly DIY aesthetic.

★ PUNK, SLIP-SYNC, AND EXPERIMENTAL FEMINIST CINEMA

As stated earlier, many of the punk musicals I will discuss feature a female punk lead character as a performer. It therefore seems important to contextualize this primarily female take on punk slip-sync with a related and simultaneous tendency in experimental feminist cinema. During approximately the same period of the punk-musical film cycle (1978–1986), several important experimental and international feminist films offered their own versions of slip-sync.

Indeed, much feminist film criticism since the late 1970s has focused on the body-voice dialectic. Generally speaking (and this is a simplification), the female voice is seen to possess potentially subversive properties in relation to the fetishized female body and patriarchal narrative structure at large (Silverman, *Acoustic Mirror*; Lawrence, *Echo and Narcissus*; and most recently, Sjogren, *Into the Vortex*). A spate of provocative films emerged that seem to mobilize such a critique: Yvonne Rainer's *Journeys From Berlin/1971* (1980), Bette Gordon's *Empty Suitcases* (1980), Julie Dash's *Illusions* (1982), Lizzie Borden's *Born in Flames* (1983), Chantal Akerman's *Golden Eighties* (1986), and Tracey Moffatt's *Nice Coloured Girls* (1987). Each of these films, in different ways, deconstructs classical Hollywood's patriarchal body-voice coherence. These experimental feminist films undo traditional cinematic sound-image synchronization, furnishing instead a filmic approach in which image and sound are more conspicuously distinct, dialectically offsetting each other. Disembodied voices critically comment on images as images, rather than images as windows onto reality, typically resulting in a liberation of woman's literal and figurative voice from the confines of patriarchal stereotype.

Not coincidentally, this critical revision of patriarchal representation through sound often involves a subversive focus on the female performing body. In a variety of ways, these films dissociate body from voice so as to expose Hollywood's construction of the fetishized female performer. But they also open up a new representational time-space, a new or other kind of synchronization that resonates with punk slip-sync. In many punk musicals, performance becomes a gendered site of contestation over new technologies of spectacle. Bringing experimental feminist film practice to bear on punk slip-sync thus enhances our appreciation of the gender-inflected stakes of punk films. It also underlines the fact that many of these punk and experimental filmmakers belonged to the same community of artists, mostly in New York, where avant-garde film, political activism, and the punk subculture cross-pollinated and overlapped, forming a kind of slip-sync zeitgeist.

The disjunctive formal approach to sound in the early-1980s wave of experimental feminist films also challenges traditional racial hierarchies and categories of ethnic identity. That is, these experimental feminist films question the very notion of identity, whether sexual or ethnic, emphasizing identity as an intersection of sexuality, gender, and race, among other facets. They also articulate identity as intrinsically multiple and dislocated, never fully coherent or stable.[15] Such an intersection of race and gender, as articulated through experimental sound, helps expand the interpretive stakes of punk slip-sync. In analyzing punk slip-sync in later chapters, we will take a cue from these feminist experimental films and assume that questions of literal and figurative synchronization bear on race as much as on gender, even if the latter occupies more of the filmic foreground. Two films that illustrate the relationship between slip-sync sound design, race, and gender are Julie Dash's *Illusions* and Tracey Moffatt's *Nice Coloured Girls*. Let us turn to them briefly as part of our historical and theoretical overture to punk slip-sync performance.

Illusions proves to be an intriguing riff on *Singin' in the Rain*; like that film, it furnishes an indirect instance of punk slip-sync. Set during World War II, it focuses on a black female singer hired by a movie studio to dub in her singing voice for that of a white actress in order to repair a synchronization error in a musical. The head secretary for the studio is herself a light-skinned black woman who apparently passes in the studio-office world as white. In a way, she therefore functions as both black and white, "slipping" from one to the other, depending upon context and the perspective of those around her. As the one who orchestrates the dubbing process, she represents a racialized slip-sync, a visual counterpart to the sound-music slip-sync enacted by the black singer. This latter character, in contrast to the secretary, is dark skinned, with stronger Negroid features. And while her appearance in a Hollywood film is essentially not permissible, her voice is a usable Hollywood commodity—but only if disembodied from her, then sutured to the performing body of the white actress in the film. As in *Singin' in the Rain*, the dubbing sequences of *Illusions* emphasize her voice matching up, but not quite matching up, with the white singing female Hollywood body.

By portraying Hollywood's need to sync up voice and body as an effort that can never be entirely successful, *Illusions* alludes to the slippage in synchronization always present in any cinematic representation, but especially around musical performance. On a more broadly cultural level, the film's slip-sync sequences highlight how black talent becomes appropriated by white culture. While the black singer's voice is treated as fodder for enhancing a white performance, the visible and audible seams of traditional lip-sync become exposed here as a slippage, one that in turn reveals Hollywood's racial and gender hierarchy. A powerful political critique of Hollywood's insidious racism, the film possesses another slip-sync double excess, one that parallels those that occurred behind the scenes of *Singin' in the Rain*'s production, mentioned earlier: the black woman's voice itself has been dubbed. She obviously lip-syncs to some other voice during her own dubbing-performance scene. The sequence, which prefigures the effect of punk slip-sync, intimates a provocative undoing of the notion of original voice in order to challenge white patriarchal structures of entertainment and representation.

Nice Coloured Girls similarly engages in a slippery sound practice as a means to interrogate patriarchal and colonial historical representation. This compelling short film deconstructs the British and Australian legacy of colonialism in modern Sydney by focusing on three "nice coloured girls" of Aboriginal descent who typically go out at night to seduce well-off white men ("captains," they call them). After dinner, dancing, and much drinking, they steal one man's money and leave him barely conscious. Employing overall a striking collage style and juxtaposing past and present, the slip-sync approach to sound occurs primarily in the women's "voices," which are not voices at all, but printed text near the bottom of the frame. Thus, their cultural and political silence becomes literalized on the sound track (no voice), but returns as printed text, expanding the film-viewing experience to include a reading experience. In a sense, their voices have slipped from sound (whether sync or nonsync) to writing: we hear their voices in our own heads as we read, which perhaps in this case is a more effective, critical form of reception than hearing them aloud.

The omniscient nonsync voice we do hear, on the other hand, is that of an educated British male colonialist, which, in a documentary-like voice-over, recites from conquest journals of first encounters with Aboriginal peoples. Here too a kind of slip-sync is deployed, since the historical patriarchal voice from the past we hear is made to overlap with, and reinhabit, present-day urban Sydney. The film insists that the disembodied singular male voice (first-person "I") be understood in relation to the silent actions of the captain; likewise, the silent written collective voice of the "nice coloured girls" (first-person "we") is made to relate to the treatment of Aboriginal women in the distant past, as recounted in the voice-over. In this way, the film synchronizes disparate voices across time; political critique in the film becomes a gesture of hearing and reading voices, voices not synced up with bodies but resynced up with history.

Such sound-track strategies, involving various forms of disembodied sound, are quite relevant to the punk slip-sync gesture. I do not contend they were consciously imported into the punk films. Rather, both the punk films and the experimental feminist films were caught up in an avant-garde trend of the early 1980s, one that played around with synchronization and the sound-image relationship generally and more or less deconstructively as a means of problematizing dominant cultural forms.

✳ PUNK AND 1980S NEOCON CULTURE

Speaking of dominant cultural forms: in the opening scene of *The Terminator* (1984), a black garbage-truck driver becomes an unsubtle surrogate for the film audience as he observes, awestruck, a late-night spectacle of electro-lightning—the arrival of the nefarious android Terminator, sent from the future into the past (talk about slip-sync!). His mission: to annihilate Sarah Connor before she gives birth to her son. After scanning the nighttime skyline of Los Angeles from above (and offering the film audience a backside peek at the imposing physique of ultra-hard-body actor Arnold Schwarzenegger), the Terminator's first order of business is to get some hip threads.

Not coincidentally, his first encounter with humans is with a group of three punks. Swiftly caricatured as brash and obnoxious, clearly hanging around in the middle of the night with nothing to do but make trouble, they fully deserve, in the film's vigilante logic, the superhuman violence to which the Terminator promptly submits them. Additionally, a certain irony lingers as the Terminator acquires his signature costume from hapless punks, as though he embodies both an extreme version of punk as well as punk's nemesis. Punk slip-sync indeed.

But this first encounter of the Terminator's is not coincidental mostly because of punk's status in the early 1980s as a disposable icon of the "bad attitude" demonized by the new neocon political culture. To fully appreciate the scene, let us link the loaded political subtext here with that of the opening sequence of the progenitor blockbuster, *Jaws* (1975). In that scene (the primal scene of the New Hollywood blockbuster as well as the New Right?), conservative antipathy toward the counterculture is neatly symbolized in the shark mauling meted out to the pot-smoking hippie girl who engaged in "free love." With the Reagan 1980s in full swing, bringing to mass fruition that shark-attack mass spectacle, *The Terminator* features another set of jaws, Schwarzenegger's, that likewise maim the grossly overinvested vestiges of the punk subculture.

The Terminator's opening engages in a kind of negligent rewriting of punk history, tossing up throwaway stereotypes for popular consumption. But we can also look three years earlier to Australia and *The Road Warrior* (1981), which enjoyed wide circulation during the punk-musical cycle and helped inaugurate the blockbuster-sequel Hollywood formula. Mel Gibson's Mad Max, a stoic loner brimming with revenge, wanders a postapocalyptic wasteland, besieged on all sides by roving bands of wildly macabre survivalist punks. Although a brief voice-over at the top of the film assigns blame for the global disaster on the excessive greed of oil corporations, what we see for the next two hours are these out-of-control punks, implying that really they caused the end of the world. Punk rock being rendered as a ghoulish spectacle of "no future" by a film that bridges Dirty Harry and the Rambo-Terminator Hollywood trend is not without significance.

In other words, the last framework I will evoke for situating the punk-musical film cycle is more broadly cultural but no less pertinent: the Reagan and Thatcher regimes, and the neocon enterprise culture that emerged and thrived during their tenures. Much has been written on British and American cinema during the 1980s, and much of it makes explicit the numerous links between the conservative ideology and economic policies bolstered by Reagan and Thatcher, and Hollywood film, finding those links in "hard body" films (Jeffords, *Hard Bodies*); yuppie road movies (Hark, "Fear of Flying"); horror films (Grant, "Rich and Strange"); time-travel fantasies (Nadel, *Flatlining*) and serialized, juvenilized science fiction (Biskind, "The Last Crusade"). British cinema of the 1980s has proved also to be a ripe landscape for unearthing multifarious responses to the Thatcher era, whether in the heritage film, best embodied by the Merchant-Ivory productions, or the multicultural Frears-Kureishi films that oddly celebrate the entrepreneurial spirit of the times (Quart, "Religion of the Market"). We should note that most of these studies uncover not a transparent celebration of Reagan-Thatcher values and policies (though many films do contain that), but rather a tension, some degree of critical resistance to these values.

This tension surfaces more noisily in the punk-musical cycle, which presents a theatrically negative response to 1980s neocon culture. At the same time, some of those films covertly or unconsciously reinforce aspects of neocon cultural agendas. I am especially interested in exploring some of the insidious ways these punk films disseminate Reagan-Thatcher ideology—as opposed to their more obvious and palpable subversion of it. Such an ambivalent relation to Reagan-Thatcher nationalist-military rhetoric is suggested, for example, in punk's neonationalist racist-skinhead strains. Another uneasy alignment between traditional conservative culture and punk is noted by Stacy Thompson in his comments on the Sex Pistols' signing in 1977 with A&M Records, which was staged as a spectacle in front of Buckingham Palace: "The juxtaposition of a punk band with English royalty suggests some parallels: both lack depth and are figureheads, for an industry or a nation. Both are types of spectacle" (*Punk Productions*, 26).

As a foreshadowing of future discussions, let us sketch some of the awkward links between punk and neocon cultural politics as they occur in the films of the punk-musical cycle. These links become visible in, for example, the revisionist Elizabethan nostalgia in Jarman's *Jubilee*; in the cutthroat, self-centered greed marking punk characters in *The Great Rock 'n' Roll Swindle*, *Smithereens*, and *Liquid Sky*; in the iconic and narrative embrace of television throughout the films; and in the ambivalent portrayal of people of color, which generally aims for inclusion but tends to undermine this aim with stubborn marginalization effects. Most significant and consistent throughout the films is the figure of the band manager, often portrayed as a money-focused visionary who is both friend and foe, both outside and inside the freshly corporatized music industry. My analysis of these punk films teases out such contradictions, arguing that the films uniquely function both outside and within Reaganomics, both against and for the new conservative ideology.[16]

Another aspect of the 1980s cultural landscape crucially relevant to the punk-musical film cycle is what might be termed the "MTV effect." On one level, this effect designates the advent in 1981 of the music-video channel MTV, which brought with it numerous drastic changes to rock and pop music culture, especially the relationship between sound and image. According to Will Straw, MTV heralded a rejuvenated neocommercialism that in its early years emphasized the single as opposed to the album, which was more indicative of 1970s rock culture; intensified the uses of publicity; and ubiquitously and fervently celebrated the "look of the sound," a look more disposable and superficial than ever before ("Pop Music and Postmodernism," 4–12). He goes on to clarify that the "relationship of songs to visuals is obviously not simply one of narrativization or visualization," but one in which the demands of form, structure, and closure deriving from the music "hold in play" the often wildly heterogeneous visuals (15).

Andrew Goodwin notes that the institutional and aesthetic changes on MTV through the 1980s reflect its "efforts to ally itself simultaneously with the major record companies and national advertisers" ("Fatal Distractions," 49). Both Straw and Goodwin characterize the first phase of MTV as having been dominated by postpunk New Pop, "music whose stress on style and artifice perfectly suited marketing through video" (Goodwin, "Fatal Distractions," 49). For David E. James, MTV's attempt to co-opt punk sparked a reaction within the punk subculture to dig further underground, to radicalize its position of resistance to such corporate co-optation (*Power Misses*, 226). Our punk-musical films don't go this far, but they do represent a direct or indirect reckoning with MTV, figuring punk's anxiety toward such assimilation. Many of the films seem prophetically aware of the encroaching MTV effect and attempt either to hijack it or to spit in its face.

On another, broader level, the MTV effect signifies changes in music technology that MTV indeed epitomizes. The technological shift MTV represented is illustrated by the spread of new electronic technologies of reproduction and communication. Paving the way for the fully digitized Internet culture of the 1990s, the early 1980s firmly established the foundations of multimedia synergy and convergence, transforming film viewers into televisual viewers through the sales of millions of VCRs, the widespread availability of cable and satellite television, and the symbolic as well as literal centrality of the remote-control device (Friedberg, "End of Cinema," 915).

The early 1980s were also the time, according to Jeff Smith, when the "trend toward conglomeration" forever transformed both the film and music industries by intensifying the synergy principle as the cross-promotional engine of the multimedia, multinational corporate structure (*Sounds of Commerce*, 190–191). To this scenario we might add the first wave of personal computers and the proliferation of multiplex theaters. Most cultural histories see a neat interlocking of the new corporate culture of the merger, deregulated business practices, the rise of the Hollywood "hard body" blockbuster, and the increased dissemination of televisual screens.

It was as though, in the wake of the Reagan and Thatcher political machines, there emerged in the early 1980s lots of highly visible, high-energy economic and cultural activity; yet the flash emanating from such visibility, energy, and activity obscured some rather narrow and insidious ideological forces at work.

Although clearly at the margins of these transformations in the broader social environment, the punk-musical cycle becomes a fleeting critical reflection that stings, that does not entirely sync up. So one of my aims in the following chapters is to unpack the relationship between the slip-sync motif of the punk musical and the sociopolitical tensions that distinguish this early-1980s acceleration of hyperreal neocon synergy.

CHAPTER 3

THE QUEEN IS DEAD

JUBILEE

THE OVERARCHING CONCEPT of in/authenticity put forward in the previous chapter is intended to help us appreciate slip-sync in the punk-musical film cycle. It is no coincidence, therefore, that in/authenticity dramatically marks the first film in our cycle, one of the first feature films to address punk, Derek Jarman's *Jubilee* (1978). The film has been hailed as one of the best and truest punk films, and derided as a shrewd, unfaithful appropriation of punk. I don't mean to be cagey when I say that the clearest stance is to accept it as both, since being both captures the paradoxical, schizophrenic heart of punk.

 ## DEREK JARMAN, PUNK AUTEUR?

Before entering the text of the film, let us step back from it a bit. Somehow, Derek Jarman's appearance as an audience extra in Michelangelo Antonioni's *Blow Up* (1966) during the Yardbirds' gig scene and his iconoclastic, visionary contributions to the set design of Ken Russell's *The Devils* (1971) and *Savage Messiah* (1972) all foretold his emergence as a feature filmmaker immersed in the late-1970s British punk subculture. In fact, Jarman attended the London art schools where punk was thriving; his Renaissance-man successes in the plastic and literary arts further underlined his relationship to the "high art" side of punk (Frith and Horne, *Art into Pop*, 124). The fact that Jarman's films have been roundly condemned by mainstream British culture as filthy and disgusting testifies to Jarman's debt to the vulgar trash sensibility of punk.

In the mid-1970s Jarman was living in Chelsea, just off King's Road, very much in the heart of the fermenting London punk scene. *Jubilee*, his second feature film, was developed from a short experimental Super 8 film featuring punk insider Jordan. A clerk at SEX, Malcolm McLaren's King's Road boutique, she was a close friend of the Sex Pistols as well as the first manager of Adam and the Ants. Her role in the film, Amyl Nitrate, a punk intellectual and schoolteacher, gradually became the main character, the first bona fide punk film narrator. She got Adam and the Ants, unknown at the time, involved in the film; Siouxsie Sioux and members of *Rocky Horror* also came on board. The recent anthology of writings about punk films *No Focus* devotes an entire chapter to Jarman, whose author claims that *Jubilee* is "probably the finest punk film of all and much more besides" (Barber, "No Future Now," 52).

However, it becomes clear from the supplemental materials found on Criterion's DVD of the film that its punk reception was hotly contested. At the film's premiere at the Gate Two theater in London, several of the punk musicians involved in the film walked out in apparent disgust. The film's "intensely private core and somewhat uneasy mix of exuberance and bleakness" put off both left and right, mainstream culture and the punk subculture; most reviews, including those from the music press, were negative (Peake, *Derek Jarman*, 251). Punk fashion designer Vivienne Westwood, one of punk's highest-profile figures as well as Malcolm McLaren's partner in SEX (later known as Seditionaries), produced a T-shirt protesting the film. The shirt was covered by a long handwritten screed explaining her disgust at the film as an exploitive work that did not understand punk, yet used it to insidiously celebrate the Elizabethan golden age (O'Pray, *Dreams of England*, 95).

There is no doubt that Jarman himself embodied the somewhat aloof art-school outsider who observed punk through a kind of ethnographic perspective inspired by genuine interest but also skepticism and opportunism. He mixed socially with members of the punk scene and recruited many of its key figures (Peake, *Derek Jarman*, 247). But he also brought his own sensibility to bear on the punk scene he was investigating. *Jubilee* mixes authentic punk participants with professional theater actors, many carried over from Jarman's first film, *Sebastiane* (1976), aiming to perform punk. But if authentic punk is itself a performance, one can fault *Jubilee* only so far. Indeed, most histories of punk point out over and over that many of the original, authentic participants in the early punk scene were middle-class public-school-educated art-college students posing as working-class gutter toughs. This, I think, lends credibility to seeing Jarman's film as in/authentically punk.

In fact, Jarman very deliberately studied the punk subculture for the film, especially utilizing the look and tone of the punk fanzines of the time as the basis for the film's production design and overall narrative structure (*Jubilee* DVD supplement, "A New Wave Movie"; see also Peake, *Derek Jarman*, 245).

More importantly, his entire approach to filmmaking perfectly embodied the DIY spirit of punk. Indeed, as Jarman's second feature, *Jubilee* not only deals with punk but also marks the start of the director's feature-film career in and through the contemporaneous punk scene.[1]

As evidenced by *Jubilee* and by his entire oeuvre, Jarman was the ultimate film auteur because his films are so intensely personal in subject matter and intensely amateur in production quality, which is not at all to say they are poorly made. Like many of his other films, *Jubilee* was shot primarily in found, nearby locations with friends, in 16 mm with some Super 8 (later blown up to 35 mm). His distinctive guerrilla style of filmmaking—he had no permits to shoot at Butler's Wharf or the Southwark and Victoria dock areas—freely and often irreverently mixes narrative, documentary, and essay. Rowland Wymer notes how Jarman's emergent approach to filmmaking had much in common with punk's approach to music (*Jarman*, 55). Discussing Jarman's attraction to these "apocalyptic" locations, Tony Peake likewise emphasizes the affinity between punk and Jarman's "impulse" to "rehabilitate what would otherwise be discarded" (*Derek Jarman*, 248). Its punk subject matter notwithstanding, *Jubilee* overlaps with punk to the degree that it was produced, distributed, and exhibited beyond traditional funding sources and commercial networks.

Also like punk, *Jubilee* came out before MTV but seemed to see it coming. In retrospect, the film has been celebrated—by critics and by Jarman himself—for possessing a keen prophetic quality. *Jubilee* envisions the corporate image-oriented rock that punk despised and that prevailed throughout the 1980s; it also offers an incisive critique of the emerging punk subculture itself.[2]

✱ *JUBILEE*'S "RULE, BRITANNIA": BEGIN THE SLIP-SYNC

The film's title refers to Queen Elizabeth II's Silver Jubilee celebration in 1977, which was scandalized periodically by various punk outbursts (shot during 1977, *Jubilee* premiered early in 1978). Noting its punk "home movie" aesthetic and mode of production, as well as its "paranoid and hysterical" visions that came true, Michael O'Pray situates the film at the center of the burgeoning London punk scene (*Dreams of England*, 94–97). *Jubilee*'s "English Renaissance structuring device" (95), which irked some punk pundits, is as follows: Queen Elizabeth I (Jenny Runacre), seeking knowledge of the future, is escorted through time by the alchemist John Dee (Richard O'Brien) with the aid of Shakespeare's sprite Ariel (David Haughton) to present-day England. This time-traveling trio observes the exploits of a group of punks surviving in and around postapocalyptic London, where buildings appear bombed out, baby carriages are left burning, crime runs rampant, and the police are fascist thugs. Most significantly, a demonic media czar has apparently inherited the top position in the government.

It is in the context of an audition in front of this media czar that slip-sync gets its first, and perhaps most vivid, articulation in our punk musical film cycle. Borgia Ginz (Orlando), who oversees a rock-music television station the punks listlessly watch, has agreed to audition Amyl Nitrate for a "Eurovision song contest." Beyond being the key slip-sync sequence in the film, this performance of "Rule, Britannia" is significant for other reasons. Apparently, the "starting point for *Jubilee* was Jarman's fascination with Jordan" (Wymer, *Jarman*, 54), which confers a certain auteurist overinvestment in the scene as well as in the earlier "Jordan's dance" sequence, discussed later.[3] Wymer goes on to describe "Rule, Britannia" as the film's "most memorable set piece" (59), suggesting, as I contend, that the sequence is overdetermined on a narrative and thematic level, and linking it structurally with classical-musical film-performance sequences. From another, entirely different angle, "Rule, Britannia" seems to be the one sequence in the film Vivienne Westwood liked, according to the text on her infamous T-shirt.

The scenes leading up to the audition performance of "Rule, Britannia" contain several details notable for how they anticipate the slip-sync effect. First, in the flat where the punks hang out, most are watching television (Siouxsie and the Banshees on *Top of the Pops*), while Bod (again Jenny Runacre, who has two roles), the leader, or "queen," of the mostly female punk gang, chants staccato verses from "Diamonds Are a Girl's Best Friend." Musically speaking, we hear a kind of song collage, two songs overlapping: a premier punk band in the background, mediatized on television; and in the auditory foreground, an ironic vamp on Marilyn Monroe and Hollywood female glamour. The film pushes the gold-digging subtext of the song to excess, since throughout these women scavenge and pillage and murder to get whatever they want. Such a music montage not only anticipates Madonna's postmodern pop appropriation of Marilyn, but also intimates the way punk's subversive stance depends upon taking to a perverted extreme everything at the conventional center of capitalist culture.

In any case, while they watch, Ginz rings on the phone, calling Bod to his studio for her opinion of his new act. Amyl, sitting there with Bod as she takes the call, asides to the camera that Bod is "in for a surprise" (unaware that Amyl herself is the new act). The sound of Ginz's demonic laugh bridges over a jarring straight cut from Amyl's knowing wink at the camera to the concert stage. As Ginz continues his laugh, now diegetic on the sound track, the camera reveals that both Bod and Amyl are already there. This transition creates a slippage, or at least an ambiguity, regarding the passage of time—a more typical sound bridge would more clearly convey the passage of time. Like the film's portrayal of Elizabeth I, such sound bridges come off as loosely "out of time" or unhinged in time: a slip within synchronization.

Before the audition begins, a tight close-up exposes Ginz concluding his laughter, then verbalizing a bemused, pernicious discourse. Apparently speaking to no one in particular (thus, by default, to the film-viewing audience), he pontificates on "the generation who forgot to lead their lives . . . too busy watching my endless movie . . . The media is their only reality; without me, they don't exist." He continues: "I sucked and I sucked and I sucked; I don't create power, I own it . . . If the music is loud enough, they won't hear the world falling apart." Probably inspired by Malcolm McLaren, the notorious punk impresario who would make similar pronouncements a few years later in *The Great Rock 'n' Roll Swindle* (discussed in the next chapter), this hyperbolic monologue frames Amyl's punk performance as being "short-circuited by a culture of Devourers" (James, *Power Misses*, 201). But it also intimates punk's complicity in its own exploitation. Additionally striking is Ginz's histrionic delivery of various acronyms, all suggestive of tyrannical corporate or governmental power: "IBM, BBC, MGM, KGB." The fact that "MTV" fits so perfectly here illustrates the film's uncanny foresight.

Once the audition begins, aspects of the mise-en-scène emphasize in/authenticity, further preparing for the slip-sync moment to come. Amyl appears on an oversized stage with a tacky fog machine, bombastic flashing lights, and a huge warped mirror behind her. No musicians are visible; Amyl "sings" (lip-syncs) to recorded music, a punk-metal version of "Rule, Britannia" (actually sung by Suzie Pinns). The only sense of this being "live" derives from the disturbing presence of Amyl's body—a wonderfully excessive, pretentious masquerade, to put it mildly. Decked out in a plastic Union Jack flag around her waist, black underwear, pink dishwashing gloves, a gold gladiator helmet, lime green tights, and garish Ziggy Stardust–style makeup, she struts about dispassionately, striking absurd, contorted poses. Her dance gestures combine striptease and military marching, mocking both. Such costuming and gesturing forcefully convey how punk pits its own excesses against and within those of mainstream nationalist commodity culture.

Close-ups reveal that Amyl makes little effort to lip-sync convincingly. She looks almost directly into the camera as the enigmatic, ominous "air raid" roars enter the hall and engulf the sound track; we also hear excerpts from Hitler's speeches. Other than suggesting the general specter of World War II–era fascism, it remains unclear under what pretext these ambiguously synchronized sounds intrude on the performance and the sound track. Near the end of the

3.1. *Losing track of the track: Jordan as Amyl Nitrate in* Jubilee *(1978),*
lip-syncing "Rule, Britannia" to someone else's voice.

song, visibly irritated, she completely loses track of the vocal track and stops moving her lips; yet her voice in the song continues without her.

While the camera style is relatively straightforward, the set design, acting, and audio mix invoke the double excess underlying slip-sync: on the one hand, her exaggerated, ironic costume and body gyrations; on the other, the technological artifice of the spectacle proceeding without her, rendering her a kind of extraneous, decorative accessory. Amyl ambivalently embraces this status. She snarls and glowers, annoyed at the performance exceeding her. But it becomes hard to distinguish such frustration from every other pose she strikes. She angrily and rudely displays her buttocks as she walks offstage before the song is done, her voice lingering without a body, the music fading conspicuously before she ducks behind the curtain.

✳ SLIP-SYNC, POLITICS, AND IN/AUTHENTIC PERFORMANCE

This ambivalence around sound track and performance, though distinctive to punk slip-sync, is mirrored in the scene's larger political tone and argument. Much of the disturbing, perhaps confusing effect of this music performance derives from the overlapping air-raid sounds and aural snippets of Hitler. Most readily interpreted as a virulent parody of British nationalism, these sound effects might also convey a longing "for a lost period of authentic national identity which can be contrasted to the sleazy and fake forms of patriotism circulating in the year of the Queen's Jubilee" (Wymer, *Jarman*, 60).[4] This exemplary slip-sync scene thus encapsulates some of the political contradictions within and around punk. But it also sketches a sound-image relation that dramatizes a disturbing erasure of any original sound presence.

Appearing over ten years before the authenticity scandals of the 1990s (and the postmodern theoretical essays they inspired), *Jubilee's* slip-sync mobilizes a deconstruction of film musical performance by rupturing lip-sync's implicit hierarchy of original to copy. By conspicuously slipping out of sync, Amyl exposes her voice as a copy, one that precedes and produces her "live" performance. The fact that it is not Jordan's but another singer's voice further deconstructs any originality or authenticity, invoking the sonic in/authenticity we discussed in *Singin' in the Rain, Blank Generation*, and *Illusions*. At the same time, her momentarily unsynced performing body becomes a remainder, a punk excess that stains the spectacle of simulation and the simulation of spectacle.

In his general discussion of authenticity in the film, Wymer makes a similar back-and-forth comment, which I see as accurate, about Jarman's take on punk in the film: "The authentic artistic individuality which he asserted so strongly against the sellout represented by punk could be found within punk itself" (*Jarman*, 67). The slip-sync performance strategy in the film crystallizes such in/authenticity, portraying punk as both utterly authentic in "its collapse of the distinctions between art and life" and utterly inauthentic in its "status as a repeatable performance, to be turned on and off at will" (66). Wymer, who links the question of punk authenticity with cinematic representation, comes down on the authentic side of in/authenticity. Riposting to the film's conclusion, mouthed by Ginz in the company of the punk gang and an aging, sequestered Hitler, that "they all sign up in the end one way or another," Wymer observes: "Except they don't *all* sign up," pointing to Viv, the "one true artist in the film," who is not present (67).

Ensuing scenes remix this slip-sync performance, further elaborating a collision between a resurrected avant-garde (punk) and the highly accommodating and insidious media culture of the approaching 1980s. This time in a recording studio, Ginz observes Amyl's friend Mad (Toyah Wilcox) and her band auditioning behind a glass booth, yielding the peculiar but appropriate effect of watching them inside a television monitor. Near the end of Mad's song, slip-sync occurs as she snarls her song lyrics furiously, losing her place and control, finally spitting on the glass.

In contrast to the previous "Rule, Britannia" number, this audition performance is more about Ginz's side of the glass; Mad's band, and by proxy punk music itself, is tightly contained, to be toyed with or observed from a safe distance. Indeed, there is a sense, in both Mad's and Amyl's audition performances, of Ginz as a "Grand Ventriloquist" figure, orchestrating the voices he appropriates (or insidiously causes to be disembodied) as spectacles of entertainment. The slip-sync moment marks a rupture in the fabric of such spectacle, a moment when Connor's active and passive ventriloquism become confused: who is singing and who is being sung?

During Mad's song, another member of the punk gang, Crabs (Little Nell), arrives with her discovery, Kid (Adam Ant), an aspiring punk singer she picked up in a diner. However much Mad's performance is rife with typical punk rage, pounding music, and screaming into the camera (at Ginz), Ginz himself has his hands coolly on the controls of the sound-mixing board, sliding the knobs up and down. Likewise, his eye drifts to the side, calmly evaluating the prize that Kid might turn out to be. In fact, Kid insists that he does not want to get "ripped off" while Mad slip-syncs in the recording booth that he would like to occupy. As in the previous slip-sync performance, live music, here at its rawest and most violent, is coded as highly mediated and manipulated. While Grossberg might view this and other punk films as co-opting authentic punk music by inauthentically visualizing it, one could argue that musical co-optation is precisely what these slip-sync performances critique.

Later, Kid will be both ripped off and ripped apart physically. Before the two gay punks in the gang, Angel (Ian Charleson) and Sphinx (Karl Johnson), warn him of this, we see another slip-sync performance sequence, another in a string of auditions for Ginz: Kid with his band, performing "Plastic Surgery Disaster." The filming and sound style is a bit different here, with a fluid, arcing camera that circles outward on a soundstage, first around the band, then behind the onlookers, Ginz and his entourage. The slip-sync effect is less visible or pronounced here, since much of the time Kid's back is to the camera. We hear the song but do not clearly see his voice coming from his spasmodically writhing body. Additionally, the clumsily tracking camera foregrounds the bodies that periodically obstruct our view of the performance.

An additional level of reflexivity in the sequence derives from Adam Ant basically playing himself as a rising punk–New Wave pop star, here rocking out in a performance that extratextually promotes Adam Ant (who, a few years later, as the film envisions, did become a huge New Wave star).[5] Another extratextual, or reflexive, dimension to this performance is that Jarman himself makes a cameo appearance as one of the observers. Along with the conspicuously moving camera, the presence of the auteur is not without import for the sequence, coding it as a more authentic moment of punk performance.

The fleetingness of such authenticity, however, is intimated just after the performance. And here too a kind of slip-sync occurs, suggesting Kid's future absorption by the media machine that will disembody him. When Angel comments, "You're great," Kid responds by uncertainly muttering, "Plastic surgery." Although perhaps a mistake in line delivery, his absurd response, very punk, yields the effect that this is all he is capable of saying, or that he is still "in the song," even though it is over. Angel and Sphinx go on to warn him of what awaits, using vocabulary that invokes slip-sync: Ginz wants to "steal" his voice, and Kid will become just another face on another album cover.

In the next scene, an unclear continuation of the previous one, bridged again by laughter (this time Kid's), Angel makes the significant statement "My generation is the blank generation," referencing not only the Who's prepunk mod anthem but also the Amos Poe documentary film with the same title, as well as the Richard Hell and the Voidoids song that inspired it. Most significant is Kid's reaction: he laughs at him, seems uninterested, and starts mimicking him with lip movements. Later, Kid will be punished for failing to heed their warning, when he is beaten up by cops. More importantly, his flippant punk lip mimicry foretells the contours and stakes of the slip-sync struggle during performance: to resist yet exploit the society of the spectacle.[6]

Another slip-sync scene later in the film pushes this idea further. Bod and the gang see drag queen Lounge Lizard (Wayne County) performing her hit "Paranoia Paradise" on television. In the film's characterization of her, Lounge Lizard seems to embody a gloating superfluous success, one that rides the back of punk but is not truly punk. The gang decides rather whimsically to go find her and murder her. We then cut to Lounge Lizard in her own dwelling, also watching herself on television. Lounge Lizard becomes so enthralled with her performing image (the exact contrary reaction to Bod's disgust) that she picks up a mic and sings along with herself, effecting yet another variation on the slip-sync motif.

Here, she doubles her vocals, slipping in and out of sync with the televised version and improvising some additional lyrics. It is a provocative slip-sync moment, since she does not lip-sync but actually sings over the televised vocal, exaggerating both the slipping effect and the fractured yet serialized postmodern identity it signifies. Not to be overlooked is the line she keeps repeating: "Paranoia paradise is gonna be the death of me"—which, of course, quickly comes true when the gang arrives and Bod lasciviously strangles her. Whereas previously discussed slip-sync scenes are driven by a punk perspective, here slip-sync becomes more conveniently associated with a certain narcissistic celebrity excess coded as utterly contrary to punk but also potentially as punk's ultimate fruition.

✴ OTHER SUBVERSIVE SLIPPAGES

Let us back away from these concrete illustrations of slip-sync performance and trace the more general notion of "slippery," or ambiguous, synchronization across the film. On a variety of levels, the film plays with synchronization in ways that elucidate the punk sensibility and the more general postmodern milieu of the late 1970s. The idea, for example, of discontinuous or fragmented time, or of a schizophrenic present tense, has been theorized as characterizing postmodern culture (Bruno, "Ramble City," 243–244). Therefore, the slip-sync performance gesture we observe in Amyl's audition is a musical incarnation—"musical" as medium but also as genre—of a more general sense of disordered time. One might justifiably invoke the "disordering of the senses," championed by Rimbaud (certainly a punk of his own time), to help explain how postmodern time disseminates a sanitized version of the modernist avant-garde sensibility throughout consumer culture, and how punk slip-sync reflects this.

Put differently, the recurrence of slip-sync in these punk films as an aesthetic strategy and a broad theme reflects the disordered time (perhaps the "new time-space compression," as David Harvey famously puts it) at the heart of late-1970s modernism as it evolved into the full-blown postmodern popular culture of the early 1980s. It is in the spirit of exploring this relation—between punk slip-sync and a broader cultural and theoretical context—that we turn to some other details of *Jubilee*.

Several casting choices create a kind of problematic doubling of characters and actors. Much of this derives from Jarman's commitment to a home-movie or amateur approach to feature filmmaking, for example, by utilizing friends in the cast and crew. But such ambivalent doubling can also be understood as an extension of the slip-sync concept, a kind of slippage in synchronization whereby body, actor, and character do not entirely unify or cohere as they do in traditional representation and narrative. As noted in the previous chapter, Jarman was able to employ two key actors from *The Rocky Horror Picture Show*: Richard O'Brien, who played Riff Raff and who wrote the original stage play and all of the music, and Little Nell (Nell Campbell), who played Columbia. Given the correspondences suggested previously among *Rocky Horror*, punk, excess, and cult film, one can confidently surmise that these "antistars" brought a reflexive resonance to *Jubilee*, a kind of underground celebrity buzz not unlike that fostered by Andy Warhol during the 1960s and 1970s. More pronounced than that regarding Adam Ant, who was still largely unknown at the time, the interpretive play, or slippage, between recognition and unfamiliarity becomes specially enhanced by the presence of these *Rocky Horror* faces within Jarman's "no future"–heritage mise-en-scène.

But let us also look at the first image of the film: the queen's dwarf (Helen Wellington-Lloyd), with dogs, in a high-key garden. Besides the fact that this actress will show up a few years later in *The Great Rock 'n' Roll Swindle* (discussed in the next chapter), her figure can be seen as a kind of cross-temporal link between Elizabethan imperial England and the punk milieu: the queen did keep a dwarf in her court, and her "freakishness" fits right in when they time-travel to punk England. Plus, the actress herself is an inside member of the McLaren-Pistols punk scene (Wymer, *Jarman*, 58).

I think she embodies a kind of slippage in time, an odd synchronization that is not entirely seamless. This notion is further enhanced when Ariel, granting the queen's request for knowledge through time travel, reveals to her "the shadow of this time"—again, a doubling, a synchronicity that is also a split, a difference within sameness. We cut to modern punk England and are greeted by the graffiti "post-modern" on a wall, insightfully underlining the link between Renaissance England as the dawn of the modern period (science, progress, capitalism, democracy, etc.) and late-1970s punk as a period after ("post") modernism, the concluding dissolution of the progressive aspirations associated with the modern era.

A more pronounced slippage effect regarding casting can be seen with the two brothers who are also lovers, and the female artist Viv (Linda Spurrier), who looks like them. Conspicuously defying casting as well as moral conventions, this aspect of the film articulates a profoundly disturbing slippage from fraternal kinship to homosexual romance via incest. Perhaps the film's most enlightened characters, the three mirror one another a little too much, suggesting a contrived resemblance, a bodily synchronization that is nevertheless slightly off. They form a circle of triangular reflection in which sameness haunts difference.

This casting feature—actors who look too much alike and who portray siblings as lovers—is itself doubled, as an inversion, in the actress who plays two roles. Jenny Runacre plays both the punk queen Bod and Queen Elizabeth. Perhaps influenced by the two actresses randomly alternating in the female lead role of Luis Buñuel's *That Obscure Object of Desire* (1977), Jarman implicitly proposes commonalities between Bod and Elizabeth by having both characters share the body of the same actress, a notion all the more disturbing because each characterization is so diametrically opposed to the other.

Not unrelated to the ambiguous identity of actor and character that concludes Nicholas Roeg's *Performance* (1970), the effect here is to unhinge the anticipated coherence between character, actress, and body; conventionally, these all need to fit together distinctly to form a fictional individual, and here they do not quite. Traditional, classical film performance relies upon clear demarcations of individuality and character. *Jubilee* undercuts, or slightly pries open, such individuality and, thus, the very notion of performance.

Other notable scenes illustrate further varieties and meanings of the slip-sync motif. For example, let us look into Amyl's opening monologue and the transition to the ensuing dance sequence. She speaks directly into the camera, though the rest of the punk gang is lounging around the flat, intermittently and listlessly responding to some of her comments. She introduces all of them to the camera but also pontificates on her punk idea of history and politics. The key concept, she explains, by directly citing *Rocky Horror*'s thesis, is "don't dream it, be it." Cognizant of significant theoretical roots reaching back beyond *Rocky Horror* to Dada, surrealism, and Antonin Artaud, Amyl tweaks the notion of "live your imagination" for the punk milieu, disaffectedly insisting on erasing the difference between art and everyday life, and between performance and authenticity. She recalls her first days of realizing this punk philosophy and of wanting "to defy gravity" by becoming a dancer.

A sound bridge of elegant classical music brings us, via a jarring straight cut, to a Super 8 film sequence of Jordan donning traditional ballerina tights and skirt and then performing ballet moves. However, the setting for her dance shocks with Dadaistic paradox: a bonfire in an industrial wasteland, where naked masked men stand around watching as books are burned. In this poetic, abstract sequence rife with potential meanings, I would emphasize the way an ambiguous, seductive impression of synchronization occurs, then gradually unravels (or slips apart). The music seems to go with her dance, but she very well may not have been dancing to this music at all. The effect being, in my interpretation of the sound mix, a distinct ambiguity whether it is sync or non-sync music, mobilizing but also dismantling the viewer's impulse to see and hear it as synced up. This is further underlined by the somewhat random use of fast and slow motion during certain portions of the dance. The cinematography enhances the subtle artifice of the sound track and mise-en-scène. The sequence is loosely coded as a memory or a flashback, but it does not really make sense as either.[7] Again, I see all these aspects as a kind of lateral articulation of the film's more realized slip-sync approach to musical performance: things appear to be in sync (coherent, unified), but are slightly not so.

Teasingly undoing synchronization while loosely preserving it creates a conspicuous textual fissure that resonates effectively with the punk-pastiche sensibility: imitating something, but with a difference. The aftermath of the dance sequence, to my mind, is relevant here. We return to the present in Amyl's room, where she continues her monologue. But now her voice is a nonsync voice-over instead of, as in the previous approach, a sync sound directly addressed to the camera. Now she does not look into the camera, and her voice has become disembodied. Interestingly, this voice seems to speak even more directly to us, coming apparently from within her inner ear and ours. It is as though her voice, having passed through the dance sequence, has slipped beyond her body, though it remains connected to it, since we view her body while hearing her voice.

Some sequences near the end of the film can also be read through the slip-sync lens, that is, as being indirect or conceptual variations on slip-sync. One sequence occurs inside the "palace of heavenly delights," a cathedral that has been transformed into a disco nightclub. Initially, the music we hear is a punk version of William Blake's "Jerusalem." The scene features characters dressed up and acting like Jesus and his apostles, moving almost Kabuki-like, artificially slow. Again, it is ambiguous whether this music is coming from the club or is playing nonsync on the sound track. When we cut back inside from a scene outside (Ginz's arrival to a fanfare), a more conventional disco song is now playing, and the camera moves around to show dancers and poseurs of all subcultural stripes, dancing together. Yet, again, a second look and listen reveal that the music and dancing do not sync up; the music seems to be dubbed over the sequence. Thus, we are confronted with a playful attempt to suggest sync sound—dancing to the music—within a disjunctive sound-image design that is fundamentally though ambiguously contrapuntal.

We also might note a related scene, one of the penultimate shots, quite fragmentary and obscure in nature. Chaos (Hermine Demoriane), the "French maid" for the punk gang, walks across a tightrope, alone in their flat. As she balances, she disrobes, appearing to be singing the Edith Piaf classic "Non, Je Ne Regrette Rien." But closer scrutiny reveals that in fact her singing voice is nonsync; her lips do not move, despite the low camera angle and the long shot distance working to imply that the voice comes from her. This is yet another ambiguous relation regarding synchronization that articulates a slippage or disconnect within the apparent unification of body and voice. This "slipped" or sloppy synchronization may simply reflect budgetary restrictions or unprofessional training; the casting of Jenny Runacre in two roles may be due to similar reasons. Such a materialist explanation of the slip-sync effect mitigates but does not minimize its vital expression of the punk aesthetic.

✳ "THE TIME IS OUT OF JOINT"

It comes as no surprise that the final sequences of the film emphasize disembodied voices, both within and outside the narrative. Let us consider how certain aspects of the film's sound track drift away from synchronized sound. In another intriguing variation on slip-sync, the sound track opens up and out, whereas the narrative folds together punk, entertainment, and fascism.

Chaos's song bridges and fades into the scene in which our punk girl gang rides with Ginz in his limo, arriving at his militarized mansion in the Dorset countryside. We learn at the checkpoint entry that blacks, homosexuals, Jews, and even Elvis have been banned ("to keep the riff raff out," Ginz's offscreen voice explains). Over several shots looking out from the car (though not clearly point-of-view shots), we hear the offscreen voices of our punk heroines uttering various sardonic and ironic comments about where they have ended up. Most of these express admiration for the impressive fortress: "It's wonderful, Borgia"; "Not all the good things have disappeared"; "It's a tragedy that fascism and freedom weren't compatible."

The next rather heavy-handed scene features all of them lounging alongside a retired Hitler in Ginz's salon, watching television, drinking, eating, laughing. Here the dialogue is clearly diegetic, crisply insinuating spatial and political complicity through sonic immediacy and intimacy. In this respect, we should note that a Nazi speech is also heard on the sound track, possibly but not clearly coming from the television. Perhaps the slip-sync strategy, which started out as an in/authentic form of punk resistance ("Rule, Britannia"), has devolved into an in/authentic form of punk collaboration (Nazi voices in and beyond the television).

This interpretation is further underlined by the Hitler character, who sports an abstract expressionist blazer while speaking directly into the camera, in German, about "artists" and "Leonardo da Vinci." Here too Ginz utters one of the film's most scathing lines, a kind of punk incrimination of punk: "They all sign up in the end, one way or another."[8] While the scene is a clear indictment of punk's embrace of its two "inner demons," popular culture (the television) and fascism (Hitler), I would also draw attention to the potent ambiguity obtaining in the scene, one not unrelated to the slip-sync strategy and motif. Bod gets up and leaves the room as all the rest laugh, toasting the television, not taking Hitler's babbling too seriously. Bod also toasts, shooting a glance directly into the camera, perhaps "confronting" the audience, perhaps exiting the scene to suggest another destiny for punk.

As it turns out, this scene is the film's penultimate scene; its real conclusion shifts to idyllic, glistening high-key images of the English coastline. The actress playing Bod, Jenny Runacre, indeed becomes the transition from one scene to the next, perhaps from one form of punk to another; her body slips across time and space from one role to the other (and one pole to the other). Here, Runacre's Elizabeth and her entourage (Dee, Ariel, and the lady-in-waiting dwarf) seek refuge from the "no future" they have entered.

Like the previous scene, this concluding sequence mixes diegetic and disembodied voices rather conspicuously, beginning with Dee and the queen conversing over extreme long shots of them. An ambient electronic score by Brian Eno furnishes the aural setting for the film's final slip-sync: Ariel's fully disembodied, nondiegetic voice-over, a lyrical Shakespearean monologue beginning with the brief chant "there and back, there and back"—a phrase that can be read as an intriguing distillation of the slip-sync formal gesture.

This gesture occurs most vividly at the close of this final monologue, which is also the close of the narrative, when Ariel narrates "the Phoenix" calling to Dee and Elizabeth: "Come—away!" Both words uttered in a dramatic whisper, the first part of the call, "come," is heard as the film fades to black; the second part of the call, "away," is heard as the cast credits appear. Thus does Ariel's voice—and in many ways the "voice" of the film itself—slip from his speaking lips, away from his body, across the scene, and beyond the narrative.

This is an antidote coda, most critics agree, to the previous scene's punk sellout to fascist mass media (Pencak, *Films of Derek Jarman*, 132–140)—a hopeful vision of the past in the future, and the future in the past. Perhaps we are meant to read the inscription of authenticity in the film's concluding in/authentic slippage, or movement, from sync to nonsync sound, from dialogue to voice-over, from speaking bodies to voices ambiguously outside history and beyond time.

Indeed, *Jubilee*'s slip-sync performance strategy engages a deeper challenge to linearity and synchronization. This is signaled within the "Rule, Britannia" sequence by the overlapping World War II air-raid sounds, invoking the end of imperial Britain and the commencement of the postwar consumer culture that culminates in the fulminating punk subculture. But it also permeates the film's time-travel framing device.

Queen Elizabeth traveling into the future with the help of her muse Ariel (who was borrowed from *The Tempest*—Jarman's next film, by the way) suggests a visionary power, a way for literature to harness the imperialist project. In this way, the queen slips out of her own time and her experience of political power into an other future time; Jarman here displays a distinctly Blakean sense of insight.[9] Conversely, Amyl, in postapocalyptic London, looks back to the past via her first-person narration and diary, deconstructing history from a punk or queer perspective.

In other words, the film's core dialogue and dialectic (Elizabeth and Amyl) trace an historical arc that is unhinged from conventional linear time. Chris Barber keenly relates this "retrogressive" notion of time to the punk motto "no future," a cyclical, Nietzschean sense of time that "does not look back to the past for solace," but that challenges consumer society's myth of progress ("No Future Now," 52–54). Attali's notion of noise as prophetic music likewise seems oddly dramatized here: punk noise breaks through the time barrier and breaks open timing—just as Elizabethan poetical-alchemical noise does, creating a circle of noise, of composing, that exceeds time itself.

As our consideration of *Jubilee* draws to a close, let us recall that the "sync" in slip-sync (or lip-sync) denotes synchronization and connotes a unified, coherent stitching together of elements (that is, a simultaneity, whether of voice and body or sound and image). *Jubilee*'s narrative and temporal displacements, its slippages across time, become a portal to the film's larger political critique and articulation of difference. The film in this way sketches a temporal disjunction or slippage in relation to music, reproduction, and the body that in turn is rearticulated in the ambiguity of the time-travel narrative as well as in some of the narration devices (editing, sound bridges, etc.).

In fact, *Jubilee* might be seen to engage in a kind of "transtextual" slip-sync, a concatenation of refracted personas outside of time: Ariel, a slave to Prospero's power; Prospero's lament over the power of representation; Elizabeth's Shakespeare; Shakespeare's Elizabeth; Jarman's Elizabeth; punk Caliban; Amyl as Prospero; Riff Raff as John Dee; and so on. Again, with *Rocky Horror* as a crucial ur-text in mind, let us note that this transtextual slipstream also possesses a transsexual dimension. The film's female-feminist-gay point of view is crucial here as a revision of patriarchal history, with Elizabeth, Amyl, and most of the other girl punks, as well as Ariel and the gay punks, all coded through a feminized, alternative masculinity.

In one of the first and best critical discussions of punk, Simon Frith and Trevor Horne conclude by emphasizing the space punk made for women, or, rather, the space women made for themselves inside punk. They also emphasize that punk's devotion to artifice and visual style was intricately linked to its challenge of straight gender codes (*Art into Pop*, 155–161). This helps us appreciate how and why most of the punk musicals feature highly unconventional female protagonists. As radically illustrated in *Jubilee*, the punk slip-sync performance gesture pokes subversive fun at the gender norms that enclose classical narrative and that establish the borders of dominant cultural attitudes.

Jubilee's slip-sync therefore reverses conventional textuality and language, unhinging the mechanisms of spectacle, Elizabethan and otherwise, and disrupting the flows of commodity fetishism, consumerism, and celebrity culture. Slip-sync renegotiates the tension underlying musical performance, the tension between visual spectacle as display, as ritual of power, and prophecy as voice, narration, discourse—a different, vocalized kind of "vision." As articulated here in *Jubilee*, and as a critical overture to ensuing variations, punk slip-sync breaks into and breaks open the very fabric of representation, dramatizing the disjunction between body and voice that history and representation must—but can never fully—repress.

CHAPTER 4

THE PUNK MEETS THE GODFATHER

THE GREAT ROCK 'N' ROLL SWINDLE

J UBILEE'S SLIP-SYNC articulates a music-image sensibility that critically comments upon new aesthetic, technological, and promotional music-industry practices. *The Great Rock 'n' Roll Swindle* (1979), Julien Temple's experimental documentary on Malcolm McLaren and the Sex Pistols, shares its formal sensibility and cynical, self-reflexive tone with *Jubilee*. Incorporating a collage of cinematic modes (animation, documentary, mockumentary, music video, narrative, diary, etc.), the film focuses on Malcolm McLaren's narration of his creation of the group.[1] Like Amyl's in *Jubilee*, his confrontational and irreverent first-person address makes several subversive links between punk, rock history, and official British history, many of them loosely illustrated with makeshift, playfully staged sequences. More significantly, the film contains numerous mock-musical numbers that extend punk slip-sync in a very different direction from that of *Jubilee*.

In many ways, *Jubilee* and *The Great Rock 'n' Roll Swindle* (hereafter *Swindle*) belong next to each other. Released in the UK in 1979 and the United States in 1980, *Swindle* was in production when *Jubilee* had its London premiere. Indeed, Temple and Jarman could be considered artistic kin, both emerging from the same milieu of late-1970s experimental British film. More significantly, both directors had formative early encounters with the Sex Pistols. Jarman's proximity to punk and the Sex Pistols we have read about previously; apparently, he shot the earliest known footage of the band, from their first gig, which Temple used in *Swindle* (Savage, *England's Dreaming*, 498).

But Temple too was hanging around the London docks where the Sex Pistols were rehearsing for their first gigs. Coming across one of these rehearsals, he immediately got the inspiration to film them and their scene. It thus makes sense that both films possess an irreverent tone and a DIY filmmaking style. And yet both films have been criticized for being inauthentic appropriations of punk. Again, for us, it is better to view them as in/authentic.

Most histories of punk tell more or less the same story, which I vulgarize here: Malcolm McLaren, while hanging around New York's underground punk scene near Greenwich Village in the mid-1970s, was impressed especially by the New York Dolls, whom he offered to manage. They said no thanks; but he took what he learned from this earliest New York punk-rock scene, which included Patti Smith, Blondie, Iggy Pop, Television, and Talking Heads, back to London, where he "manufactured" the Sex Pistols, galvanizing the London punk-music scene, around 1976. The accuracy of this mythology has been hotly debated, especially by band members, including Rotten and McLaren, and other punk-rock celebrities of the time. Such difference of opinion is well evidenced in Temple's more recent punk documentary, a sort of sequel to *Swindle*, *The Filth and the Fury* (2000), which purports to give the band's side to the story told in *Swindle* by McLaren. Nevertheless, McLaren's legendary success as a maestro of punk led to a 1988 exhibit at the New Museum of Contemporary Art in New York, titled "Impresario: Malcolm McLaren and the British New Wave."[2]

From the start of the Sex Pistols phenomenon, McLaren apparently had always envisioned a film as part of the spin. Temple, at the time attending the National Film School, had filmed many of the Sex Pistols' earliest gigs, as described above. He approached band manager McLaren, who initially rejected the young novice in favor of hoped-for film deals with Warner Bros. and Twentieth Century–Fox. These fell through, as did various other configurations for a film crew as exploitation-cinema names like Russ Meyer, Jonathan Kaplan, Roger Ebert, and Pete Walker came and went.

Finally, after the band broke up in 1978, McLaren agreed to work with Temple to complete the film. It is interesting to note that the film was financed primarily with music-industry money from the Virgin label, and attracted producers Don Boyd, who would later produce some Jarman films, and Jeremy Thomas, an art-cinema producer working with Nicholas Roeg and Bernardo Bertolucci, among others. To me, this signifies punk's peculiar, perhaps paradoxical status as being both inside and outside, both for and against, the music-culture industry.

In any case, McLaren is clearly the dynamic, tyrannical "visionary" here, overseeing the completion of the film. Temple explains on the audio commentary on the *Swindle* DVD that McLaren, involved in all kinds of lawsuits involving the film and the rights to the band's music, threatened to fire Temple, but then agreed to keep him on as a "slave." Somehow they continued to

slap the film together, adding more recent footage shot without Rotten's participation, to come up with the brilliantly mishmashed (and, thus, brilliantly
punk) final product. Hailed upon its release by *Variety* as the "*Citizen Kane*"
of rock movies (McGillivray, "Twenty-five Years On," 16–20), *Swindle*, according to Temple, was McLaren's attempt at producing a kind of anti-pop-music
film, although he had his name removed from the film's credits. For Temple,
the film sets out to destroy the Sex Pistols' revered mythological status by ruth-
lessly exposing how the whole phenomenon was a spectacular sham, a sick joke
played on the music industry.

Regardless of how it came into being or what its intentions were, *Swindle* reflects punk in all its contradictions, and on multiple levels. Like *Jubilee*, *Swindle* can be characterized by an overall punk-filmmaking sensibility:
excessive, amateur, DIY, underground. Also like *Jubilee*, *Swindle*'s approach to
music performance can be described as anti-Hollywood or mock-Hollywood.
This indeed is what K. J. Donnelly means when he calls *Swindle* a "punk anti-
musical," one that "offers an updated and postmodern image of the end of
utopia through a dissolution of the film musical as a form" ("Entertainment
and Dystopia," 171). Donnelly reads the film's articulation of "the essence of
punk—its attitude" through its parody of the musical film genre as well as its
bricolage of musical and documentary forms (173). His close and lucid analysis
of the film emphasizes how it disingenuously inhabits the musical and documentary, how it is, thus, a swindle in its formal features, suggesting an unten-
able status both outside and inside the genre.

★ "IT'S A SWINDLE": MUSIC-IMAGE MISMATCH

Swindle at its core is McLaren's macabre walking tour through the phenomenon of punk. Taking full pompous credit for it, he also paints punk as intrinsically a sellout.[3] Donnelly puts it this way: the film "destroys punk in order to
launch the solo career of renaissance man McLaren, who . . . narrates the story
as a succession of aphoristic lessons and is the final animated figure seen in
the end title sequence" (173). Corresponding to this sham attitude is the film's
overall sloppy, rowdy approach to the editing and the sound mix, which often
enhances the slip-sync effect, as we will see.

The opening credit titles, in distinctive punk cut-up lettering, introduce
McLaren as "the embezzler," Sid Vicious as "the gimmick," and Johnny Rotten
as "the collaborator." The eerie, rather disturbing opening of the film foretells
the slip-sync approach: a tight close-up of McLaren donning a rubber bondage mask and looking directly into the camera: a striking mock close-up or
anti-close-up, since we cannot see his eyes or face at all behind the mask. On

the sound track: low, atonal nondiegetic music; heavy breathing; his raspy, loudly whispering voice-over. But no (or perhaps no): it may not be voice-over, since he may be speaking (sync) from behind the mask. That is, this image-music mix emphasizes slip-sync ambiguity and exaggerates the aural excess of a potentially disembodied voice, one that seems as if it should and perhaps does belong ("perhaps" being the operative term here, for slip-sync) to this strange face without a face.

The first scene from *Swindle* I want to discuss in terms of slip-sync is the film's title-song sequence. This, the film's first musical number, was filmed after the Sex Pistols' dissolution in 1978. Rotten and McLaren had had a severe falling out, and Rotten would have nothing to do with the film, unlike the other three, who appear throughout.[4] Presumably written for the film, the song is performed by the three remaining Sex Pistols plus a couple of backup singers as a "1978 Audition," with the subheading "Anyone can be a Sex Pistol."

During the song, one singer after another comes up on stage, takes the mic, and sings a verse or two. The first singer wears a life mask made from Rotten himself; at the close of the song, all the singers collect on stage, one of them, Edward "Tenpole" Tudor, spasmodically shouting rock history tidbits at the camera. Apparently McLaren and Temple had posted a trade-paper ad to replace Rotten, and many of the singers we see were actual respondents; supposedly, some of the lyrics were created by them on the spot (Temple and Salewicz, DVD audio commentary). A gag spectacle staged specifically for the film, the performance is intercut with the credits: Helen of Troy (the dwarf who appeared in *Jubilee*, here McLaren's mute confidante) scrambling to put together the letters of the film title—at the end correcting "swine" to "swindle" (in perhaps an instance of slip-spell).

This "audition" sequence mobilizes slip-sync from a kind of flip-side angle: instead of one singer losing the vocal track, here multiple singers create a "rotating" vocal track, "slipping" in and out of sync. In another synchronization twist, it appears that the band is "play syncing," or miming, to a pre-recorded instrumental track. At various points we clearly see drummer Paul Cook and bassist Sid Vicious blatantly faking it; in a playful blip echoing *A Hard Day's Night* and *Head* (1968), one quick shot has Vicious on the drums, Cook on bass! The wild spontaneous energy of the amateur lead vocalists lends authenticity, dramatizing the DIY theme so prevalent in punk. Yet the sporadic rotation of singers, combined with the miming band, evokes a more cynical flaunting of artifice through sound-image disjuncture. The droning refrain "rock-and-roll swindle" reinforces the ironic tone underlying, and undermining, such "audience participation," the last singer stating directly into the camera as the song ends, "It's a swindle."

But aesthetically too, it is a swindle: the image of live music performance is false, a good illustration of Auslander's "liveness"; or at least there is a gap, a slippage, between image and music. For Donnelly, the number "seems to be a reconstruction": "It is not a reality but a possible reality being presented as an aestheticised history" ("Entertainment and Dystopia," 174). This is especially enhanced by the cinematic presentation of rotating singers, a kind of jump-cut pasting of image over music that is not quite logical. Further coding such punk in/authenticity as ultimately a gag, a gimmick—a swindle—is the way the singers ape Johnny Rotten, Elvis Presley, and other rock stars. Temple him-self has commented that the film was intended as a joke to mock the earnest critical reception of the Sex Pistols, and that possibly McLaren ended up tak-ing such "spoofing" as "reality" (McGillivray, "Twenty-five Years On," 20).

The sequence also invokes larger questions of punk performance and the tension between the visual and the aural—a tension underlying the slip-sync moment, when sound and image, focalized on the performing body, come slightly undone. Donnelly, for example, sees the sequence as having to com-pensate visually for the absence of Johnny Rotten's singing ("Entertainment and Dystopia," 174). The various conundrums of the sequence are also sug-gested by David Huxley, who vacillates regarding *Swindle*'s take on punk, stat-ing on the one hand that the vocals are essential to punk sensibility, and on the other that visuals are the "*key* elements in the construction of 'punk'" ("'Ever Get the Feeling,'" 95).

Such comments invoke Grossberg's general derision of visualized rock, since *Swindle* as a film constitutes a second swindle, the first being the content of the film, McLaren's story of theft. I am contending instead that punk music (and perhaps all rock music, but that is another matter) can and should be seen and heard as essentially visual. In this sense, whether by design or not, *Swindle* and all the punk films of our cycle are authentic expressions of punk, meaning, more accurately, in/authentic expressions of punk, since one of the distinctive things punk does is to problematize authenticity itself (Huxley, "'Ever Get the Feeling,'" 82–83).

✗ PUNK SLIP-SYNC AS MOCK-MUSICAL PERFORMANCE

Many of the other musical-performance numbers in the film employ a some-what different variation of slip-sync, though one still understood as a punk take on lip-sync that blatantly does not sync in some way. In this film, such punk slip-sync often becomes specifically an effect of the overall mock-doc and mock-musical approach. For example, throughout the film there are musi-cal numbers in which the singer "sings" along to a music sound track that is

4.1. *Malcolm sends up the musical: flannel bathrobe, "Cash from Chaos" T-shirt prominently on display, and some flamboyantly sloppy lip-syncing. It's a swindle.*

entirely beyond or outside the fictional logic of the scene; not only are no instruments visible or relevant, but the singing voice itself seems to belong to someone else. In this sense, *Swindle*, like *Jubilee*, anticipates the tone of the soon-to-be MTV; it also hooks up formally with the unnerving though amusing slip-sync excesses of *Pennies from Heaven* (1981), in which the actors lip-sync to famous singers' versions of the songs.[5] *Swindle*'s playful, reflexive slip-sync parodies the musical genre, according to punk's distinctive cut-up look and feel, with all the seams of classical song and dance exposed.

The first of these mock-musical numbers, not surprisingly, is enacted by McLaren himself. While pontificating to Helen as the two put up flyers in a downtrodden mausoleum, an orchestral jazz score absurdly arrives on the sound track. McLaren takes his cue and "bursts into song," "You Need Hands," with Helen as his mute Ginger. Considering the song's politically conservative associations (Donnelly, "Entertainment and Dystopia," 176), McLaren tries too hard to achieve a camp effect: he pretends to seriously lip-sync to his own voice, slipping out of sync—such slippage being the point.[6]

This mock-musical approach aptly conveys the crucially irreverent punk pastiche-parody sensibility that also distinguishes, for example, punk fashion (Hebdige, *Subculture*, 106–109; Donnelly, "Entertainment and Dystopia," 174). It likewise serves as a carnivalesque framework for dramatizing punk's paradoxical attitude toward the mainstream music industry and rock-and-roll culture in general. Paradoxical because McLaren and the Pistols incorporate this culture they despise, pushing it to subversive excess; carnivalesque because they employ a theatrical mimicry to achieve an inversion of roles and expectations.[7]

Slip-sync becomes part of this imitation of musical convention, but with a difference. For example, as Steve Jones mimes a private dick trying to track down McLaren (the main fictionalized thread running throughout the film), record-company executives are repeatedly ridiculed. One sequence featuring a series of their shocked reactions to the band is followed by Jones having an absurd "red light" encounter with a stripper, slip-syncing to his own version of Eddie Cochran's "Lonely Boy." It becomes over-the-top ridiculous: the song not only plays nonsync, but also belongs to another time, the 1950s (and is thus doubly nonsync); he pretends altogether listlessly to be singing while he tumbles with her. A joke from a musical-performance standpoint, the scene also mocks the earnest reactions of music-industry insiders.

A similarly silly example occurs earlier, in the cartoonish sequence mocking the band's record deal with EMI. This time drummer Paul Cook plays a baby in a crib in a gingerbread house, slip-syncing to a song he and Jones recorded after the band's break-up, "Silly Thing" (it looks as if either Jones or McLaren is dressed up as Santa Claus, trying to break into the house). Whether conceived by design or not, the formal attitude here is that the musical genre, and visualized music generally, is a sham, yet one to be ludically and lewdly embraced. Appropriately, the cartoon-style mise-en-scène and slip-sync sound design lead directly into one of the film's animation sequences.

Yet another brazenly absurd example of mock-musical slip-sync occurs near the end of the film, in an oddly reflexive film-within-a-film sequence. Still supposedly tracking McLaren, an exasperated Jones enters a theater to watch a film called *Who Killed Bambi?* This film within a film, whose title refers to one of the original titles of the *Swindle* film project, purports to mock-document how, after the band's break-up, Jones and Cook ventured to Brazil to jam with the famed criminal Ronnie Biggs and hang out with fugitive Nazis while Sid toured France.[8] In the lobby of the theater, Tenpole Tudor appears again as the concession clerk; he periodically "performs" the absurd title song to the film, "Who Killed Bambi?" The nostalgic, entirely inappropriate, classical Hollywood-style orchestration clashes with his flamboyant slip-syncing. His apparently signature performance style of flailing about epileptically very much underlines the "slip" in slip-sync. Donnelly sheds much light on the performance, which for him is emblematic of the film's excessive parody: "Tudor has a highly idiosyncratic singing style, which can be characterised as punk or a parodic 'punk,' while his visual demeanour burlesques the singing process. Tudor's voice is like a sampler of vocal effects. The song itself is a spoof" ("Entertainment and Dystopia," 176–177). We might also note how the song that belongs with the film being projected is heard (and "seen") in the lobby adjacent to the screening—another kind of slippage in music-image synchronization.

But surely the best, or at least most spectacular, examples of these mock-musical slip-sync performances are those involving Sid Vicious in France. Sid slip-syncs to his own surprisingly faithful versions of different Eddie Cochran songs. He performs the first, "Something Else," in a small dark apartment, sporting only his slinky underwear (as Nancy looks on, sneering). The number in no way pretends to identify the music source, evoking very much an amateur, "home movie" musical number. Like the sequences of Jones watching himself in the film—indeed, he is watching this scene—here the reflexive dimension becomes excessively over the top. Mainly, Sid performs for himself, admiring himself in a mirror while mock singing, slipping his lips around a voice that does not seem to be his. The few quick cutaways to Nancy watching him add an acerbic and ironic commentary. Embodying punk mimicry, Sid basks in his foolish, lewd attempt at playacting. As in many other numbers in the film, the excessive slip-sync here becomes doubled in that it mocks the whole idea of staging a filmed musical number as well as his own idiotic attempt; a kind of carnival nihilism pervades this punk destruction-cum-deconstruction of filmed music performance.

A few scenes later, Sid rides a motorcycle through the French country-side, slip-syncing to Cochran's "C'mon Everybody." Wistfully alluding to the motorcycle sequences of *The Wild One*, *If. . .*, *Girl on a Motorcycle*, and *Easy Rider*, Sid's lip-sync is so feckless and reckless it becomes one more spectacle of slippery silliness, not unlike similar scenes from pop musicals like *A Hard Day's Night* or *Head*, though with none of their innocence. The blatantly non-synchronous sound track creates what I would describe as a parodied synchresis (again, Michel Chion's term for sound and image appearing to naturally go together). Like the Johnny Rotten mask the first fan rips off his face in the film's credit sequence described above—only to be "doing" Johnny again, beneath the mask—here Sid's performing, "singing" body becomes a mask that willfully slips across the visual surface of the film as well as the aural surface of the sound track.

Sid's "C'mon Everybody" is crosscut with McLaren at a train station, still lecturing Helen about the wisdom of his exploits. On the train, a bizarre narrative digression seems at least tangentially related to punk slip-sync. Vividly recalling the Lounge Lizard scene from *Jubilee*, McLaren has a campy pop star strangled so that he can "hide" in the persona of the pop star and evade Jones and the authorities as he flees the country. When Jones discovers the body in a bathroom on the train, a tape deck is in the corpse's mouth and McLaren's voice is coming out—yet another kind of slip-sync, one in which lo-fi technology literally displaces a human voice and identity, yet also covers over (while exposing) his slipping away. Also of note are the oblique references to Nicholas Roeg and Donald Cammell's *Performance* (1970): a fleeting shot of McLaren disguised in the back of a limo recalls the Mick Jagger–James Fox confusion at the end of that film. Additionally, one of the actors from *Performance* makes a cameo appearance a few scenes earlier. One might consider *Performance*, in its play with identity and its use of music, as a kind of modernist proto-slip-sync film. Indeed, according to Donnelly, this murder sequence on the train is detritus from the original *Who Killed Bambi?* script, which called for rock star "M. J.," based on Mick Jagger (star of *Performance*), to be murdered by the Sex Pistols. So these *Performance* allusions seem somewhat contrived ("Entertainment and Dystopia," 172–173).[9]

Sid's performance of "My Way" in a Paris nightclub, near the very end of the film, is perhaps the most famous scene in the film—partially because of Alex Cox's remake of it for his biopic *Sid and Nancy*. We will consider Cox's version in Chapter 9; for now, let us note that, ironically, Temple's original version does not really partake of slip-sync. The performance does partake of the film's mock-musical approach: Sid's grotesque mimicry of Sinatra; the musicians not being visible; Sid firing a gun on his audience; the whole stagy, artificial context of the song. Yet the synchronization is pretty tight and not especially foregrounded. As we will see, Cox's version turns out to be much more intriguing, as one of the best and most famous articulations of slip-sync.

★ SLIP-SYNC, RACE, AND "THE REAL"

One last example of such mock-musical slip-sync performance we should take note of is the disco sequence, especially interesting for how it invokes issues of race more overtly than previously discussed numbers do. McLaren enters a nightclub called The New Oldies Club, where disco is blasting. Up on stage, a black singing group, the Black Arabs, is "performing" a disco version of the Pistols' "Pretty Vacant." It soon becomes clear that slip-sync is at play, since the group's vocalizing gestures variously mismatch the sound track. McLaren has positioned himself up in a rafter, overlooking the mayhem, singing along and having a ball. Jones is outside trying to get into the club, to no avail. The MC of the disco group voices another one of McLaren's lessons, number 5, about "BS-ing the record company."

No doubt the filmmakers probably conceived of the sequence as yet one more carnivalesque absurdity poking fun at punk. Moreover, this musical performance is one among many throughout the film in which the Pistols' music slips into another musical genre—whether orchestral, piano lesson, disco, or

French street music. Such radical disjunction between original version and cover version suggests another stylistic variation on slip-sync. But it also betrays McLaren's brazen and perhaps ludicrous self-promotion, his insistence on inserting "his" punk music into a canon of recognizable standards.

In this particular disco-hip-hop scene, the canonization of the Sex Pistols dovetails with another hierarchy—the hierarchy of the racial other. I do not deny that there may be some affection and respect for black music here, or even a suggestion of how punk and disco could come together under the same musical-political agenda. There is also a kind of inversion of the slip-sync operation we discussed in Julie Dash's *Illusions*: there, the black voice and talent was appropriated, made invisible in the service of the visible white female performer; here, the white punk voice and talent is appropriated, revised by a black musical style that is visibly and audibly privileged.

And yet, the sequence cannot quite shake associations with some of the same old stereotypes: McLaren is above the black singers, and behind the scenes, orchestrating everything (the editing and low angles emphasize this); the detective-noir narrative pursuit likewise interrupts the musical performance, thus in some way framing it. Especially here, this film noir imagery evokes the whole *Chinatown* legacy in which the detective antihero ventures into a dark (dark-skinned), exotic, and dangerous part of town.[10] Glancing back to *Jubilee*, we can link this scene with the church disco scene, although there, a more sexually and racially diverse crowd intimates a merging of disco and punk. We can also link this scene to the overinvested moments when black characters appear in *Sid and Nancy*, especially at the end, when black disco-dancing kids precede Sid's entry into Nancy's limo of death.

My point here is to ask that we not lose sight of the insidious sexual and racial politics at work within all this carnivalesque mockery and parody. McLaren, Jones, and Vicious portray themselves as white, big-boy punk celebrities; Helen becomes McLaren's silent (silenced?) listener, a kind of surrogate audience in the film for the audience of the film; Nancy is given one shot; blacks are given one token scene of disco dancing; indeed, no female characters are developed in the slightest, most of them luridly associated with hard-core sex.[11] Such radical mockery becomes not so radical if we hold the film up against this tradition of patriarchal white "bad boys." It is perhaps no coincidence that both films in this study featuring male slip-sync are grandiloquent biographies of the Sex Pistols: *Swindle* and *Sid and Nancy*. Such persistence of white patriarchy within punk, reflected to a degree in most of the punk musicals, is precisely what *Nice Coloured Girls* overturns in the context of urban Australian nightlife. Testifying to that film's more progressive politics, we should take note of the one punkish male working at the nightclub, who helps the "coloured girls." Though fleeting and oblique, his appearance seems to be feminized, possibly coded as gay, offering a visionary counterpart to the punk masculinity of *Swindle*.

In the vein of highlighting the conservative within the subversive, I would conclude by questioning much of the supposedly real concert footage that appears throughout *Swindle*. For example, when the band plays on the boat for the queen's jubilee celebration, we seem to be hearing the original studio recording; yet the concert footage is "live." Though most of it does convincingly sync up, there are a few moments when the song does not sync with the players. Perhaps for convenience, or for some technical reason, the director chose to synchronize the original recordings with these performances of them. There is nothing wrong with that, but it adds yet another layer to the slip-sync phenomenon I am analyzing.

In questioning the veracity of some of the concert footage, Huxley ponders whether "the sense of audience excitement at the group's performance may be totally manufactured" ("'Ever Get the Feeling,'" 94). Donnelly too phrases carefully his descriptions of the so-called documentary portions of the film, which "try to give an impression of unmediated honesty, reconstructing the group as if live on stage" ("Entertainment and Dystopia," 175). An effect of punk's anti-record-company attitude and DIY production values, this flaunted ambiguity around the "real or live" question also articulates the simulation effect overtaking the music and image cultures generally—the advent of "liveness" and the predominance of sloppy contrivance or obvious artifice as the norm. Such in/authenticity hovers around Jon Savage's characterization of the film as a "stress nightmare," citing McLaren's explanation of the purpose behind the film: "To lie incredibly. We did it quite successfully. The irresponsible nature of it all was the key to it" (*England's Dreaming*, 499–500).

CHAPTER 5

YOUR FACE IS A MESS

BREAKING GLASS

"**S**TEREO TV: An Idea Whose Time Has (Almost) Come," by Martin Porter; opposite, an ad for Scotch brand audiocassettes with the tagline "When we were breaking new ground in cassette sound, others were still breaking glass." The article and advertisement face each other on opposing pages of *Rolling Stone* (September 17, 1981). Not surprisingly, the content of the article and the ad complement more than oppose each other. Porter's piece reports the utopian projections of industry insiders regarding the advent of stereo television, especially since MTV just debuted on cable in early August of that year. Taking a poke at competitor Memorex, recordings on whose cassettes could supposedly break glass, the Scotch ad sings the praises of its new Metafine tape, "the world's first metal tape," promising to bring "true, pure sound."

Both texts might appear charmingly old-fashioned to us today (though one wonders whether someday cassettes will make a retrochic comeback similar to that of LPs). Yet both articulate the progressive paradigm driving developments in high-fidelity sound quality and its connection to visualized music, anticipating today's enhanced CDs, DVDs, and podcasts.[1] Given the ad's coincidental mention of "breaking glass"—the title of the British punk film discussed in this chapter—I will make use of these texts as a stepping-stone to what both implicitly reject and repress: the punk-rock movement.

Waning and probably dead by 1980, transmogrified into one of its many afterlives (techno, New Wave, LA hardcore, etc.), punk nevertheless stood brazenly as the rabid antidote to MTV, high fidelity, and everything stereo television stands for. Punk ironically achieved the "true, pure sound" the ad alludes to but misunderstands: the true, pure, raw sound of punk rock's noisy music. Punk proudly embraces its status as Other (let us capitalize it), "still breaking glass," according to the ad. The ad and the article look forward, beyond punk, to new technologies of sound and image. The punk films coming out around this time conveyed frustrated suspicion of and irreverent resistance to this dominant trend, even while they became rather unwillingly swept up in it.

In rather distinct ways, both *Swindle* and *Breaking Glass* embrace the "breaking glass" attitude implicitly dissed by the ad and the article. "Breaking glass" characterizes both films' celebration of music as loud noise that potentially shatters the "glass" of mainstream high-fidelity televisual culture. Slip-sync proves to be a crucial strategy for each film's deployment of such "noise." Attali's core sense that "noise is violence" is relevant here. Let us think of "breaking glass" as noise that "disturbs": "To make noise is to interrupt a transmission, to disconnect, to kill. It is a simulacrum of murder" (*Noise*, 26). Such a conception of noise, while perhaps theoretically exaggerated, helps us appreciate the operations of slip-sync throughout these punk films.

Unlike *Swindle*, *Breaking Glass* taps more clearly into the classical narrative tradition of the Hollywood musical, tracking the tragic arc of a postpunk diva. Despite being so little known, the film deals incisively with punk's fusion with New Wave and techno, and contains numerous compelling musical performances. Additionally, the film's postpunk distance and stronger narrative development yield a more elaborate and lucid critique of punk. As we will see, slip-sync occurs most dynamically in the opening credit sequence, yet transpires more loosely throughout the narrative.

Breaking Glass also offers a vision of punk on the cusp of the Thatcher 1980s that is as sobering as that of *Jubilee*, and much less ludic or parodic than that of *Swindle*. In his distinctly unimpressed overview of the British punk-film cycle, Donnelly gives the film a few sentences, noting that it "demonstrates vividly the iconography of post-punk music," but that it "dressed up a rather traditional story in punk apparel" ("British Punk Films," 110). I invite us to push a bit further this accurate but parsimonious description. Let us reconsider how the film might intriguingly apply punk aesthetics to the musical genre and independent film in its portrayal of punk–New Wave singer Kate, played effectively by Hazel O'Connor, who composed and performed all the film's songs.

On paper, *Breaking Glass* does seem to represent a kind of sellout by punk to mainstream commercial cinema; or, conversely, popular cinema's appropriation of punk in the diluted form of a New Wave musical. The film reflects a confluence of independent sensibility and commercial production values, a confluence that distinctly marks the British film renaissance of the 1980s.[2] It was produced by entertainment financier Dodi Al-Fayed (son of the billionaire owner of Harrods), who the next year would coproduce *Chariots of Fire* (1981) and who would famously perish with Princess Diana in a car crash in Paris in 1997. Other financing came from Film and General Productions (also producing around this time *Gregory's Girl* [1981] and *Britannia Hospital* [1982]).

Breaking Glass also bears the distinction of being Brian Gibson's first directing feature; he also wrote the screenplay. After rising through the ranks of British television, working on both documentaries and dramas, Gibson became a notable (though underrated) director of rock- and pop-music films, among them *The Josephine Baker Story* (1991), *What's Love Got to Do With It?* (1993), and the clever mockrockdoc *Still Crazy* (1998). While *Breaking Glass* had a fairly wide distribution, coming in strong at Cannes and also playing at the Los Angeles International Film Exposition, it was not received too well by the press or audiences. It did, however, generate a few very popular radio singles, this probably partially due to the involvement of Tony Visconti, David Bowie's producer, with the music. The sound track remained among the UK's top 20 best-selling albums for several weeks, making Hazel O'Connor temporarily a postpunk pop star. Like many a rock-music film before and after, the film is remembered mainly for its coveted cult sound track.

Despite its weak reputation, *Breaking Glass* is a smart though dated film that integrates punk and New Wave into the musical-genre paradigm without completely making over its musical inspiration. More importantly, it elaborates the slip-sync concept on multiple levels. The first few sequences illustrate how Kate is savvy about the need to promote her image. Yet we also learn right away that she sings about issues like racial tensions and the impact of new computer technologies because she is fiercely committed to making a social difference through her music. Kate's persona and performance style is techno-robotic, yet her songs critique such a mode of identity. In this way, she neatly embodies both punk political resistance and punk media flamboyance. More than a formal sound-track technique, slip-sync becomes articulated across the narrative as Kate struggles to retain authority over her (literal and figurative) voice while the new corporate music industry gradually consumes her.

✶ SLIP-SYNC: SOUND AND VISION

As it turns out, the film's opening credit sequence offers the film's most vivid and instructive slip-sync performance. It also works well as an overture to the major slip-sync conflicts within the narrative. This extradiegetic performance sequence should be read not only as a framing device, but also as an evolution of *Jubilee*'s slip-sync. That is, the sequence takes the slip-sync sensibility of *Jubilee* to a new terrain, one where punk merges with more conventional narrative as well as techno–New Wave. Welcome to 1980.

5.1. *Breaking the fourth wall: Kate (Hazel O'Connor) in* Breaking Glass *(1980), slipping into sync with her singing voice on the sound track as she confronts the audience.*

After the film's first establishing nighttime shot of London, we find our-selves, via dissolve, inside a train car of the London Underground—no doubt intended to code Kate's punk artistry as "underground" and therefore authen-tic, street credible. As the camera dollies forward down the aisle to a close-up of Kate, the song "The Shape of Things to Come" begins playing on the sound track. Yet, as with *A Hard Day's Night*'s "I Should Have Known Better" (also on a train), there is a notable ambivalence regarding the source of the music. She seems to hear the song (in her mind's ear?), rocking her head slightly in time with the music. She gets up and starts walking down the aisle, her steps also in time with the song's rhythm. But the other passengers show no sign of hearing the music. With no apparent music source inside the fiction, she is neverthe-less somehow "with" the music.

This music-source ambivalence is given another twist when she physically slips into the next car via a match cut. Here, she is singing the song, obviously lip-syncing, looking directly into the camera and performing for us, the audi-ence of the film. The camera dollies back, "pushed back," as it were, by her forward movement, exaggerating both the overall direct performance mode and the power of the vocal track she now possesses—or is possessed by. As she moves into the third train car, the camera match-cuts to a perspective outside the train looking in, tracking alongside her as she continues moving through the train, audaciously putting up stickers and spraying graffiti. But now, let us note, she has stopped lip-syncing, though her voice continues on the sound track. The slip-sync here has a rather different tone and form from that of Amyl's "Rule, Britannia." Yet Kate does slip or shift from hearing her own voice to singing or lip-syncing it. Exuding considerably more agency than Amyl, Kate alternates from sync to nonsync with each train car during her smartly choreographed slippage in and out of sync.

Yet the last shot of the sequence undercuts such agency, linking up with Amyl's frustrated sense of being overtaken by the music sound track. Standing on the back ledge of the last car as it pulls away into a dark tunnel, Kate is barely visible in the extreme low-key light, now again lip-syncing the final lyrics. Her receding from the camera into the tunnel's blackness becomes an apt figuration of the ensuing narrative motif of her body slipping away from her voice. Treated with a slight reverb to convey an echo effect within the tunnel, her voice exceeds her (we still hear it for a few seconds) as her lips disappear from view.

This last slip-sync moment, and the entire credit sequence, foreshadows the traumatized, mediatized fate awaiting her. Though extradiegetic, this musical performance anticipates her success, interestingly, by coding it through the slip-sync strategy whereby body and voice dissociate. Her musical art, when it becomes commercially successful, will carry her into the void: her body will become separated from her singing voice, such fissure or slippage demarcating her loss of musical and artistic identity.

On both formal and thematic levels, the film's slip-sync narrative is not unrelated to Mary Ann Doane's conception of the synchronous voice as a guarantor of the "phantasmatic" unified and coherent body upon which classical cinema depends. As she notes, when asynchronous sound, disembodied voices, or voice-off come into play, as they do in slip-sync, the "risk" of "exposing the material heterogeneity of the cinema" arises, a risk that classical film works to contain ("Voice in the Cinema," 373–378). A punk musical like *Breaking Glass* (or *Jubilee* or *Swindle*, in different ways) is less concerned with containing than with mobilizing this risk, in which such "material heterogeneity" becomes a music-image tension around performance that in turn comments upon new modes of spectacle.

In this vein, I think the slip-sync double-excess effect of the *Breaking Glass* credit sequence comes into sharp historical and cultural focus if we consider the formal relationship between the sound track and the moving camera. Self-conscious and even a bit clumsy at times (no Steadicam here), the tracking and panning camera movements reflect the film's modernist stakes, the challenge to convention that Kate enacts throughout the film. Though the film contains very few hand-held camera moves, often the dollies, as in the credit sequence, feel hand-held: conspicuous and perhaps reflexive, they are in any case a throwback to modernist art-house cinema (including the Adam Ant performance sequence in *Jubilee*, for example).

On the other hand, the sound mix is postmodern, looking forward to music videos and a more innocuous, perhaps insidious reflexivity. That is, the music track here has an overdetermined relation to the fictional space: the music, including her voice, exceeds her acting and performing body. The music is everywhere and nowhere; the narrative context and her bodily presence work "inside" the music track, in its service, a sort of postmodern-punk revision of classical musical performance. Thus, the sequence keenly demonstrates the double excess or ambivalence of punk slip-sync: refusing yet sometimes embracing synchronization's move into a slippery, postmodern kind of spectacle.

Likewise suggestive of modernism struggling within and against the postmodern—that is, punk struggling within and against corporate co-optation—is how this slip-sync sequence articulates her relation to her public. The cross-section "audience" of train passengers does not hear her music, barely acknowledging her as she prances around spray painting, glaring at them, sometimes "singing" at them. The slip-sync strategy serves to overlap two worlds or spaces: the world of musical performance, which in the narrative she will aspire to and finally reach, and their space in a banal conveyance of transportation. As numerous scenes later in the film will demonstrate, Kate feels some antagonism toward her audience. As she struggles to reach them, they don't appreciate her; when she does reach them, they misunderstand her; often, she sings or screams at them, whether they are fascist punks or middle-class businessmen. Such antagonism is, of course, a signature of punk musical performances; it is also a historically consistent cliché of pop-music narratives (and the narratives of most artists). Yet here in the credit sequence on the train, slip-sync uniquely codes this cliché, as she tries to "wake them up," to affect them.

In the first narrative sequence in the film, Kate meets Danny (Phil Daniels), her would-be manager and eventual love interest. After trying to hustle his way backstage to what appears to be a Wings concert, Danny comes across Kate, who is putting up posters on the street for her upcoming gig. Striking up a conversation, he challenges her to sing for him, right there in the street, to sort of prove herself worthy of him coming to the gig. She finally agrees, singing a few lines from one of her songs. Impressed, he agrees to come.

Notably, the scene culminates with a kind of inverted slip-sync, quite the contrary of that in the credit sequence. She is on the street, at night, thus lending a certain punk credibility to her voice and to the film's first narrative turn ("street credibility" is mentioned cynically later by a record-company hack as a desirable attribute). Moreover, she sings solo, with no music, likewise coding an authentic point of departure for her trajectory into the drama of slip-sync and commercial success. Here, perhaps for the first and last time, she fully possesses her voice, her voice is fully present, her voice is the music (Doane's phantasmatic voice)—the utter contrary of slip-sync, as exemplified in the credit sequence and later in the film.[3]

Further supporting this reading of the scene is the fact that Kate articulates her punk "vision." First, she explains to Danny that her music is not punk or New Wave, but is "inspired by punk." After singing at him, "You're a program!" (a line from her song), she explains that although she can't change the world, she can write and sing about it; also, she is developing robotic movements for her performances. Her desire to sing about new technologies and how they affect society further deepens the resonance of the film's overall slip-sync aesthetic and theme.

The fact that she mimics these new technologies in her performance style, however, sets up the bind whereby she ends up becoming what she criticizes. This bind is very much at the core of the slip-sync moment: punk's struggle to assert its voice within new technologies of music production and performance spectacle. If the credit sequence encompasses the film globally, foreshadowing where Kate will end up, this first narrative scene establishes her authentic, punk-inspired launching point, most crucially signalizing her voice as a coherent and unified expression of her vision. This is the voice—center stage and conspicuously isolated, yet coded as real—that slip-sync throughout the film will problematize.

But there is still more to this first narrative scene's relevance to slip-sync's cultural politics. Let us note at the outset how *Breaking Glass* opens rather conventionally with Kate performing for the camera, invoking a solid classical-Hollywood and patriarchal legacy. And let us then note how the narrative proper begins with Danny: we actually follow *him* as he stumbles upon Kate, thus framing her story as a female punk artist within his story as the visionary manager of her talent. Perhaps a convention of the pop-music narrative formula (in which managers typically figure as exploitative characters), such a framing device privileging the male manager should be read as a cipher of 1980s Thatcher culture. Indeed, not only *Breaking Glass* but also *Jubilee* and *Swindle* feature manager figures who loom large in a variety of ways: hyperpowerful, demonic, seductive, duplicitous, creative. Put differently, one effect of punk rock's inscription within the rock-music narrative film is the articulation of a more intensified role for band managers, reflecting the new corporate culture that celebrates and depends more on them. This is perfectly illustrated in Danny's character, who has a central role in the film as a "good manager" and who comes, like her, from the streets.

These punk musicals thus articulate an odd, contradictory circle in which punk's fervent anticorporate, antimanagement sensibility becomes filtered through nihilism and a flamboyant pop-cultural pastiche into a surprising merger with management. Perhaps an accidental banner for the early 1980s, punk's DIY suddenly stands not only for artists becoming producers but producers becoming artists. In any case, we will argue that slip-sync always bears crucially on this artist-manager dynamic, expressing in performance sequences the conflict between punk as antispectacle social critique and punk as superspectacle whore to mass culture.

✗ SLIP-SYNC AS MUSICAL SOUND BRIDGE

With the next scene, in which Danny arrives at her gig, the film initiates a formal pattern of musical sound bridges. Now, these in themselves are common enough in almost any mainstream narrative film and are especially prevalent in musicals and musician biopics. Sound bridges typically take two forms: from offscreen to on-screen sync sound, or from nonsync to sync sound as one scene cuts to a new scene. For the first form, we might think of a shot of one character in one room hearing another character in another room—then cut to a shot of that second room. For the second form, the audience will hear nonsync sound over one shot, which becomes sync after a cut to the next shot reveals the source of the sound. In both instances, the sound bridges two shots (either two shots in the same scene, or two shots of two distinct scenes).

However, as with its moving camera and direct address, *Breaking Glass*'s musical sound bridges torque these conventions slightly, opening up surplus territory in which the slip-sync style and theme can operate. In the second narrative scene, as Danny enters the bar, we hear Kate before we see her, a technique not exactly unrealistic and, again, not exactly original. Nevertheless, the sound track exaggerates the aural presence of her singing voice. A kind of indirect or soft version of slip-sync occurs: her voice exceeds her body for an initial moment. As her popularity increases, such musical bridges become more elaborate, developing the slip-sync motif whereby her visionary voice dissociates from her body and image.

A good stylistic example of a slip-sync musical bridge takes place during the sequence when Kate and Danny audition musicians for their band, Breaking Glass. The scene starts with Kate playing a bit of her music on her portable keyboard-synthesizer, then bridges via a cut to a quirky sync music montage of different musicians, each playing to the song. Done for comic effect, the jump cut–montage editing emphasizes discontinuity in time by compressing time. Each of the auditioning musicians plays in sync to the music, but the sequence itself is out of sync regarding plausibility and the laws of physics. We saw the same kind of rotating slip-sync in the "1978 Audition" title sequence of *Swin-*

dle. But here, the jump cutting and time compression are more pronounced, since not all the musicians are in the room together (as they are on the stage in *Swindle*). As in *Breaking Glass*'s credit sequence, the music here forms the scene's foundation, and the players slip in and out of sync with it. Unlike a more conventional approach, in which the subject-performer expresses the music, here the performing bodies are subject, and subjected, to the music.

Another, more politicized example of a slip-sync musical bridge occurs a bit later, linking the scene of Breaking Glass recording its first single with the scene of the band trying to get it played on the radio. First, a touch of backstory: in the lobby of the apartment where Danny lives, Kate notices some graffiti on the wall: "Black Man." In a reiteration of her visionary punk street credibility, she then writes a song called "I Am the Black Man," which reflects upon racial strife at the time in Britain. We see the band in the studio recording the song, the music clearly sync, diegetic. The scene concludes somewhat comically with the band bursting into the mixing room, harassing the engineer to intensify the sound by making everyone louder. At a certain point, Kate seems happy with the mix.

As she listens, we straight-cut to a new scene, a shot of a black homeless man slumped in the street, apparently illustrating the point of the song, which continues over this new scene, nonsync (thus, the musical sound bridge). The camera cranes diagonally up the building to the window where Kate stands staring out, implying her mystical affinity with the black man outside, the social inspiration for the song. Yet this frame-within-a-frame mise-en-scène and disembodied sound track also foreshadow her alienation as a rock star, soon to come. Before moving on, we should also note how the figure of the homeless black man on the street ultimately becomes a token pretext for Kate's white, privileged, "homeless" alienation on her way (up, literally and figuratively) to stardom. Like *Swindle*, *Breaking Glass* engages in an insidious though well-intended dialectic around punk's whiteness, which appropriates people of color to heighten the "authentic" in in/authenticity (a problem we will return to later).

In any case, when we cut to inside the office, the song now slips back to sync, playing on a small tape deck on the desk of the two talent agents whom Danny and Kate are desperately trying to please. I would underline how the use of the song to bridge the scenes conveys formally the theme of her voice slipping in and out of the grasp of her own agency. In the studio mixing room, she struggles with a recording of herself, trying to get her voice right; then, this "correct" disembodied voice floats across, via the crane shot, and comments upon a relevant social situation, the black homeless man. As Kate stands framed alone in the window, her voice is further alienated from her as she attempts inside to promote her voice (that is, her punk vision of the social) into commercial circulation. These musical bridges suggest her new artistic struggles: as she becomes more mediatized, she loses, and loses control over, her voice.

The next several sequences in the film employ a more elaborate montage–musical bridge format as the police, after raiding one of Breaking Glass's rehearsals, begin to hound the band as it travels around gigging, building up their popularity. The song "Big Brother" grounds the entire montage, seamlessly slipping from sync performance scenes to nonsync narrative scenes. This music-video-type montage emphasizes that her disembodied singing voice is a way of giving voice to the band's outsider, punk status. That is, the sound track privileges her music, and especially her voice, by consistently cutting back to sync-sound medium shots of Kate singing the song on stage, "narrating" these random, discontinuous narrative scenes of police harassment. During these sync music-performance shots, again, she sings directly into the camera, adding a reflexive, perhaps political edge to her performance. But according to the slip-sync musical-bridge format, her sync voice gradually slips away from her as she provokes the police and as she becomes a celebrity.

✳ SLIP-SYNC, BREAKING GLASS, AND THE SOUND MIXING BOARD

The musical sound bridge, as we have seen above, serves as an effective though indirect formal device in Breaking Glass for elaborating slip-sync as a tension within the interwoven tropes of popularity and performance. Another dimension more specifically of the mise-en-scène and the narrative further enhances slip-sync as a critical concept—critical of the film's characters and critical to the film's form. I am referring to the sound mixing room. Such a location recurs throughout the film as an overinvested narrative space where the conflict between live punk music and recorded, simulated music as a commodity comes to the foreground. Such a space is more or less a staple of the pop-music film. Let us recall the scene in Jubilee in which Mad's band performs inside the recording booth, behind glass, with Ginz's hands on the mixing board as he considers his next potential pop-star commodity. But like the musical sound bridges, these pop-music film clichés are given a special twist within the punk slip-sync framework.

Indeed, Breaking Glass makes elaborate narrative use of this mise-en-scène device. The film's title itself resonates with this connotation, alluding to the glass window of the recording booth, which divides the band playing live, representing visionary inspiration and immediacy, from the mixing board, where its sound is being recorded (reproduced and commodified)—"stolen," if you will. The name of the band of course aims to connote loud punk music that breaks glass, but perhaps also loud critical ideas that break the glass houses of conformity and hypocrisy. In the spirit of slip-sync, "breaking glass" likewise suggests transgression of the glass divide between musicians and engineers, producers, and managers. Such a transgression is distinctly punk in its DIY ramifications, that is, that musicians *are* producers. But it also is easily compatible with postmodernism's blurring of boundaries as well as with new corporate configurations that prioritize distribution over production and that intensify streamlining and downsizing. I think the mixing board stands in for a larger theme in the film related to how the music industry that punk rock encountered was becoming hypercommercialized, digitized, and somewhat hyperreal, blurring together more than ever the live and the recorded.

Much of the middle section of the film uses the sound mixing room as a literal and figurative site of the punk articulation of slip-sync. This articulation, as we have seen, involves both resistance and submission to the music industry's intensified embrace of visualization and simulated spectacle. Not surprisingly, these scenes start to recur as the band becomes more popular and enters the professionalized music-industry world.

In one of these mixing-board scenes, while recording the song "We're So Unreal," Kate appears to be imprisoned by the recording booth. The framing emphasizes her body inside an enclosed space, whereas the mixing board, hovered over by producers and engineers, appears larger in the frame. As Kate's star rises, as she successfully disseminates her social message, so too she is perpetually seen behind glass (and not breaking it), smallish in the background, while the foreground carries the mixing board and its entourage of industry producers. Awkwardly among the latter is Danny, who moves from the mixing room to the recording booth to converse with the band; he is the go-between. Closer to the camera are the new music producers. Audible to us, they secretly confer about how they don't like this new music and how Danny represents a "new animal" who plays aggressive on behalf of the artist but who also wants all the cash reward; they correctly predict that he "won't last."

Later mixing-board scenes further develop such antagonism, expanding the slip-sync concept beyond a formal strategy. After a traumatic experience during a race riot at one of the band's concerts, Kate again finds herself behind the glass of the recording booth, convulsing and sobbing silently. Significantly, she can no longer sing, she cannot find or summon her voice. The slip-sync effect here relates to her losing her voice at the moment of her becoming an object of consumption. Danny has to bring her out of the recording booth and into the sound mixing room, where the producers arrange for her to get medical help; she can only grunt. The mixing room becomes a crucial site for this slip-sync trauma: she is slipping out of sync with herself, ironically, while sitting around the sound mixing board.

A later sound-mixing-board scene further articulates her descent into the commercializing machine as a major crisis. Her new producer, Bob Woods (Jon Finch), is at the controls in the mixing room. Not surprisingly, two band members complain that the music is "crap" and threaten to quit. The music has gone soft, more pop than rock. Ensuing scenes can be viewed as a kind of reverberation of this conflict. The band is shooting a music video: all artifice, all posturing and contrivance, cameras and monitors roving everywhere. That is, the glass of the recording booth, which links the mixing board with the musician, and the image with the sound as a spectacle in the making, becomes incisively unpacked by the film as images of Kate proliferate on billboards and magazines and in videos. Her image exceeds her in the same way that her voice exceeds her, dramatizing the punk slip-sync conflict: resisting but moving through new technologies and new commercial economies.

★ SLIP-SYNC, MASS MEDIA, AND DRUGS

Another audiovisual pattern that punctuates *Breaking Glass*, one not unrelated to these mixing-board scenes and to slip-sync generally, is what I will call for convenience the recurring radio scene. These brief, usually transitional, and internarrative scenes expand the scope of the mixing-board scenes by extending the slip-sync theme to an explicitly mass-media realm. Throughout the film, we periodically cut to an establishing shot of the city while on the sound track we hear a radio announcer making various typical but pertinent comments: the popularity of disco (which Breaking Glass will soon change), sound bites reporting racial strife, unemployment, strikes, etc.—tidbits of the 1979–1980 social milieu. This voice connotes both sync and nonsync sound, since it is obviously being broadcast and heard in the city we are looking at; but the sound, more like a voice-over, rarely seems to come from any specific source in the shot.

This disembodied voice, perhaps too familiar a convention to be called slip-sync, is a prime example rather of Michel Chion's "acousmatic" voice: a non-sync voice not yet seen, a voice that does not yet possess a body but that possesses a magical power of narration: "It's as if the voice were wandering along the surface, *both inside and outside*, seeking a place to settle" (*The Voice in Cinema*, 23). Typically either a "voice of god" narrator or a privileged voice-over from within the fiction, this "ubiquitous," bodiless voice can also be sourced in "media," which "send acousmatic voices traveling," as the radio announcer's voice does for most of the film (24). These radio sequences thus enhance the slip-sync theme, articulating Kate's identity crisis through the mass dissemination of her voice.

Near the end of the film, Kate is interviewed on the radio show we have been hearing throughout, a scene that finally embodies the radio announcer's voice (we see him speaking), yet further disembodies Kate's voice. Exaggerated by conspicuous green-tint lighting and a slowly arcing camera, Kate is framed by the shot–reverse shot editing as isolated from the announcer but also as inhabiting his isolated space. Her makeup and acting are quite striking, suggestive of the conflation of icy stardom and robotic dehumanization. She looks and acts like a kind of empty mask; perhaps once inspired to make social commentary, she now exudes rock star decadence. This radio sequence cuts periodically to the familiar extreme long shots of the city, but this time, uniquely, we see the source of the broadcast voice as we cut back to her face as she speaks. This intensifies the film's slip-sync theme and effect as her voice becomes disengaged from her body and disseminated as an excess beyond her body, over the airwaves.

Indeed, most of the punk slip-sync moments in all these films are elucidated, but not fully accounted for, by Chion's acousmetre, though his emphasis on "both inside and outside" resonates. In the above slip-sync examples, a voice that belongs to a body becomes acousmatic by virtue of performance, recording technology, or, as here, media broadcast. That is, in a disturbing riff on the acousmatic, the singer's voice disengages from the body, reversing Chion's trajectory of "a voice that seeks a body" and becoming instead a voice that leaves a body—or else a body that seeks the voice it has lost, now an acousmatic excess.[4]

A further slip-sync dimension to this radio-interview scene is supplied when we hear callers suspiciously questioning her new, supposedly more commercial sound and popularity. The moment is effective, since a discussion of Kate's artistic authenticity takes places between her and her audience as a conversation between broadcast voices. The disembodied voices of her fans challenge her for being controlled by "the record company," which she denies. One caller is especially vehement, calling her "a poseur"; she thinks it is Danny, but the caller only laughs at her. It sounds like him, but we cannot be sure—yet another instance when the film mobilizes an effective ambiguity around body-voice identity.

Equally relevant in this respect is the sound bridge out of this scene and into the next: looking again at the city skyline, we hear bassist Ken (Jonathan Pryce) ask Danny, "Have you seen Kate?" Then we cut to the next scene, in Danny's new club, where Ken has joined him and the drummer, in exile, so to speak, from the Breaking Glass phenomenon. Inside the radio station, trapped by her own popularity, Kate has drifted more to the "in" side of punk in/authenticity. In contrast, Danny and some of the other band members have become more authentic, nonbroadcast outcasts.

These radio scenes, along with the mixing-board scenes, form part of a larger narrative articulation of slip-sync, namely, the collusion, rather typical of celebrity narratives, of the mass media, stardom, and drug addiction. This dimension of slip-sync becomes especially pronounced during the second half of the film, when Kate's rising popularity is accompanied by her loss of control of her music, her voice, and her body. The new, corporate music industry gradually overtakes and invades her performing body. Much of this begins with the "Rock Against 1984" concert, a crucial turning point in the film.

First of all, the film's Rock Against 1984 concert sequence seems explicitly modeled on the actual Rock Against Racism shows from the late 1970s, for which punk, ska, reggae, and dub music artists joined forces to protest the rising tides of racism accompanying Thatcherism. In the film, Overlord Records, which signed Breaking Glass, conceives of the band's appearance at the benefit as good publicity. Then, at the concert, the record company insists on flying its banner onstage, much to Kate's chagrin. So this is a special contradictory moment in the context of slip-sync: she has compromised by signing, but the contract permits her to fulfill her vision by performing at a benefit concert politicized by racial tension. But the overly enthusiastic intervention of the record company at the concert provokes Kate's negative capability: she refuses to play.

However, the narrative mitigates this refusal by having a huge mob of fascists barrel toward the stage to protest the band's protest. When Kate sees them, she chooses to recant her refusal, defiantly leading the band into "I Am the Black Man." A violent riot ensues, culminating in Kate's traumatized vision of a young white teen, bloodied and screaming; she too starts screaming, which the film "freezes" and silences with a freeze-frame of her face. This image in turn becomes a photo in a newspaper headline about the riot and the death of the young man. Here, as another kind of inverted slip-sync, her screaming face, mediatized, becomes silenced.

The entire sequence, one of the most intense dramatically and formally in the film, may be understood through Paul Gilroy's discussion of the images generated by the Rock Against Racism campaign. These images, according to Gilroy, were greatly influenced by the punk aesthetics of bricolage, collage, montage, and pastiche. Gilroy argues that these image strategies became instrumental to the antiracist struggle of the time, this struggle in turn politicizing the punk cut-up approach to images (*Ain't No Black*, 122–129). This sequence from *Breaking Glass* suggests a corresponding film practice that rewrites sound-image relationships so as to open up the text, and punk, to political interventions around ethnic identity.

In a slick and poignant scene transition, the freeze-frame newspaper photo of a screaming Kate, it turns out, is hanging framed in Overlord's office. The management team is discussing how the fallout from Kate's involvement in the riot actually presents a great opportunity to seize popularity. But Kate can't bring herself to sing or perform; she is too sick from the experience. Kate's singing body is becoming a commodity, subject to company control. Overlord's co-optation of a vital political point for commercial ends foreshadows the fate awaiting Kate's visionary punk social commentary.

The band's decision to take on whiz producer Bob Woods is a kind of antidote to this crisis, purportedly to help her recover. At his English manor home, he agrees to audition Kate. But it is notable that Kate is at first outside on the lawn, viewed in long shot, tiny in the frame, while Bob, Danny, and others discuss her—again, the "behind glass" imagery, her body being viewed as performing object. Accompanied by a piano, Kate comes in from outside and does her new song for him; it is much more pop and commercial than her previous work. Appropriately, strings and other instruments appear magically on the sound track, nonsync, to back her up, a contrivance reminiscent of classical musicals. Such formalistic contrivance is relevant here as she enters the final phase of her highest stardom and endures the most misery and abuse.

Indeed, the song becomes a slip-sync music bridge, bringing us via a straight cut to her recording the song in the studio, suggesting that Overlord's sway over her is a foregone conclusion. Here, other band members deride the sound of the new song; during the session, Ken complains to her that "it's out of sync"—but she cannot hear him. Especially with the lengthy artificial sound bridge (the multiple instruments heard in Woods's parlor), the sequence is highly conspicuous, demonstrating formally her absorption into music-industry conformity. Not surprisingly, the next scene is the one mentioned previously, of Woods producing a music video of her. The slip-sync here, unlike its modernist, punk manifestation in the film's opening segment, results from obvious lip-sync, overproduction, and simulation, a spectacle of entertainment. During the shoot, her voice on the sound track intones certain lyrics in a certain way; but these vocal intonations do not match her lip-syncing for the taping. That is, her voice literally does not match her image, but more important is the figurative mismatch resulting from the highly commercialized context. Notable for taking place a year before the advent of MTV, the scene anticipates the look and feel of the music-video culture in the pipeline for the 1980s generation of youth.

What the corporate music-industry machine does to her exterior performing body, drug addiction achieves on its interior. After the authentic members of the band, Danny, the bassist, and drummer, quit—the more superficial, stardom-hungry guitarist and keyboardist hang on—Kate becomes more dependent on drugs, more distant and miserable. The film equates her rising popularity not only with her disembodied image and voice, but also with her body's invasion by drugs, suggesting a kind of double slip-sync, from within and without.

First of all, let us note the degree to which the band's image has gone high tech, megaspectacular, and ultrarobotic. Kate's startling makeup and gestures are seductive and precise—but too much so. "Pretty vacant": she seems to have become that which she wanted to critique. Incorporating obvious characteristics of David Bowie and Devo, her persona has also gone androgynous, evoking Annie Lennox and Lene Lovich (an early punk-techno crossover artist who was originally offered the role of Kate). But this change seems to be a corporate packaging effect, erasing more than extending her artistic identity. Filmed with tight close-ups that convey a subtle slip-sync, she is obviously lip-syncing. A "live" variation on the music-video sequence discussed above, such obvious lip-sync, soon to be standardized by MTV, becomes a dystopian foreshadowing of punk's potential susceptibility to the encroaching culture of hyperreal spectacle.

Equally important is the scene before she goes onstage: she once again refuses to play. As with the Rock Against 1984 concert, her refusal is overturned, this time by the Overlord lords, who bring in a doctor to inject her with drugs. The scene is staged as a pseudorape, with the record-company hacks holding her down while the needle is forcibly injected into her backside. Rather than suggesting punk resistance, here her sick, drugged body more aptly conveys the dimension of slip-sync in which the machinations of spectacle overwhelm and overtake the performer. She is forced to go on stage and embody—become synced up with—the commodified excesses of mass media entertainment.

And yet, for the punk musical, such synced-up embodiment apparently cannot fully hold. This seems reflective to me of how punk itself, as we have discussed throughout, is internally torn in two opposite directions. Kate enacts one final slipping out of sync, with mixed consequences. In an implausible and melodramatic climax, Kate dashes from the stage after the first song, traumatized and hysterical, ripping off her headgear; she runs down the street, into a tube station, and onto a train car, bringing the film full circle.[5]

This train ride becomes a kind of nightmare inversion of the opening slip-sync sequence. The passengers become all the characters in the story of her rise to stardom. One of her songs is playing, nonsync on the sound track. Significantly, she does not slip into sync and sing, as in the opening segment—she

5.2. *Out of sync: Kate becomes a robotic punk pop star near the conclusion of* Breaking Glass *(1980). Photo courtesy of Photofest.*

apparently has lost her singing voice for good. Both train sequences have a dreamlike quality, related to the predominance of the music track. But here she is subjected to it and objectified by it, her role not that of an active agent, as in the opening credit sequence. While the first car contains her fawning fans, the second car she moves into contains only the "ghost" vision of Danny, who morphs into the youth murdered at the concert race riot. The scream-ing figure shifts (via jump cuts) from one persona to the other while charg-ing her, pushing her back into the first car. Note how in the opening credit sequence she seemed to "push" the camera back as she moved forward; here, she is pushed back by the nightmare vision figure. Finally, overwhelmed, she screams in response to his screaming; the close-up of her screaming face (no freeze-frame or silence here) fades to a white screen as the sound of her scream bridges us to the film's coda.

Danny visits her in hospital: she is catatonic, unable to speak. She tries to mouth "help," but no sound comes out. So the final slip-sync sound bridge of her scream—a culmination of her drug-addicted popularity and the loss of her body-voice unity—takes away her voice. But the sound track gives it back. Over the final two shots of the film—a close up of Kate, perhaps faintly inspired by Danny's gift of a keyboard, and a long shot of Danny leaving the hospital—one more of her songs begins and continues over the final credits. One last time her singing voice is fully disembodied, here with a special sense of finality.

★ SLIP-SYNC, MALE MANAGERS, AND THE FEMALE PUNK STAR

The end of the film, which culminates visually on a long shot of Danny and aurally on Kate's voice, becomes a portal into several subtextual aspects that further illuminate the punk slip-sync dynamic. The conclusion of the narrative features him as active, her as passive and silent: voiceless. We see him moving on, while she is stationary, captive. When her nonsync singing voice begins, it bridges us out of the narrative. Part of the nonsync music sound track, her voice can be said to have now become fully disembodied from her.

A closing song over end credits is common enough, perhaps here empha-sizing the tragedy of the loss of her voice. Yet the film also ends with Danny's redemption, which can be unpacked in terms of various gender contradictions that relate to both punk slip-sync and the larger cultural context of the new entrepreneurialism of the 1980s. It is true that the film overall demonizes new corporate commercialism and technology as exploitative. But Danny's charac-ter presents a more complicated angle on this issue.

While Kate is obviously the central character of *Breaking Glass*, Danny represents many of the film's intriguing cultural contradictions, all of which bear at least indirectly on the punk slip-sync historical moment. I am thinking especially of the film's insidious gender dynamics and how these signify the advent of Thatcher culture. Before turning to those, let us first take note of Phil Daniels, a compelling young actor at the time of the film's release, mainly known now for his work on British TV, including more than 200 episodes of *East Enders*. Just before playing Danny in *Breaking Glass*, Daniels gave a powerful performance as Jimmy, the lead character in *Quadrophenia* (1979), a film based on the Who's 1973 rock opera that, though a period piece about Mods in the 1960s, resonates lucidly with the burgeoning late-1970s punk movement. Daniels perfectly captures Jimmy: the ultrasensitive, tormented teen outsider who adores the Who; who can't fit in with family, work, school, or even his own Mod identity; and who is eventually driven to self-destruction. Then, just after *Breaking Glass*, Daniels appeared in Mike Leigh's *Meantime* (1984), alongside Gary Oldman and Tim Roth, again portraying a frustrated working-class youth. The film is notable for Leigh's hard-core realism and trenchant social critique of both the emerging Thatcher culture and the declining punk subculture. My point is that Daniels brings a loaded persona to Danny, one that helps legitimize and authenticate his role as small-time, would-be rock-star manager.

The subtext of the narrative arc further enacts this backdoor validation. Let us recall that although the credits feature Kate performing, the narrative proper begins with Danny.[6] Moreover, the first part of the film articulates Danny as a typical Thatcherite character: a relentless entrepreneur, starting from the bottom, determined to climb upward and into the music business (Quart, "Religion of the Market," 20–21). Initially, he comes off as somewhat evasive; when Kate questions his motives, he replies, "I like to promote." Likewise, we quickly learn that he works secretly for Overlord, buying up mass amounts of the assigned discs, thus helping manipulate the market. Initially a disposable extension of the new corrupt music industry, he nevertheless displays from the start a stubborn determination to strike out on his own.

Some of the radio news comments further elucidate the film's political ambivalence regarding Danny and the new Thatcherite culture. One report reflects a cynical antiunion sentiment, reporting in sarcastic tone that there will be "no news today" because news journalists are on strike and that "the news is all strikes anyway." Another report comments on the prime minister (Thatcher is not named) asking the unions to back down, insisting she will "fight anarchy everywhere," alluding to both union and punk resistance. Then the record-industry slump is mentioned; the only stability is in the disco market, which Kate's postpunk sound challenges yet extends through the new music technologies of the 1980s (Straw, "Pop Music and Postmodernism," 7–8). The political ambiguity around these sound-bite details is itself a reflection of Thatcherism.[7]

Later, as his discovery, Kate, becomes a popular music-industry insider, Danny becomes a disgusted outsider. As Kate loses control over her music and her voice, slipping out of sync with herself, Danny gains control over his independent musical vision. If Kate starts as the figure of audience identification, Danny comes to supersede this figuration: he becomes the more sympathetic casualty of "her" tragic narrative (my quotation marks suggesting it is not really hers). We come to agree with him, frustrated with her decisions.

In her exhaustive history of women in rock, Gillian G. Gaar notes how *Breaking Glass* "reflected none of the progression women had made in the realm of punk and new wave, for 'Kate' turns out to be just as easily manipulated as any stereotypical female musician . . . becoming just the sort of musician her character is supposed to despise—a blatantly packaged 'image'" (*She's a Rebel*, 208). On this note, Gaar explains a bit of interesting backstory to the film: the role of Kate was originally written for a man, but after the film's producers saw a Lene Lovich concert, they offered her the role. Lovich declined, so Hazel O'Connor was given a seemingly golden opportunity to star in the film and write all the songs. She enjoyed a brief popularity with a few hit singles from the film, then disappeared from the radar, oddly though obliquely mirroring Kate's fate (207–208).

The final and overriding aspect of Danny's redemption is through the film's romantic subplot. As Danny becomes legitimized as the manager-rebel, he also becomes the unfairly scorned lover who is devoted to Kate's art and affection. She ends up betraying him, even though she appears not to intend to. But the pressures of the industry (and the film's narrative ideology?) prove too strong—for her, but not for Danny, who resists, who seems to take over her visionary impulse as she loses track of it. Thus, when Danny comes to visit her in hospital at the end, he is "proved" right. Yet he is not bitter, but still devoted to her, thus haloed as a humble hero. She is ravaged, abused, catatonic, and mute: she has no choice but to listen to him, and he is all gracious savior.

Thus, Kate's tragic arc as a punk visionary stampeding through the new Thatcherite landscape becomes vitiated on one side by a ruthless corporate record company, which eventually consumes and destroys her, and on the other side by a slick entrepreneur who becomes better suited to navigate this new terrain than she. Ultimately, Kate suffers the conventional fate of the female performer, objectified and edified by the lead male's erotic gaze and by the narrative as a whole. Kate's earlier punk sister Amyl, in *Jubilee*, likewise displays visionary, rebellious punk tendencies, but eventually becomes consumed by the media machine run by Ginz.

Such ambivalence regarding punk and feminism is reflected in, for example, Lauraine Leblanc's ethnography of the experiences of young women in the punk subculture: "For a brief moment, all forms of transgression had free rein, and women in punk took full advantage of this atmosphere of permissiveness and rebellion. Yet, despite the doors that opened for women in the underground New York punk rock scene, the subculture was heavily male dominated, and remained so when exported to the United Kingdom" (*Pretty in Punk*, 36).[8] At the same time, the fact that *Breaking Glass* centers on Kate's tragic downfall from visionary punk outsider to commercialized robot is a notable concession to the potentially progressive feminist strains within punk.

The racial politics of *Breaking Glass* are equally insidious and slippery: Kate uses with good intentions the racialized image of the black man just as Danny uses with good intentions Kate's credentials as a female punk musician. When Kate sings, "I am the black man and you are the white" at the fascist, racist crowd, a provocative, perhaps disturbing slippage in gender and race occurs. She appropriates male identity to confront and criticize whiteness, but she also appropriates black identity by deploying the privilege her own whiteness affords.

As we conclude, let us revisit the racial contours of the traumatic outcome of this most crucial scene. The British people of color who come under attack are represented as a vague, chaotic blur, an aspect of the mise-en-scène. In contrast, the young man killed in the stampede is white, apparently an innocent bystander, a music fan. Isolated by repeated close-ups, he seems as unlikely and historically misleading as D. W. Griffith's Reconstruction-era black male rapist Gus in *The Birth of a Nation* (1915).

Then, Kate's scream in reaction to this white boy's crucifixion—fades to white. In a way, Kate becomes the "noble savage" female punk artist whose visionary aspirations become reinscribed within the institution of whiteness and through the ideology of white romance. The latter is notably underlined by her nightmare vision on the train at the end, when Danny and this anonymous, thus mostly symbolic, white youth merge as victims of her sellout as a punk artist.

Such are the subtextual slippages of punk slip-sync in the film. Both *Breaking Glass* and *Jubilee* portray punk music's attempt to disrupt or slip up a new, conservative corporate culture. Both also submit a female punk to the task, with mixed results.

CHAPTER 6

AMERICAN SLIP-SYNC REMIX

BLANK GENERATION, ROCK 'N' ROLL HIGH SCHOOL, OUT OF THE BLUE, SMITHEREENS, LIQUID SKY

AS WE RECROSS THE Atlantic and move forward into the early 1980s, let us establish a loose overview of punk's influence on American films. The last American punk film we took note of was Amos Poe and Ivan Kral's *Blank Generation* (1976), a film I consider crucial for its formative articulation of a slip-sync aesthetic in the context of the original, late-1970s New York punk scene. The film's overall unsynced presentation of punk bands performing in dingy nightclubs such as CBGB perfectly launched the punk musical's slip-sync sensibility.

 ## REFLEXIVE REPRISE: *BLANK GENERATION*, AGAIN

But there is another *Blank Generation* film, this one released in 1979 and directed by Ulli Lommel, that more directly anticipates the style and sensibility of the American independent punk narrative film.[1] A German émigré director, previously a protégé of Rainer Werner Fassbinder, Lommel would go on after *Blank Generation* to establish a cult reputation for directing bizarre low-budget slasher films. For *Blank Generation*, the director employed Richard Hell as his leading punk rocker–cum–movie star. A founding member of the band Television, Hell is most remembered in punk history as the leader of his second band, the Voidoids. It is with this band that he wrote and recorded the punk anthem "Blank Generation." A formative player within the original New York punk-music scene, Hell more or less plays himself in Lommel's *Blank Generation* as punk musician Billy, who struggles to retain artistic authenticity while maintaining an ill-fated romantic relationship. In this respect, we should note how the first *Blank Generation*, a slip-sync documentary, confers a raw, utopian authenticity on the punk bands playing at CBGB, whereas this second *Blank Generation*, shot only a few years later, is marked in its slip-sync narrative by a more cynical, haunted, and slightly nostalgic quality.

More specifically, the film contains early variations on some of the hallmarks of punk slip-sync musicals. For example, early in the film Billy walks off the stage at CBGB in the middle of a song, for no clear-cut reason; in a scene near the end of the film he explains that he walked off because he knew he would never be able to connect with the audience, that they were watching him as if he were "a car wreck." Not uncommon in performance films generally, this melodramatic gesture nevertheless resonates with the punk slip-sync idea. Resembling what we previously noted in *Breaking Glass* (released one year after *Blank Generation*) about Kate bolting from the stage during the film's concluding concert, Billy leaves the stage also in the middle of a song, frustrated with the audience and with the performance spectacle overall. Of course, the setup also recalls Amyl's "Rule, Britannia" slip-sync, in *Jubilee* (released one year earlier).

Lommel's *Blank Generation* also leans rather heavily on reflexive motifs and strategies, another aspect of punk slip-sync. Lommel appears in the film as a German television personality trying get an interview with Andy Warhol. The interview finally occurs near the end of the film, Warhol appearing as himself, intimating the historically significant Warhol-punk connection (Sargeant, *Deathtripping*, 28–29). A pretentiously cool send-up of television's fascination with celebrity, the sequence is literally "blank," thanks to Andy's minimalist non sequitur replies, quietly conveying punk's in/authentic take on television as "pretty vacant." Indeed, throughout the film people seem to be filming one another or viewing one another on monitors, and speculating frequently, via references to Godard, on the meaning of cinema.

The somewhat forced tone of this reflexivity refers us to the broader tension in the film between art cinema (with its meandering plots and self-conscious style) and lowbrow exploitation cinema (with its bad acting, awkward scripts, and poor production values). This tension, an important characteristic of the American punk films discussed below, comes across in the film's strong visual and thematic emphasis on the Lower East Side of Manhattan as the place of punk. It likewise comes across in the film's music: Billy's sync punk-music performances versus the nonsync modernist-jazz score (very *Taxi Driver*).

Most of the actual punk-music performances featuring Billy seem tightly synced. But there are scenes in which the sense of punk slip-sync looms. For example, Billy plays his new single in a bar while he tries to reconcile with his French girlfriend; or his music is mysteriously, ambiguously playing in the background (sync or nonsync, it is not clear) at an apartment above CBGB, where he is temporarily staying. These scenes code the overlap of private and public space through music, itself doubling as both simulated performance and ambient noise. They also suggest Hell's persona drifting in and out of sync with his role as Billy.

Speaking of punk drift, we should also mention a good companion piece to *Blank Generation*, Jim Jarmusch's first feature, *Permanent Vacation* (1981), for its New York punk sensibility about young, would-be Beat-punk philosopher Aloysius Parker (Chris Parker) wandering around the Lower East Side. No-wave punk filmmaker Eric Mitchell makes a cameo in the film, which was shot on 16 mm for around $12,000, just after Jarmusch finished film school.

One intriguing incorporation of the punk slip-sync approach occurs during the credits when slow-motion sequences of busy New York pedestrian traffic at one point focus on the performance of a street-musician sax player. On the sound track, nonsync, we hear a jazz score featuring saxophone, which loosely syncs up with the street musician.[2] In other words, a sort of audio interzone is opened up here between sync and nonsync music: the two are closely matched, but slightly yet crucially mismatched, anticipating the punk slip-sync performance moment. The slow-motion cinematography, combined with the slip-sync sound track, nicely conveys punk's difference, or distance, from everyday life and mainstream culture. Other notable traces of slip-sync in the film include an early sequence of Parker dancing in a friend's apartment, in a kind of slippery, punk-spasmodic frenzy, to a Charlie Parker record, as well as his voice-over throughout the film, which is particularly distant, disruptive, and self-conscious.[3]

★ SLIP-SYNC SILLINESS: *ROCK 'N' ROLL HIGH SCHOOL*

Another attempt in 1979 at bringing punk into film narrative was *Rock 'n' Roll High School*, both a sensationalistic musical and a precursor to teen comedies of the 1980s like *Fast Times at Ridgemont High* (1982) and *The Breakfast Club* (1985). Indeed, the film partakes of Timothy Shary's delineation of the youth film of the 1980s, the diverse flourishing of films about teenagers that coincided with the advent of the multiplex mall, cable television, and VCRs (*Generation Multiplex*, 6–7). Thus, the film anticipates *Times Square, Ladies and Gentlemen, the Fabulous Stains*, and other early-1980s punk films as offbeat and idiosyncratic narratives about young people. We might note, however, that Shary's useful and exhaustive study makes scant mention of punk films about youth, a lacuna that testifies to these punk films as being rebellious within a "rebellious" genre. That is, they did not integrate into the mainstream youth-genre categories of the time, because they are punk as well as cult and independent.

Produced by shlockmeister Roger Corman and released through his New World Pictures, *Rock 'n' Roll High School* bears the distinctive Corman stamp. Director Allan Arkush had worked for Corman before, but this was his first feature. Arkush's original idea was to focus on a heavy-metal band and a high school rebellion. When he first discussed the idea with Corman, the latter proposed calling the film *Disco High*. The disco motif stuck through several drafts of the script, but eventually Arkush talked Corman out of it, insisting on something more authentically rebellious like the punk band the Ramones (*Rock 'n' Roll High School*, DVD audio commentary; Whitely and Dvonch, "Essay by Screenwriters," 18).

Rock 'n' Roll High School has become a cult classic. Based on a story by Arkush and Joe Dante, the film reaches outward from the hermetic New York focus of *Blank Generation* to deal with fan culture and punk's impact on suburban teenagers. In contrast with *Blank Generation*'s earnest art-cinema pretensions, *Rock 'n' Roll High School*, permeated by a tongue-in-cheek tone, comes across as a goofy exploitation film and a boisterous promotional vehicle for the Ramones. Arkush apparently aimed to inspire the cast and crew by screening *A Hard Day's Night*, going for a "manic blend of comedy and rock and roll" (Whitley and Dvonch, "Essay by Screenwriters," 19). Clearly also a spoof of films like *Blackboard Jungle* (1955) and *High School Confidential!* (1958), the narrative centers on Riff Randell (P. J. Soles), an obsessed Ramones fan at Vince Lombardi High School, and the havoc she wreaks, especially in attempting to see their concert and give them a song she has written for them.

The punk theme and iconography is tenuous in *Rock 'n' Roll High School*, since none of the main teenage characters or almost any of the other kids look or act punk. They seem rather middle class, wholesome, and suburban. The look and feel of punk is mainly localized in the Ramones themselves, so when they finally enter this primarily clean-cut, small-town fan-base milieu, the otherness punk aspires to becomes amusingly highlighted. We might note also that punk is rarely mentioned in the supplemental material and commentary accompanying the 2001 DVD release of the film; instead, the cast and crew talk about "rock and roll." At one point on the audio commentary, director Arkush situates the film at the dawn of the "LA scene," which included the punk bands Fear, Black Flag, and X—though, again, he never uses the term "punk." In any case, all this contributes to the lighthearted, comic tone of the film, which contrasts sharply with that of *Blank Generation* and most of the other punk musicals, linking *High School* best with *Swindle* (on the audio commentary, Arkush also cites *The Girl Can't Help It* as a strong influence). The

6.1. *Slip-syncing down the hallway: the Ramones "performing" with their fans in* Rock 'n' Roll High School *(1979). Photo courtesy of Photofest.*

playful reflexivity and cultural critique of the film's slip-sync sequences is thus best understood through the prominent tropes of spoof and parody.

Indeed, one side effect of this aspect of the film's mise-en-scène is that it situates punk within the onset of conservative Reagan culture. This becomes apparent at the start of the film, when the new female principal pontificates on the "new decade" and the need to put a stop to all the "permissiveness" on campus. American flags and Uncle Sam posters adorn the school offices. Yet future yuppies inhabit the student side of the story too: one enterprising kid, Eaglebauer (named after a character from Ernst Lubitsch's *Design for Living*), has set up a makeshift service "company" in the boys' bathroom. Perhaps most excessively, the principal at the end comes up with a "final solution" to the problem of teen resistance: burn all the rock records. Such fascistic extremism becomes an easy rationale for the film's climax, when the students and the Ramones together blow up the school.

More significant is the film's emphasis on the narrative motif of the fan, which focuses on Riff's adoration of the band; it is her fandom that leads the whole school, and the film itself, toward the rebellion it unabashedly celebrates. Perhaps not coincidentally, this gets articulated in a couple of interesting slip-sync sequences. During gym class, Riff switches the tape to a Ramones song while the teacher is out; the students break into a play-sync song and dance, miming rock instruments, while Riff slip-syncs to Joey Ramone's vocals.

A later slip-sync sequence features Riff waiting at the head of the line to get tickets to a concert. As the Ramones arrive by car to greet their die-hard fans, one of their songs starts, and Joey listlessly slip-syncs while Johnny Ramone play-syncs on an unplugged electric guitar. The song is clearly playing non-diegetic on the sound track, but the band playfully pretends to be performing it, continuing while getting out of the car, entertaining the fans in line. The drummer simply clacks his sticks together (which we do hear on the music track). When the band's manager arrives and says something to one of the groupies, we can see that his words are clearly out of sync with his lips as the song and scene end. On the audio commentary, Arkush talks about the mis-matched sound in this scene and about the very tight reins Corman kept on the budget and the shooting schedule. This parsimony contributed greatly to the slippery and sloppy production design of the film, especially regarding sound-image synchronization. My point being that the half-baked, rough-around-the-edges sound mix and editing reflect a B movie sensibility that in turn reso-nated particularly well with punk performance and music aesthetics.

An even more vivid slip-sync sequence occurs when Riff is alone in her bed-room, apparently getting stoned. She puts on a record of the Ramones, and the band magically appears, slip- and play-syncing to the record. Her mind-altered state serves as a justification for several playful, silly slippages in synchroniza-tion: Johnny's acoustic guitar suddenly becomes electric; Riff's costume sud-denly changes; the bass player appears in her shower, etc. A bit like similar she-nanigans in *Swindle*, these scenes come off as comic punk riffs (her name!) on previous pop musicals, the band flaunting slip-sync throughout.

6.2. *Playing around with slip-sync: the Ramones in* Rock 'n' Roll High School *(1979)*.

An intriguing in/authentic parallel occurs later in the Ramones' live performances, during which they did not lip- or slip-sync. Here, the director
chose to print the lyrics as subtitles on the screen, partially undermining the
performance authenticity by coding it as contrived, at least by the filmic presentation. Related to this is how certain shots of the hysterical audience were
accidentally recorded in fast motion, and then left that way for comic, reflexive effect (and also probably because the producer considered reshooting too
expensive). In any case, we should note in turning away from *Rock 'n' Roll High
School* how all these slip-sync performance examples emphasize the fan narrative motif, which became more significant in the American punk films of the
early 1980s.[4]

✕ A PUNK CINEMA OF LONELINESS: *OUT OF THE BLUE*

We move into 1980 with a somber contrast to *Rock 'n' Roll High School's* goofi-
ness: Dennis Hopper's *Out of the Blue*. Released in West Germany under the
moniker *Dynamite Punk*, the film was shot in Canada, supposedly takes place
in Texas, and finally received a minimal U.S. release in 1982, with the tagline
"She's 15: The only adult she admires is Johnny Rotten." The film focuses on
antiheroine Cebe (Linda Manz) and her embrace of punk, and rock culture
generally, as a reaction against her dysfunctional parents, especially her father,
Donny (Hopper), who sexually molested her.

Clearly inspired by the early-1970s independent-film movement that Hopper actively helped foster, *Out of the Blue* possesses that period's signature
disenchanted, drifting quality as well as a top-heavy rock sound track. Linda
Manz's Cebe, very much an older sister to her *Days of Heaven* (1978) character,
seems a victim and product of her lower-class small-town environment as well
as the depredations of her alcoholic father, who at the start of the narrative is
in prison for crashing into a school bus full of children. Cebe's mother is likewise portrayed as irresponsible, sexually loose, and addicted to heroin. Yet the
film is notable for its peculiar appropriation of punk. On the one hand, punk
in the film becomes relatively superficial, almost trendy. On the other hand,
and in line with the narrative tendency in American punk musicals that I am
outlining, the film engages in an ethnographic exploration of how teenagers get into punk, how they "make it matter" (Grossberg, "Media Economy,"
205–206).

Like the kids of *Rock 'n' Roll High School*, Cebe does not look punk at all.
Yet she talks about it a lot, as does her father. Rather unconvincingly because
she is so young, Cebe is also taken with Elvis, who in the film's narrative time
frame has just died—and 1977 is the year most associated with the beginning

of punk. The film is peppered with awkward lines about punk: how Elvis was a punk, how punk is here to stay, etc.

Out of the Blue's variation on slip-sync is intimated in one of the first scenes, which features Cebe sitting in the abandoned big rig her father plowed into the school bus. She is talking on the shortwave radio, reciting punk maxims: pretty vacant, anarchy, subvert normality, disco sucks, kill all hippies. Combined with the slow, arcing tracking shot that eventually frames her in the driver's seat, her rant about punk comes off as a voice-over, yet is in fact sync sound. This effect not only obliquely invokes slip-sync but also foreshadows the importance in the film of music and sound track.

Indeed, a few scenes later, in another languorously long take, she is walking around outside the house, then sitting in the dilapidated greenhouse; Elvis Presley's "Heartbreak Hotel" is playing, but we do not discover that it is sync, coming from her portable tape player, until very near the end of the scene. Again, an ambiguity around sync and nonsync sound obtains. Additionally, we hear her humming and singing along with the song, but closer inspection reveals that this is heard only on the sound track; her lips are not really moving.

This and other slip-sync effects are no doubt partially due to sloppy or underfinanced production values. And yet I would encourage us to see, or hear, such miscues and slippages in aural-visual timing in aesthetic rather than fiscal terms. The film clearly embraces a documentary, reflexive sensibility as well as a low-budget exploitation tone, which of course harks back to Hopper's own filmic upbringing under the tutelage of Roger Corman. This is not to say that such slippages are intentional—rather, that they are not entirely accidental, reflecting a certain stylistic and historical moment when punk and indie film came together.

I would thus like to consider some other aspects of the film's use of music, which might appear secondary to the plot but in fact is quite central, especially to an appreciation of how slip-sync operates here. First, almost every scene in the film is accompanied by music, either diegetic or nondiegetic; the title of the film in fact comes from a Neil Young song that recurs. The film's heavy use of music seems to go beyond trendy shorthand characterization, instead complementing the distinctive use of long takes and sequence shots in the film, defining the space of the characters as determinants in the narrative. One interesting scene, evocative of slip-sync, occurs when Cebe walks the streets downtown, an oddly nonnarrative, documentary-type shot that is also boldly yet playfully reflexive. She is walking along with a strange man in a blue cape, accompanied by a woman on crutches (there is no narrative accounting for these characters); he is singing along to a tape playing in a boom box he is carrying. The shot concludes with Cebe—or rather, Linda—missing her mark, then coming back to the camera, asking, "Is it okay?" Offscreen, we hear Hopper and the production crew mumbling and laughing.

But a more relevant slip-sync occurs when Cebe finally gets to see a punk band in a nightclub. The band play-syncs and slip-syncs: the music track is very loosely matched, or mismatched, with the image track. It is a Ramones-type song, and the audience in the club overacts ridiculously and is, as well, much too old and bearded to be pogo dancing (one suspects that Hopper does not mind such silly contrivance). After the song, Cebe ventures backstage to meet the group. We should note the scene's visual emphasis on all the punk groupies hanging around in the hallways, doubly underlined by a filmmaker walking around asking people, "What does punk rock mean to you?" and "What are you doing here?" That is, there looms here a sense that punk is a readily available trend as well as a community with a brief history.

After befriending the drummer, Cebe comes out onstage for the band's next song, standing behind the drummer and carefully watching him play. Finally, he lets her sit in on the drums, dramatizing punk's DIY philosophy whereby the punk fan participates in punk music. The song's refrain is "You're some-body." It is interesting that this music-performance scene comes across as more live, more tightly synchronized than many other slip-sync scenes. We might speculate that her participation as a fan helps sync up the performance and the sound track. In any case, all this further contributes to the fan narrative structure I contend characterizes many of the American punk films.

One of the film's striking though obvious dimensions is its insistence on her obsession with punk as refuge from her identity crisis within her family. In many ways, punk becomes a vehicle, a language, that the characters use to indirectly talk about the disturbing family issues at the core of the narrative. As suggested above, Cebe's embrace of punk is strangely distant, intangible: punk for her is more an idea that she decides to sport rather than a musical or subcultural lifestyle.

However, near the end of the film, Cebe does finally dress up more like a punk than before—with a touch of early Elvis and James Dean thrown in. When her parents see her, they are horrified that she "looks like a dyke." But the film is ridiculing their homophobic perspective, invalidating it: drunk and high, they had just previously agreed to let Donny's forty-something friend Charlie have sex with Cebe. Cebe goes into a rant about "hating men," because, we soon discover, of what her father did to her as a child. After the next scene, in which she kills her father, she sits with her mother in the abandoned rig, a stick of dynamite burning. A safety pin in her cheek, she starts talking about punk to her mother, who doesn't understand and who notices the safety pin just before the explosion that ends the film.

6.3. *Divided by glass: her dysfunctional family drives Cebe (Linda Manz, right) to punk rock, in* Out of the Blue *(1980). Photo courtesy of Photofest.*

This terrifyingly pessimistic conclusion is one of the few scenes that vividly incorporates the look and ideology of punk, further suggesting that punk primarily serves as a facile costume for Cebe's isolation and rage. On the other hand, unlike the end of most other punk films, this conclusion takes punk's "no future" nihilism most seriously, pushing it to fruition with self-destruction. It also fuses a self-destructive feminist critique of patriarchy with a lateral version of Judith Halberstam's "punk tomboyism" ("Oh Bondage," 170). Indeed, the parents' horror at Cebe's desperate dyke look highlights the scene's indictment of straight family culture. It also harks back to earlier scenes of Donny and Charlie engaging in some oddly excessive homosocial bonding that seems ripe for a queer reading. At the same time, as Halberstam might point out, such rebellious tomboyism becomes overly pathologized by the film, that is, shown as a facile result of her being sexually abused as a child.

✳ NEW YORK DOLLS: *SMITHEREENS* AND *LIQUID SKY*

In the period 1982–1984, three films came out that made significant though peripheral contributions to the punk-musical cycle we are describing: *Smith-*

ereens (1982), *Liquid Sky* (1983), and *Repo Man* (1984). The first two films have the most relevance for us: they feature female punk protagonists and an ambivalent or problematic feminist perspective. Both focus on the allure and façades of the hip, urban New York punk scene; Wren (Sue Berman) in *Smithereens* tries to break in as band manager, and Margaret (Anne Carlisle) in *Liquid Sky* tries to make it as a New Wave fashion model. As with *Blank Generation* and *Out of the Blue*, both films push more toward the independent- or cult-film mode, giving little emphasis to any musical-genre influences—though the punk-music scene is still clearly the narrative milieu for each film.

Distinctive about *Smithereens* and *Liquid Sky* is that each codes its punk female protagonist as coming from elsewhere (the New Jersey suburbs and the Midwest, respectively). Their punk identities become articulated through an alienated sense of displacement. While Wren and Margaret live in the Village and the Lower East Side, respectively, they both are somewhat desperately searching for a figurative place in the New York punk scene. That is, a sense of belonging: Margaret's confessional monologue near the end of *Liquid Sky* forcefully conveys this, as do, in *Smithereens*, the scene of Wren visiting her sister in the New Jersey suburbs, and the closing shot of Wren wandering the highways, on the brink of prostitution. *Smithereens* exaggerates Wren's slip-space displacement by showing her getting evicted at the start, then rambling from one living space to another. Contrarily, *Liquid Sky* exaggerates Margaret's slip-space by having her be too much a part of her loft's décor; the overbearing New Wave environment, like the aliens, comes to overtake her; this assimilation is best emblematized by the horrific fashion shoot that occurs near the end—inside her apartment.

Additionally, again like *Blank Generation* and *Out of the Blue*, both films possess a keen, excessive approach to mise-en-scène. More than any other film technique, mise-en-scène defines a film's characters and overall style: *Smithereens* is open form and gritty in its washed-out and dingy locations, *Liquid Sky* is closed form and baroque in its garish costumes and colors. Both films emphasize the leading punk female's alienation by place, frame composition, long takes, and long shots.

Beyond this visual and narrative emphasis on space and place (which is not so important to the British punk musicals), both films engage an overinvested discourse about punk's historical relation to the previous counterculture. In *Smithereens*, Wren bounces back and forth between two men: the punk rocker Eric (Richard Hell, again), more desirable because he is part of the scene she wants to enter, and the nerdier but more authentic Paul (Brad Rinn), who clearly represents the counterculture—he lives out of his van and leaves Wren at the end for a commune in Vermont. *Liquid Sky*'s trope of the counterculture

6.4. *Alienated slip-space: Wren (Sue Berman) in bed with the New York punk scene, including Richard Hell,* right, *in* Smithereens (1982). *Photo courtesy of Photofest.*

is similarly embodied in Margaret's acting professor, Owen (Bob Brady), with whom she has an on-off romantic relationship, though "romantic" is hardly the right term for any relationship in this film. Indeed, Owen, from his pompous 1960s pedestal, repeatedly berates Margaret about her punk crowd for its dispassionate, dehumanized lifestyle; but the film harshly exposes his own hypocritical posturing.

Both films convey a "pretty vacant" nihilistic quality, one that exhibits certain punk attributes but that also reflects, perhaps indirectly and even insidiously, the politically and socially conservative culture of the early 1980s. Embodying some of the demonic manager traits of Ginz, McLaren, Danny, and Bob Woods, Wren is a brazen self-promoter and cutthroat entrepreneur whose scheming could easily be assimilated to neocon capitalism. But it is also her "speculative" pillaging that echoes the speculation-driven real estate scandals that came a bit later in the decade: lacking talent and a product, she just wants to exploit the punk scene however she can.[5]

The dehumanized ennui of Margaret's punk fashion circle likewise reflects aspects of the yuppie lifestyle that ran parallel to punk: intense image consciousness, devotion to designer labels, deep indebtedness, and alienated social relations. Indeed, the film brilliantly deploys its science-fiction genre markers around the concept of alienation: the humans are the aliens, whereas the aliens, invisible, feed off the humans' drug addictions, which are ineffectual antidotes to their alienation. All this, perhaps surprisingly, becomes a not inappropriate, backdoor metaphor for Reagan's deregulation policies, militaristic ideology, and Star Wars fantasies. For example, Janet Bergstrom has highlighted the film's global emphasis on conceptual design, which renders it a cult film with "too much spectacle" that nevertheless follows the cue of new "imaginative media advertising" ("Androids and Androgyny," 37). Within this tonal framework, the androgynous punk fashion models "project hostility and aggressiveness toward each other, the camera and the audience"—alienated but also aliens (48).

Not exactly *Rambo* or *Die Hard*, but not so very far from either. Indeed, Gaylyn Studlar rightly notes how *Liquid Sky* cynically portrays punk androgyny as "another capitalist cannibalization," one that pretends to subvert gender norms: "Margaret has simply replaced one assigned identity with another, currently more fashionable one, but her 'genderless' body remains irrefutably exploitable and thus defined as belonging to a specific class—female. Margaret discovers that one can cross boundaries of sexual difference but not undo them" ("Midnight S/Excess," 150–151).

In this respect, let us appreciate the insidious, conservative ambiguity of each film's ending. Each betrays a reiteration of the femme fatale's doomed fate: the freeze-frame of Wren, desolate and abandoned, wandering the high-way, poised to become a prostitute; and Margaret's high-tech, sci-fi orgasmic overdose dance of death.

Lastly, I would be remiss not to mention the superb punk film *Repo Man* (1984), Alex Cox's first feature. The film cleverly incorporates other genres like the road movie and science fiction, making it a great companion piece for *Liquid Sky*.[6] *Repo Man* focuses on the Los Angeles punk scene, carrying out a biting political parody of Reaganism along the way. On the other hand, it does articulate a funny and smart critique of punk (Goshorn, "'A Bad Area'"). As Adam Knee concludes, *Liquid Sky* and *Repo Man* are highly allusive films that ground their campy sci-fi intertexts in punk–New Wave social commentary. That is, both films, while riffing uniquely on science fiction, belong to a new genre that might be described as New York punk–New Wave and that would include *Smithereens* ("*Liquid Sky*," 112–113).[7]

Indeed, all three films figure prominently in J. P. Telotte's anthology on cult film; and *Smithereens* is mentioned in several histories of the New American independent film (Levy, *Cinema of Outsiders*, 356–358; King, *American Independent Cinema*, 225; Merritt, *Celluloid Mavericks*, 307–308), including Richard Ferncase's *Outsider Features*, which devotes an entire chapter to it. All three films thus support the speculation that the American punk-musical films fed into and off of the emerging independent sensibility: not particularly genre oriented, they are preoccupied with fan culture and with punk's social or ethnographic impact and influence. However, *Smithereens*, *Liquid Sky*, and *Repo Man* are not really about the music business or making music; we thus will leave all three films to the side of our discussion, using them more for reference and context.

✳ SLIPPERY PEOPLE: SPACE, PLACE, AND FANS

From this quick glance across the first wave of American punk narrative films (approximately 1979–1984), several codes come forward that help recontextualize the slip-sync concept. Generally speaking, these films move away from the performance motif connected to the musical and toward the ethnographic motif connected to independent or cult narrative. Such generalizing is always limited, fraught with exceptions; yet it appears that these films tend to focus less on punk music performance, as compared with *Jubilee*, *Swindle*, or *Breaking Glass*, and more on the punk-fan subculture surrounding the music. Conversely, the business side of punk seems more covert or sidelined in these American films in comparison with boldly visible personas such as *Jubilee*'s Ginz, *Swindle*'s McLaren, and *Breaking Glass*'s Danny. However, as suggested above, the rejuvenated consumerism and commercial activity of the early 1980s nonetheless seeps into the American punk musical narratives as a kind of dark mirror from the middle of the road.

These American punk films also possess some of the seeds of the mid-1980s American independent-film movement, which is typically dated from 1984–1986 with the appearance of debut films like *Stranger Than Paradise* (Jarmusch, 1984), *Blood Simple* (Coen brothers, 1985), and *She's Gotta Have It* (Lee, 1986). With its emphasis on odd, quirky characters and plots, this burgeoning American indie-film movement also foregrounds conspicuous motifs of space and place. Much of this revolves around a sort of regionalist tension between New York—the unofficial capital of independent film and the polar opposite, geographically and stylistically, of Hollywood—and suburban Middle America (Levy, *Cinema of Outsiders*, 152–183; MacDonald, *Garden in the Machine*, xx–xxi). Unlike the art-school or working-class ethos of punk in the London films, here punk becomes a vehicle of cross-fertilization, of topographical migration—an access point for rural or suburban youth seeking to explore urban bohemia. For most of these punk films, the central location either is New York City or is distinctly and self-consciously not New York City—some place clearly other than New York that is small-town or suburban Middle America.

To get a more nuanced handle on this aspect of the American punk musicals, we might turn to Michel de Certeau's distinction between space and place. Place, for the French theorist, is more institutionalized and stable, already inscribed in a category or bureaucracy; space, in contrast, is more amorphous and fluid and involves mobility and traversal—it is more receptive to transience. As suggested by the overview above, and as the next few chapters will convey, many of these American punk films represent punk-musical and identity conflicts through these two intersecting spatial tropes: the punk music scene becomes a delimited and stylized location that characters literally or figuratively pass through. More specifically for slip-sync, Certeau's notion that a place becomes a space "when it is caught in the ambiguity of an actualization" (*Everyday Life*, 117) resonates with our tension around the moment when a punk performance does not entirely fit in with its own spectacle.

Without pushing the distinction too much, since these elements do appear in British punk films, we might nevertheless proffer the idea that punk in the U.S. films is more bound up with identity—punk as both a subculture and a masquerade, in Judith Butler's sense. Though Butler focuses primarily on the philosophical genealogy of identity as a gendered construct that has haunted feminist theory, her intimations of a "political" alternative resonate with punk identity, especially as articulated in these American films: "There is subversive laughter in the pastiche effect of parodic practices in which the original, the authentic and the real are themselves constituted as effects" (*Gender Trouble*, 186–187).

Punk becomes here a costume that makes a statement, and a statement that is a costume. What makes American punk such a compelling illustration of Butler's masquerade is its self-consciousness, irony, and cynicism (expressed in different ways in all the punk films): in/authenticity, in that the punk outsider costume is both real and fake at the same time. Not unlike their British counterparts in the films previously discussed, these American punk characters make no pretense of taking seriously either the dominant mass culture of commercialism punk mines, or its own rebel-outsider position. In contrast to Butler's ideal of subversive masquerade, the slippery, elusive masquerade in these punk musicals tends to convey a depoliticized, even paralyzed ennui, a frank expression of punk's intrinsic sellout from the get-go.

A more specific aspect of this angle on punk identity is the centrality in these films of fan activity. Not surprisingly for the punk context, such fandom often results in a crossover onto the stage as a performing musician. In a sense, according to punk's essential DIY philosophy, there are no punk fans; or there are only punk fans. In the authentic, ideal music scene envisioned by punk, there are no punk stars, the fetish objects necessary for the fan relationship to exist.

In this way, just as punk music and films anticipate postmodern theories of "liveness," so too they anticipate recent theories of fandom. Henry Jenkins, for example, theorizes fandom in ways that easily, though surprisingly, can be traced back to punk. He shows how fans are typically portrayed in popular culture as psychotic, excessive, and superficial figures of ridicule: "The stereotypical conception of the fan, while not without a limited factual basis, amounts to a projection of anxieties about the violation of dominant cultural hierarchies. The fans' transgression of bourgeois taste and disruption of dominant cultural hierarchies insures that their preferences are seen as abnormal and threatening by those who have a vested interest in the maintenance of these standards" (*Textual Poachers*, 17). Though his study deals primarily with television fans, Jenkins's recuperation of fan activity, through Certeau's concept of poaching, envisions it as something creative and resistant by virtue of its very excesses and transgressions of "proper" codes of reception.

Yet such bad taste sounds a lot like the subversion of normality that punk has always celebrated. That is, early punk music and film articulated such a concept of fans as producers by radically erasing the fan-star distinction. We should likewise note that with such a valorized notion of fan activity, we have circled back to the cult-film sensibility. In other words, cult and punk film come together in the punk musicals (especially the American ones discussed in the next few chapters) around a radical audience participation, an excessive fandom that is not one. Let us therefore reinscribe Jenkins's "textual poaching" to designate the creative, proactive, and productive fandom powering these punk-musical narratives, and punk generally, by mobilizing excessive aesthetic strategies: bricolage, citation, and decontextualization (Hebdige, *Subculture*, 107–108). These American punk film musicals defy the negative representations of fandom in more mainstream films by embracing this negativity and by collapsing as much as possible the fan-star dichotomy.

Another crucial feature that links up American with British punk films: an emphasis on female leads. On the one hand, this seems to bode well for punk as perhaps the first rock culture that opened up a democratic space for women, whether as a result of "all the rules being broken" (Gaar, *She's a Rebel*, 190) or as "a refuge from femininity" (Halberstam, "Oh Bondage," 153–154). And yet it is tricky terrain: visibility in itself is no guarantee of authenticity and can often lead to a new, more insidious but equally subordinate status for women (Marchetti, "Documenting Punk," 274–276; O'Brien, "Woman Punk," 194). Many of the films focus on young women navigating the punk subculture in a variety of ways, forming a dynamic feminist articulation that generally seems progressive: in many instances, the films highlight the gender roadblocks that women face. And yet, as we saw in the British films, this emphasis on the female as punk spectacle becomes complicated, as does the representation of race in relation to punk, an often awkward and unresolved issue.

One last trope that comes up more seriously in the U.S. films, compared to the UK films, is the specter of the 1960s counterculture. Sixties activism and music repeatedly function as a kind of ghostly presence that generally provokes antipathy, though sometimes an ambivalent kinship. This may be due to the New York punk scene emerging out of an avant-garde genealogy with stronger links to the 1960s underground culture—the bloodline passing from Warhol's Factory through the Velvet Underground to Patti Smith, Iggy Pop, and the Ramones. It also may reflect the pressing cultural and historical significance of the hippie counterculture in the United States, resulting in the paradoxical sense that punk wants to dissociate itself from the preceding counterculture but ultimately belongs to and extends it.

Now, how do all these codes relate to our concept of slip-sync?

For these American punk films, slip-sync becomes opened up, yet in ways that continue to negotiate the specific (and British) music-image performance context previously discussed. Focusing on music performance and synchronization wherever possible, I will also redeploy slip-sync more broadly and loosely as a punk gesture beyond music performance, as a metaphor for the trials of punk identity and fandom, and as an analytical category for elucidating spatial dislocations and temporal disjunctions. That is, slip-sync as exilic traversal: punk characters moving from outlying suburban to in-crowd urban areas, a kind of displacement that suggests slipping into and out of place. And slip-sync as a disjunctive sense of history and time itself: not only a nihilistic "no future" refusal of a progressive course of history, but also punk's slippery position within the history of pop music and of subcultures (especially, as suggested above, the countercultural sixties). In accordance with the contours of this expansion of the slip-sync concept, we will open our focus to include punk fans, the punk scene, and punk identity in relation to punk music performance.

CHAPTER 7

TALK OF THE TOWN

TIMES SQUARE

Even the naturalistically foul language seems merely artificial and exploitative in this confused and hopelessly silly romp.

—David Sterritt, *Christian Science Monitor*, on *Times Square*

This evil, lying little fantasy has been photographed in ugly color, and a mess of mediocre rock music has been draped across it like mozzarella on lasagna. If the producer, Robert Stigwood, sells soundtrack albums with this movie, he should set up a fund for every girl mugged, raped or battered in Times Square.

—David Denby, *New York*, on *Times Square*

SUCH VITRIOL WAS typical of the reviews that greeted *Times Square* upon its release in December 1980. Conceived and produced with much studio fanfare (a big budget, high expectations), ticket returns tell us the film failed miserably. One senses this was partially due to the clumsy attempts of independent-minded directors and producers hired to make a slick Hollywood film. Or perhaps it was due to Hollywood executives trying make a quick and easy buck on independent filmmakers and the cutting-edge rock-music scene (as they had done successfully so often throughout the 1970s). In any case, beyond being remembered for its sound track, the film has been rescued from the dustbin of film history by cultural critics and cult audiences taken with its queer subtext.

For us, however, the vehement dismissal by the popular press of *Times Square* as a smarmy failure becomes a significant doorway into its status as an in/authentic punk musical. That is, its offensive qualities (bad acting, a weak script, poor directing and production values, sexploitation imagery, etc.) are not unrelated to its attempts to incorporate punk. In this sense, we can contextualize *Times Square* as a fitting example of Kay Dickinson's movies that "don't work" with their music. Full of mismatches—a noxious failure in the eyes of critics—*Times Square* intended to capitalize on punk. Slip-sync, I would argue, critically accounts for some of the more interesting textual and cultural residue of the film's audacious misfire.

Following in the footsteps of *Rock 'n' Roll High School*, *Times Square* was a sensationalistic effort at packaging teen rebellion for 1980s youth audiences. Both films import punk iconography with the apparent design of serving it up for the mainstream, probably with disco's trajectory through *Saturday Night Fever* (1977) and *Fame* (1980) in mind. We can surmise that such intentions guided *Times Square* simply by noting that the Robert Stigwood Organization was its production company. An Australian entertainment mogul throughout the 1960s and 1970s, Stigwood produced and promoted several huge rock acts in addition to blockbuster movie sound tracks, rock theater extravaganzas, and monster rock-musical films, among them *Jesus Christ Superstar* (1973), *Tommy* (1975), *Saturday Night Fever* (1977), *Grease*, and *Sgt. Pepper's Lonely Hearts Club Band* (both 1978—the latter, a Beatles–Bee Gees fiasco, anticipated the failure of *Times Square*). The film critic of the *Village Voice* opens her review of *Times Square* by noting that Stigwood is "the only mogul who'd spend $20 million on a low-budget movie," his "operative principle" being "hear the movie, see the album" (Rickey, review of *Times Square*, 50). Apparently, Stigwood insisted that certain dialogue scenes be cut from the film in order to make room for more music; when director Allan Moyle refused, he was fired, though he retained credit as director.[1]

After bombing in theaters, *Times Square* quickly became a film coveted mostly for its hard-to-find sound track, which brought together songs by several New Wave bands as well as a rare XTC song written specifically for the film. Indeed, the sound-track album was released six weeks ahead of the film. Along with its intensive and expensive advertising campaign, *Times Square* itself furnishes a vivid example of music-driven, "high concept," synergistic marketing, which was somewhat at odds with its punk pretensions (Denisoff and Romanowski, *Risky Business*, 255). Whereas *Rock 'n' Roll High School* cashed in on the in/authentic star power of the Ramones, already-established punk rockers who played themselves as if in an advertisement, *Times Square* took a more modest yet riskier approach, casting two young unknowns in the leading roles.

Yet the potential for punk in/authenticity resulting from this casting choice is largely undermined by the film's bloated sound track, described above. A rather inauthentic (sans our punk slash) excess, its wide-ranging song list includes "Talk of the Town" by the Pretenders, which nominally evokes many of *Times Square*'s problematic characteristics: "pretending" to be punk, deigning to tap into the "talk of the town" but provoking the wrong kind of talk (bad reviews and minimal ticket sales). Moreover, as we will see, another kind of "talk of the town" permeates the film: radio talk. Perhaps betraying the film's overkill confidence that an overloaded sound track would yield big box-office returns, *Times Square*'s mismatched portrayal of radio as punk friendly is crystallized in the one major star the film trades on, *Rocky Horror* lead Tim Curry, here playing the parental but hip DJ Johnny LaGuardia.

★ TIMES SQUARE: THIS MUST BE THE PLACE

The two punk characters proper, Pamela Pearl (Trini Alvarado) and Nicki Marotta (Robin Johnson), are teenagers from radically different backgrounds. This pairing proves to be the film's main strategy in rendering punk more palatable: streetwise, hard-core Nicki and pampered, middle-class Pamela. They befriend each other while sharing a room in the psychiatric ward of a New Jersey hospital, then escape to Times Square to make it on their own in the music scene.

Times Square opens with a credit sequence that deploys a variation on slip-sync for an intriguing symbolic purpose, recalling and extending the credit sequence of *Breaking Glass*. As the credit sound track plays Roxy Music's "Same Old Scene," Nicki is seen strutting down an alley, finally stopping to set up her electric guitar and amp behind a disco nightclub. Decked out in classic punk attire of tight black leather, she starts thrashing out some atonal power chords, not only as an affront to the "same old scene" at the nightclub, but also as a way to engage in a sound collision with the music sound track itself, a striking though crude narrative instance of Attali's "noise."

By creating such a conspicuous sound montage (one music track diegetic, the other nondiegetic), the film quickly establishes the antiaesthetic of Nicki's punk music identity. On the one hand, as Carrie Rickey notes, the filmmakers "use rock like program music" (review of *Times Square*, 50). Yet the scene's variation on slip-sync underlines Nicki's anomalous, nihilistic punk gesture as a reflexive spectacle, both within and beyond the narrative. That is, Nicki's musical assault is in sync, since it is diegetic; in fact, for a few seconds she actually plays along, thrash-style, with Roxy Music. But it is also out of sync, since it clashes with both the disco mise-en-scène and the nondiegetic effect of the music, playing literally against it.

As its title suggests, *Times Square* places special emphasis on place, illustrating my argument that punk slip-sync in the early-1980s American context emphasizes space and place in relation to punk identity and fan culture. Here, Times Square designates the punk place, the "scene," which becomes a space where the girls can cultivate their punk identity. Indeed, while Stephen Duncombe theorizes the punk scene as being postplace, determined by dispersed and mobile zine communities ("Let's All Be Alienated," 428–435), Stacy Thompson clearly organizes his sociological and aesthetic critique of punk around distinct scenes with distinct place locations (*Punk Productions*, 9–79). These two perspectives on the location of punk reiterate Certeau's distinction invoked earlier: places are grounded in some kind of institutionalized infrastructure, and spaces are virtual, transient, and defined by fluidity and mobility. While the specific punk-scene locations Thompson identifies are themselves fluid, terminal, and not merely un- but antiofficial, both attitudes toward the punk subculture, whether as a place or a space, emphasize the underground, ethnographic dimension of punk, which is reflected in these American punk-influenced films.

Early on, *Times Square* conveys an ambitious though clichéd and clumsy dimension of this emphasis on space and place. The mayor's urban planning commissioner is presenting his plan to revitalize Times Square; he also happens to be Pam's father, David Pearl (Peter Coffield). He has brought her to the meeting to be paraded as evidence of the need for urban renewal. When he refers to her negative experiences in Times Square, she starts mumbling over and over, "It's not true"—again, a kind of slip-sync sound montage in which her words collide with and undermine his.

The moment creates a literal as well as symbolic overlapping in synchronization that distorts one meaning, his public version of her, to convey more noisily another, her private resistance to this version. The father's plan for revitalization anticipates Mayor Giuliani's approach of the 1990s, but here with a liberal veneer; at one point in his presentation he quips, "After all, I'm a liberal." David Pearl's political solution to the problems of the place of Times Square (in Certeau's terms, a space improperly "practiced") reflects the early-1980s neocon economic strategy: speculative investment, gentrification, zero-tolerance cleanup strategies, and enforced "family values." Her father seems a clear, though caricatured, cipher of the liberal-cum-yuppie, and his gentrification plan posing as social reform will indeed take flight during the 1980s.

✳ GIRLS ON THE RUN:
SLIP-SYNC SOUND TRACK AND PERFORMANCE

Having quickly established both girls, in different ways, as supposedly out of control and mentally unstable, the film puts Nicki and Pam in the same hospital room, under observation for "seizures." Without much sophistication or originality, the film links misguided, even abusive parental authority with medical and legal authority, showing the latter's definition of normal to be highly suspect. Even though the signifiers of punk are minimal, and punk is not really mentioned throughout the film, Nicki's behavior seems very much punk in spirit and sensibility, much more so than Cebe's in *Out of the Blue*. Dropping sarcastic quips to Pam, she lasciviously munches on flower petals— a Dadaistic destruction of etiquette, a parody of consumerism with intimations of cannibalism. She likewise mocks the psychiatrist's questions with a verbal pastiche or cut-up (to use the more correctly punk term) of clichés and contrived non sequiturs. The slightly younger and certainly more sheltered Pam observes Nicki's behavior out of the corner of her eye; gradually, she becomes seduced.

After they bond, they escape their hospital-prison to the "sound track" of the Ramones blasting from Nicki's boom box. This seems like a ridiculous flaw or mismatch in the script and staging, since it draws enormous attention to them as they dash through the halls. But it also possesses the slip-sync aesthetic quality of equivocating around diegetic and nondiegetic sources: it playfully vacillates between clearly sourced music and background accompanying music. Indeed, there is a punk tonality to the musical affront, a way of saying: "I'm not trying to sneak away, I'm making a spectacle of my rebellion, I'm going to noisily expose myself to capture even as I evade it." No doubt, it is also a flimsy pretext for having the Ramones' music playing during the scene, to liven it up with a visceral, though promotional, audio track.

The film's use of the Ramones in this scene is not explicit in its articulation of punk. And this is true throughout *Times Square*, which often relies on a certain diluted shorthand, perhaps with the aim of broadening punk's appeal. Having severely failed in this aim, the film likewise possesses minimal authentic punk value; there is too much dilution, which is itself poorly executed.[2] But this sense that the film is caught between being not punk enough and too punk—a quality that it shares with *Ladies and Gentlemen, the Fabulous Stains*, as we will see in the next chapter—becomes another articulation of what we have explored so far as punk in/authenticity. Missing both its target audiences, the general youth culture and the hard-core punk subculture, *Times Square* reinscribes the punk sensibility in a terrain that is alien to punk itself, yet still beyond Hollywood's good taste.

Let us note an example that follows directly on the Ramones-fueled escape scene mentioned above: the clumsily punk aura of the abandoned Pier 56 warehouse they hide out in. Pam and Nicki squat in an industrial wasteland that is oddly comfortable and convenient, constructing a home that is fully makeshift, decorated with disposed clutter and recycled garbage. In fact, we see similar kinds of punk living spaces, but more hardcore and in black-and-white, in Penelope Spheeris's *The Decline of Western Civilization*, released around the same time, in 1981. As with the hospital-escape scene, there is no doubt an absurd implausibility to them setting up house in this location for the duration of the film's time span of several days.[3] Likewise, their "blood sisters" bonding scene, inspired by a poem Pam wrote about Nicki, seems like a sentimental cliché—not very punk. The scene concludes with a tacky punk coda as the two girls scream their names at each other.

However, the sound of their screaming voices, lingering briefly as disembodied over an extreme long shot of the dilapidated dock area, obliquely intimates the central role radio plays in the film. Whereas punk music was never too radio friendly, *Times Square* treats the radio as a progressive, populist outlet. Unlike *Breaking Glass*, which makes minimal use of the radio, mainly to furnish a sense of general political currents and the public world, *Times Square* elaborates a narrative impact for radio waves, personified in the character of DJ Johnny LaGuardia, played by Tim Curry of *Rocky Horror* fame. Such casting obviously aims to render the radio a sympathetic "space" across the place of Times Square.

Curry's DJ becomes a poet-prophet of the airwaves: somehow he gets wind of the city planner's daughter being on the lam with a dangerous punk rocker. On the air, he claims to be "tuned in" to the outlaw couple, playing what he believes to be their favorite song. Helping turn them into punk rock stars, he reads Pam's letter on the air, moralizing that the two girls "don't need antidepressants, they need understanding"; that Pam has not been kidnapped, but "soul-napped, Nicki-napped, happy-napped." This mystical kinship between DJ and outlaw harks back quite faithfully (even if accidentally) to a similar relationship in *Vanishing Point* (1971).[4] A more contemporaneous, though less interesting, parallel can be found in Screaming Steve, the DJ from *Rock 'n' Roll High School*, who sides with the teenagers throughout in their confrontations with the high school administration.

Hiding out at the edge of Manhattan, Pam and Nicki come to embody the punk lifestyle by hustling and stealing in various ways. Eventually, Nicki helps Pam get a job as a dancer in a sleazy nightclub, the Cleopatra Lounge; she sports a hooker outfit but refuses to go topless. Indeed, like *Swindle*, *Times Square* alludes to the "hardcore" link between porn and punk made by David E. James, but in a highly watered-down and unconvincing way (*Power Misses*, 224). This comes into sharper focus as Nicki makes her punk-music debut in the same nightclub, an admittedly cheesy revisioning of the original New York punk club scene, when bands debuted in East Village dive bars and strip joints. During this section of the narrative, some slip-sync performance techniques come to the foreground, detailing the start of Nicki's punk-music fling with fame.

First, a precursor to her own music-performance destiny occurs one night when Nicki and Pam run into a friend of Nicki's while walking down a busy Times Square block. They begin dancing down the street, to the Talking Heads' "Life during Wartime," supposedly emitting diegetically from her friend's boom box. I say supposedly because the music once again also clearly functions as nonsync sound track. I would not deny, or apologize for, the clumsily contrived *Fame*-type tone of the scene; as Rickey rightly points out, "They're a dancing contradiction to the lyrics" (review of *Times Square*, 50).

Yet a slip-sync sensibility obtains around the scene's ambivalence regarding diegetic and nondiegetic music. A sympathetic reading, or one attuned to the subtext of mismatch, might see this as foreshadowing the slippery struggle of the punk musician to in/authentically inhabit mass culture as music spectacle. Nicki's prancing and singing along to the song codes her as a would-be pop star in the film and of the film, a punkish outsider on the road to fame—and it is a very *Fame* scene, which is partly why it feels so wrong. It is interesting to note how all the street folks she jams with are people of color, including her friend, who follows dutifully with the boom box. Interesting for how it partakes of the use of people of color that we have already observed in these punk musicals: convenient tokens of street credibility and a kind of dark or "wild side" authenticity.

In any case, a more compelling slip-sync example emerges out of the genesis of Nicki's first song. At the nightclub where Pam dances, Nicki shares with Pam a poem she composed; Pam, quite impressed, hears it in her head more as a song. When Nicki first performs the song with the nightclub's band, the sound and arrangement are distinctly punk: fast, harsh, repetitive, with a lyric refrain of "Feed me—I'm a damn dog!" This progression from writing (private) to spoken word (intimate) to music (public) concisely builds to Nicki's slip-sync performance.

During the song, the audiovisual mix seems a bit flubbed, since her lip-syncing does not quite match her voice on the sound track. Likewise, she starts out playing electric guitar, then puts it down midway, although we still hear it playing in the song. We have seen this kind of audiovisual leeway in *Swindle* and *Rock 'n' Roll High School*. Such tinkering with realism is perhaps a convention of the musical, legitimized by the suspension of disbelief. On the other hand, this scene's performance is supposed to be live within the narrative, and thus would not typically justify such playing, which I think rather should be understood in the context of slip-sync and mismatch.

In other words, the scene's half-baked slippages in synchronization seem like an expression of the punk-inflected singer and music as well as the clumsy, amateurish effect of the production quality, itself a result of contradictory industrial

7.1. *On her way to "sleez bag fame": Nicki (Robin Johnson) slipping out of sync during her first nightclub gig, in* Times Square *(1980).*

motivations. Let us recall that with slip-sync, it is not just a question of blurring the audio diegetic-nondiegetic boundary, but of highlighting—by default or by design—this blurring. Moreover, Nicki as front woman seems carried away by her own raw energy and passion, which push the familiar boundaries of the band (the Blondelles, normally the club's lounge act), the venue, and the film's audiovisual synchronization. Perhaps more than most other slip-sync performances we have examined, this one seems like a direct expression of punk's characteristic sloppy, slippery, excessively intense delivery.

✶ RADIO, NOT TELEVISION: SLIP-SYNC AND MASS CULTURE

As with most of the other punk-musical films discussed, *Times Square* displays an unresolved, ambivalent attitude toward mass media and mass culture. At first glance, much of the film's sentiment seems anticorporate and unsympathetic to the world of mass media. But as noted above, the radio station and, especially, LaGuardia's persona are clearly coded as legitimate critical voices, aligned with Nicki and Pam. Indeed, the performance scene following upon Nicki's rendition of "Damn Dog" takes place in LaGuardia's WJAD studio: Nicki, Pam, and the band (now the Sleez Sisters) perform live over the airwaves a rather punk song; its provocative refrain, "Spic, nigger, faggot, bum, / Your daughter is one," is obviously directed at Pam's father, but is verbally dedicated by them to "Brian Jones and all the dinosaurs kicked out of bands." No slip-sync here; this is authentic radio.

This comes into sharper focus through contrast when the two girls devise a shock prank of dropping televisions off buildings. An obvious and perhaps simplistic actualization of the then-popular bumper sticker "Kill your television," it nevertheless conveys a vital punk sensibility and aesthetic, one that invokes elements of punk's prehistory—a kind of Dada-Happening-Situationist spectacle as antispectacle.[5] LaGuardia's radio broadcasts celebrate these antics, exaggerating their shock effect and theorizing their political ramifications. As the Cars' "Dangerous Type" plays (once again, both sync and nonsync, both on the radio and on the film sound track), his radio broadcasts become voice-over narration for a montage of several television explosions. His radio show urges the girls on, articulating their message for them: "a new iconoclast has come to save us"; for everyone who just "stays at home"; "let it be passionate or not at all." The film clearly prefers the radio to television, the former being instrumental in engendering the kind of publicity that leads to the almost overnight development of a huge fan base.

This equivocation around mass media (radio versus television) is given a special twist near the end of the film as fame and stardom become more problematic. Nicki seems to gradually fall under a spell, embracing the "live fast, die young" creed. When Pam protests, Nicki explains that fame is the only option for her, implicitly underlining the idea that middle-class Pam is more or less posing as a punk fugitive, whereas Nicki is for real. However, a few scenes later Nicki's authenticity is recast as in/authenticity: with Pam secretly observing, Nicki strikes air-guitar poses in front of a mirror. Pam's perturbed voyeurism is coded as rationally distant, in turn framing Nicki as the more excessive character—significantly here, through Pam's point of view. This sparks Pam to call her father on the phone for the first time since her escape from hospital, foreshadowing the film's resolution, a happily reunited father and daughter.

At a loss over Nicki's apparent loss of identity to the lure of celebrity— even if it is a punk version, driven by nihilistic self-destruction—Pam invites LaGuardia to their place. In a classic case of mistaken identity that lends the film's narrative frame a touch of the romantic-comedy genre, Nicki overhears and misinterprets the invitation. This leads into a "jealous rage" montage, which invokes the family-melodrama genre as it crosscuts between Nicki's overwrought agony and Pam's meaningful conversation with the DJ. Accompanied by a nonsync Patti Smith song, which clearly favors Nicki (who seems loosely modeled on punk diva Smith), this segment culminates with Nicki developing her "painted mask" look, soon to become her signature, imitated by all her fans. Nicki's "sleez bag" costume thus originates authentically in her own personal torment, legitimating it in advance of becoming in/authentically popularized. The delegitimization occurs later through her radio-broadcast slogan that rather keenly invokes punk: "If they treat you like garbage, put your body in a garbage bag; if they treat you like a criminal, black out your eyes."

This mass-media and celebrity theme is pursued further in a later slip-sync scene. Recalling the sound-mixing-board motif previously analyzed in *Breaking Glass*, Nicki bursts into LaGuardia's studio, flinging an object through the glass that encloses the booth he is working in. She demands that he let her make a live broadcast of her hysterical musical confession, for Pam; guitar in hand and pounding out monotone chords, she rants out her tortured revelations—very Patti Smith. However, the slip-sync twist comes as we watch the DJ secretly kill the broadcast. Thus, she is made by the film to misperceive the spectacle she believes she controls; she hears her voice as broadcast, mediatized, when in fact it remains flat and private, confined to the studio. The ruse is further conveyed when she breaks down during the song and LaGuardia has her removed against her will.

✳ A QUEER CLIMAX: SLIP-SYNC AND FANDOM

The shutting down of Nicki's performance signifies a subtle shift in the film's portrayal of LaGuardia's radio station; it becomes a space and sound not entirely friendly, perhaps a bit more like television than we thought. But the shutting down of her performance should also be read, I think, in the context of the not entirely repressed romantic-erotic bond between the two girls. Nicki's overwrought musical confession, along with the previous "jealous rage" sequence, brings this bond most fully forward. Indeed, Jenni Olson points out the queer subtext here, despite numerous references to the lesbian bond between the girls being deleted from the final script (*Ultimate Guide*, 253–254). The two girls also clearly represent the two types of tomboyism identified by Halberstam in films from this period ("Oh Bondage," 172). The film therefore must conclude with their separation: Pam the feminine queer goes back home; Nicki the butch queer disappears into the crowd. So too the slip-sync spin in this scene suggests how the gatekeepers of mass media can go only so far in disseminating punk rebellion—a punk rebellion in this case with palpable undertones that challenge normative heterosexuality.

This queer subtext continues through the film's conclusion, which offers a surprisingly upbeat and progressive vision of mass culture. Nicki's "garbage bag" outfit and painted black mask across the eyes enjoy a magically rapid dissemination and catch on "big time." LaGuardia gets the radio message out that she will be doing a concert in Times Square on the rooftop of a movie theater. All the "sleez bag" girl fans come flocking, coded not as punk delinquents but as normal middle-class daughters. "Sleez bag" vendors pop up, cashing in on the trend. Though evil commercialism looms, the emphasis here is on how authentic fan culture spontaneously forms into an audience to support its rag-doll punk idol's one big show.

Before turning to this, let us heed the in/authenticity circumscribing such authentic fan culture. This in/authenticity has more to do with race than with mediatized performance. Indeed, as we will see, much of Nicki's performance is represented as distinctly raw, an unmediated exchange between her, her fans, and Pam. Harking back to the insidious specter of racial others we identified during the "Life During Wartime" street dance, all the "sleez bags" are young white females. Clearly coded as "in sync" with New York's hip radio messages as they make their way to Times Square, they are gawked at by men and women of color, mainly African Americans and some Hispanics. The montage sets up dark-skinned people on the "dark side" (prostitutes, drug dealers, etc.) as collectively forming a titillating danger the sleez bag fans must pass through. It also aims to portray these white girls as subversive and socially other through the eyes of ethnic and racial minorities—an ironic reversal, to put it mildly. Such shorthand becomes a backhanded reiteration of an easy stereotype. In this way, among others, the film's progressive treatment of female punk performers and fans seems not so progressive.

Nevertheless, Nicki's rooftop concert valiantly deigns to cite the Beatles, ending the narrative with a carnivalesque lovefest, but one probably too schmaltzy for Bakhtin.[6] Yet a reading against the grain of the scene's mismatch (it is a highly implausible and overly sentimental scene) might yield a notable articulation of mass culture through fan agency. The hordes of devoted, inspired "sleez bags" form a crowd but also a costumed community, derivative yet passionate. A few moments into "Damn Dog," the police stop the show and make ready to arrest her. Despite, and because of, the law's interruption, a somewhat remarkable moment unfolds as a fervent female punked-up audience engages in a kind of public dialogue with its performer. In a gesture of melodramatic contrivance, the police give Nicki a moment to say a few parting words, mainly about her precious camaraderie with Pam, her "best friend."

Her expression of their bond serves to pry open, within the place of the building as stage, a spectacular space of escape, one ridiculous yet utterly predictable: she suddenly leaps off the building, into the welcoming, buffering arms of the crowd below. Fantastic and sentimental as this appears, we might glean from it utopian connotations absent from the more typical rock-star self-destruction or alienation narratives, such as those concluding *Smithereens*, *Liquid Sky*, and *Sid and Nancy*. As we will see, this conclusion also serves as a suitable companion to the festive performance conclusion of *Ladies and Gentlemen, the Fabulous Stains*.

7.2. *Rooftop punk diva: As Pam (Trini Alvarado) looks on, Nicki sings "Damn Dog" just before diving into a sea of fans, at the conclusion of* Times Square *(1980). Photo courtesy of Photofest.*

Here, Nicki literally and figuratively fuses with her fan base, disappearing into the crowd and presumably moving on to new musical horizons. According to the rock-star narrative formula, the film sets her up to be punished or captured or sacrificed in some way; but it then refuses her this destiny with a refreshing celebration of her escape to freedom in and through the concrete manifestation of her punk-music legacy—her fans. Therefore, I would think twice about Judith Halberstam's assertion that "like the tragic hero, she suffers for her ambition" ("Oh Bondage," 172). I think Nicki's leap should be read not as a tragic downfall, but as a ludic displacement of her romantic-erotic bond with Pam, which ultimately the film must repress, with a more dispersed immersion into her sprawling gang of girl groupies.

Perhaps as an antidote to, or at least compensation for, this resolution favoring the triumph—fame and escape—of the punk outlaw, Pam reunites with her father. The sheer insipidness of this occurring on a rooftop we might take as a deliberately unconvincing bow to Hollywood's demand for a conventional happy ending. Likewise underlining such cheesy falseness, Nicki's band starts play-syncing over the film's concluding number, a disco song by the Bee Gees. Obviously faking it to nonsync sound-track music, the musicians play their parts conspicuously, recalling similarly half-baked scenes from *Swindle*. The playful, silly artifice, whereby synchronization is slippery or sloppy, suggests an inside subversion of the rock musical formula. (This, again, is not dissimilar to the MTV performance sequence concluding *Ladies and Gentlemen, the Fabulous Stains*, a film we turn to next.) In the context of the punk musical, such slip-sync might be read as a campy, excessive critical gesture, articulating resistance through performer-fan fusion.

Fittingly, a detail from Nicki's attire, visible just before she leaps off the roof, seems to sum up the film's potential, far from realized, for critical slip-sync: a splashy button on her lapel, with bright red lips that shift (slip?) from open to closed, depending upon how the light hits it.

CHAPTER 8

UH HUH HER

LADIES AND GENTLEMEN,
THE FABULOUS STAINS

Ladies and Gentlemen, the Fabulous Stains *has the unlovely effect of making the music industry seem crasser and rock fans look dumber than they actually are.*

—J. Hoberman, *Village Voice*

OMPLETED IN 1981, *Ladies and Gentlemen, the Fabulous Stains* (hereafter *The Stains*) was shelved by Paramount after preview screenings did not bode well. In 1984, the film saw limited regional release, notably a brief run at the Film Forum in New York City.

But it eventually found, or was found by, a sympathetic niche audience, first on late-night late-1980s cable television, then again in the mid-1990s for its pre-riot-grrrl sensibility. Thus recovered from the garbage bin of film history, *The Stains* has enjoyed screenings since the late 1990s at prestigious film festivals in Chicago and Sidney as well as runs at New York's Museum of Modern Art and Yale University's School of Art film series. In September 2008, a long-awaited remastered DVD was released.

Like *Times Square*, *The Stains* has achieved considerable notoriety as a cult film. As suggested in an earlier chapter, it is no coincidence that these and other early-1980s American punk narrative films (*Rock 'n' Roll High School, Smithereens, Liquid Sky, Repo Man*) fit the cult-film category. Whether by design or default, the cult film, according to J. P. Telotte, hinges on its embodiment of transgressive desire, or "boundary crossing": "For the cult audience implicitly desires something unavailable in the undifferentiated world; and the cult promises a meaning different from that handed down or sanctioned by society and its privileged institutions" ("Beyond All Reason," 12).

Groping to capture the fading punk-music subculture, these American punk narrative films noisily embrace such transgressive subject matter. Moreover, they often combine Bruce Kawin's distinction between the "inadvertent" and the "programmatic" cult film ("After Midnight," 19). *Times Square* and *The Stains* are particularly marked by this tension: translating punk into accessible narrative, yet self-consciously aiming to remain faithful to its marginalized, subversive tonality. For both films, the boisterous failure of translation (leading to their status as "inadvertent" cult) seems to have been partly a result of the attempt at fidelity (which is achieved by "programmatic" cult films). Whether they are bad punk films or bad because they are punk films, we will analytically embrace *The Stains* along with *Times Square* as strangely cheesy artifacts, discovering in the process the vital contribution they make to the punk-musical cycle.

Like *Jubilee*, *Breaking Glass*, and *Times Square*, *The Stains* focuses on young female punk (or punk-influenced) musicians struggling to express themselves, the deceptively simplistic pre-Madonna tagline for *The Stains* being, "These Girls Created Themselves." Yet *The Stains* picks up where *Times Square* leaves off, widening its scope to more fully incorporate punk-music fans. Also like *Times Square*, *The Stains* shifts in style and genre to an independent- or cult-film mode, though both films contain plenty of music on various levels.

Before considering the textual details of *The Stains*, let us take note of the sense of slip-sync surrounding the film's production and distribution. Directed by *Rocky Horror* producer Lou Adler and scripted by Nancy Dowd, the film's original title was *All Washed Up*. A hugely successful rock-music entrepreneur himself, the owner of The Roxy club in Los Angeles, Adler apparently changed the title of the film after Dowd quit during production (Jonathan Demme was supposedly brought in, uncredited, to rework the script). Having just received an Oscar for the screenplay for *Coming Home* (1978), Dowd refused association with the final cut, using the pseudonym "Rob Morton" in the screen credits because she was so frustrated with changes made to her script, the overall careless directing of the film, and even some sexual harassment during shooting (Palmer, "Disappearance and Re-emergence," 219–221): "Given Dowd's feminist take on punk rock, and with her very recent experience of successful Hollywood screenwriting, it was perhaps inevitable that she and Adler, a face from rock's hippie past, would approach the business of movie-making and the realisation of *The Fabulous Stains* from very different positions" (220).[1]

Such conflicting visions during production recall the problems that plagued and doomed *Times Square*. Though there are countless similar backstories in industrial film production, I think it is more or less justified to comprehend this contradiction working within and against these two early-1980s films as a distinctly punk contradiction: between punk's repulsion by and attraction to popular culture, as well as between its nihilism and its refusal to die. This, combined with *The Stains* being buried from most public or critical attention for many years, yet eventually coming to life on late-night cable television and the cult-film circuit, suggests how the film seems to have always been slightly out of sync with itself and its cultural reception.

It is rather striking how the fan culture represented within the film eventually came to fruition beyond the film. That is, this film about punk fan culture was ironically denied an audience until almost a generation after it was made, when the audience for the film finally found not only the film, but also a stylized reflection of itself inside the film. On this note, let us listen to an evocative personification from one of the film's fan blog sites on MySpace.com:

> I am a film that Paramount Pictures commissioned Lou Adler to direct. I was theatrically screened in 1984 at Film Forum in NYC. Then I was shown on Night Flight on USA Network in 1986. Then I was shelved. I survived only via bootleg on ebay for many years. I managed to get shown on VH1's Rock and Roll show in 2001 . . . My goal is to make as many people aware of me, so that Paramount Pictures will finally go ahead and release me to DVD. I mean, it's been 25 years! I have inspired many GRRL bands and am the ultimate film that witnesses Hard Punk turn into New Wave. I PRE-date Madonna but could be the exact road map she could have followed. (http://www.myspace.com/lagtfs)

Such a slipped-up reception, not atypical for cult films, resonates in a dramatically reflexive way with slip-sync, understood as a broadly punk concept characterizing much of the audiovisual and spatiotemporal articulations within the early-1980s punk music-film intertext.

Seen today as a visionary precursor of the 1990s riot grrrl music movement, the film, we must state up front, is hardly a work of art. Permeated by low production values, especially the badgered script and acting, the film could be described as a gorgeously trashy B movie that somehow manages to incisively articulate a dark side to early-1980s American culture. Because, like *Times Square*, it failed to achieve the commercial aspirations it was forced to pursue, *The Stains* too can be appreciated and read through Dickinson's film-music mismatch. Within and beyond its bad taste, this strange cult film also possesses some striking though confusing commentary on feminist politics and the American reimportation of punk music. While the film shares many features with *Breaking Glass* and *Times Square*, both released a year earlier, it extends slip-sync beyond the context of music performance, integrating it with issues of place, history, and fan activity.[2]

MEET THE FABULOUS STAINS

The Stains focuses on Corinne Burns (Diane Lane) and her sister Tracy (Marin Kanter), who form a punk–New Wave rock group with their cousin Jessica McNeil (Laura Dern), in the wake of their mother's death from lung cancer. Apparently abandoned but under the partial care of their mother's sister, Aunt Linda (Christine Lahti), they run away to join a concert tour that passes through their town; the Stains open for a punk band from Britain, the Looters, who themselves open for a bunch of heavy-metal has-beens, the Metal Corpses. The film basically traces the rise and fall—and rise—of the Stains while on the tour.[3]

The Stains contains several interesting twists that expand the reach of the slip-sync concept. The very beginning, for example: a pronounced sound effect of a clock ticking, apparently nonsync, since there seems no logical source for this sound in the image that fades in from black. Yet a loosely ambiguous source for the sound does obtain in this first scene: a news report asks us to recall a previous news story of the televised firing of Corinne Burns from her job as a fry cook. The previous report seems to have been about the state of teenagers in the small town of Johnstown, Pennsylvania—"the town that would not die" according to the program, but according to Corinne, a town that "died years ago." The replay of her firing is shown on multiple monitors—inside the television studio? It is never made clear. Then a freeze-frame of her shouting "ago" allows the sound of the word to linger beyond the frozen image. A touch of slip-sync film style that, when unpacked, suggests that history and memory are always mediatized, thus never entirely synchronized with themselves, or at least subject to slip-sync. Appearing here as an auditory remainder, or excess, that never entirely fits into representation, slip-sync leaves behind a stain on the very process of representation.

Besides how uncannily the opening segment anticipates the reality-TV phenomenon of the early 2000s (and we will encounter other prophecies throughout the film), the segment clearly situates Corinne as already mediated, already a kind of star, but one produced by and for the "human interest" news category. In asking viewers to recall her, the news program aims to resync her up with the current program it is moving into—and also, effectively, with the narrative of the film itself. Her mediatized identity is emphasized by the multiple monitors she appears on—the kind of thing *Breaking Glass* culminated in for Kate. Moreover, her firing and its mediatization together allude to the surrounding cutthroat economy of the Reagan era, when the service sector began to completely displace manufacturing and when teenagers had few employment possibilities beyond fast-food outlets. The film codes Corinne's outcast punk identity as a clear outgrowth of these social factors.

Whereas Kate was churned up by the excesses of media at the end of her fame narrative, Corinne starts her narrative arc already there, jaded and tough. The segment thus cleverly articulates her resistance to such mediatization. For example, the freeze-frame is ambiguous: does the film generate it on her behalf, to punctuate her resistance, or is it a slick effect of the news program? The nonsync ticking of the clock likewise may have been intended as a convention for conveying a "timely" urgency, typical of human-interest news programs like *60 Minutes*. But it also intimates the broader, more critical notion that history itself is mediated, that memory is coded, and that representation depends upon a synchronization that never fully obtains.

The idea that Corinne was a news star before becoming a punk rock star continues to be emphasized as a reporter reads letters from young female viewers identifying with Corinne's plight. Lending credence to the original news story we are being asked to recall, this gesture also initiates the fan motif of the narrative, which will become significant later. We should also note that the film credits begin rolling during this fan-mail sequence, and that the title of the film appears during a long high-angle shot of the production crew during the newscast, intimating a reflexive attitude, a "stepping back" from the news, to expose the process of its production.

The Stains thus seems to be engaging in a critique of the news media from within. Corinne, however, occupies a radically unstable position within this "within": the object of the news story, yet a kind of loose cannon. Forcefully illustrating this is the mock interview segment that follows, again ambiguously coded as part of, yet distinct from, a news story. As the film credits continue to roll, the voice of a male offscreen interviewer probes her, seemingly concerned for her plight; yet we watch Corinne restlessly feigning compliance, applying makeup, and smoking. Too conventional to be called slip-sync, the voice-off interview in this scene nevertheless feels contrived and conspicuous: the camera seems to look too intently at Corinne, while the male voice is too theatrical—a slip-sync-like tension between sound and image, an excessive, perhaps poorly executed, audiovisual mix. Looking offscreen, she sarcastically warns the interviewer to stop talking to himself or he will get fired. Other punk-inspired lines she tosses out are worth citing. "We're all horny dogs," seeming to speak not just of her band, but of everyone in society. She flippantly renames herself and her band members: "My name's not Corinne—it's Third-Degree Burns"; the other two are renamed "Depleted" and "Dizzy Heights." She spontaneously declares herself manager of her own group, the Stains (thus prefiguring this film's deconstruction of the male-manager narrative thread familiar from previously discussed films). Regarding her home life: "All the furniture's gone, the lease is up"—and she doesn't care.

One stylistic feature of this segment that in my view evokes punk slip-sync is the odd dissolves that occur on her, for apparently no reason, as she speaks or listens. This comes off like a dissolve jump cut, suggesting a slight passing of time, but also a sense of her identity slipping out of sync with itself by virtue of being mediatized by both the news program and the film itself. (More prophecy: Jump cuts become commonplace hip in movies of the 1990s during mock or real interview segments—*Leaving Las Vegas* (1995) comes to mind.) The scene fades to black as she stares at him with a knowing smirk. It is an effective overture to the film's later exploration of her punk-rock-star relationship to the mass media.

The film's opening credit sequence suggests how *The Stains* will recontextualize slip-sync as a marker of fan identity as well as of temporal and spatial dislocations. Before pursuing some of these avenues further in the body of the film, let us continue to glean some of the slip-sync-inflected sequences occurring early in the narrative.

For example, in the scene at cousin Jessica's home, which features Jessica's mother, Linda, and a friend of hers, there is a long and cumbersome, rather oddly formatted sound bridge. The conversation of the two women in the kitchen is heard over a long shot of a long take of Corinne arriving at the house. For most of the shot, we are unsure where Corinne is going (all we know from the previous scene is that she has to make a phone call), or how the conversation on the sound track relates. The voices initially seem to be discussing Corinne, but it turns out they are discussing her recently deceased mother. I encourage seeing and hearing this sound bridge as another conspicuous and ambiguous sound-track feature that kind of slips across the scene as Corinne's mobile and dejected space intersects the adult's place of home upon Corinne's arrival.

Once the shot cuts to inside the house, yet another intriguing variation on slip-sync occurs. A sappy pop song comes on the radio, and the two mothers start singing along. Not only are they off-key and out of sync, but—no surprise—they also sound awful. Here expressing an obvious generation gap, their performance of the music highlights not only the commercial conformity they embody, but their hypocrisy as well. Linda taunts Corinne, calling her a "TV star," and harasses both girls during the scene; yet booze and cigarettes figure prominently on the table between the moms, and a large television looms behind them. During Corinne's phone call, Linda maliciously turns up the volume, the slip-sync sing-along burying Corinne's attempt to get a job.

As a slip-sync coda to this sequence, the next scene comes via another sound bridge, this time of industrial noise and a vague honking sound. Abruptly and quite disorientingly, we cut to Corinne standing on a hill overlooking a drab suburban landscape, another concise ethnographic and topographic exposition of the source of her punk rebellion. Rather than smoothing it over, the sound bridge enhances such disorientation: it is unclear where she is or why she is there. Similarly strange is how and why she begins talking to herself about building her own radio station, which will broadcast no commercials or news, only "rock and the truth," and about how "it's all gotta change." Her monologue is quirky and conspicuous enough, but the sound mix too seems grafted on. We don't really see her speaking, partially because of the lighting and framing, but partially because of the slippery sound synchronization. This sensation becomes most prominent when she begins bouncing in a kind of punk pogo dance and counts off "1-2-3-4"; it appears postdubbed and out of sync, yet it is more accurately deemed a slipped sync, since she is supposedly uttering the count. Rather implausibly but playfully, her counting serves as a sound bridge to the next scene: kids dancing to 1980s New Wave music in the nightclub where her life will change. Implausible because she could not possibly be counting off that music; playful because the film's slip-sync aesthetic has her do so.

✳ PUNK IN/AUTHENTICITY: FROM SLIP-SYNC TO SLIP-SPACE

As a matter of fact, the nightclub scene mentioned above changes Corinne's life by setting into motion the iconography of punk and the theme of punk in/authenticity. The bored, restless, nihilistic state Corinne and her friends find themselves in is relieved by punk music and attitude. In the nightclub, Corinne first encounters the Looters, a British punk band on its first American tour, opening for the over-the-hill Metal Corpses. Corinne wanders through the crowd, mesmerized by the punk group's thrashing energy on stage and especially by the lead singer; several shot–reverse shots emphasize their unlikely, mystical eye contact (they are "in sync") during the song "The Professionals."

Before following this narrative thread, we should note the makeup of the band: our old *Swindle* pals Steve Jones and Paul Cook from the Sex Pistols (guitar and drums), Paul Simonon from the Clash (on bass), and lead singer Billy, played by Ray Winstone, a young British punk- or working-class-type actor just coming off a powerful performance as a Rocker in *Quadrophenia* (1979) opposite the Mod Jimmy (Phil Daniels from *Breaking Glass*). So the extradiegetic star power of the Looters not only links back to *Swindle* and *Breaking Glass*, but also lends all-around punk authenticity.

Yet such authenticity becomes suspect when one considers the promotional benefits these punk stars yielded. McLaren's famous motto "Cash from chaos" starts to look more like what that phrase always really meant: good old-fashioned cash from commercialism. In this respect, we should note that Jones and Cook formed a short-lived band called the Professionals after the Sex Pistols' breakup; thus, it seems quite cagey (and very McLaren) for them to be performing this eponymous song throughout the film. Indeed, the film trades on the authenticity of the punk Looters yet, to its credit, repeatedly deconstructs this punk "authenticity" as in/authentic, primarily at the hands of Corinne's acerbic ripostes.

Beyond her simply being wowed by front man Billy, the nature of their first eye contact foreshadows her empowerment as a fan to become a performer. Through the scene's shot–reverse shot, she seems oddly crucial to the impact he is having. This harks back to a similar scene in *Rock 'n' Roll High School*, in which Riff in the audience gets close to Joey near the stage. He bends down and they stare into each other's eyes, then she hands him a note, which he reads to the audience. Just as this onstage fan-performer connection leads to Riff meeting the Ramones backstage, so too here in *The Stains* Corinne manages a face-to-face encounter backstage. The Looters are not happy about opening for an aging heavy-metal band, so when Corinne approaches Billy about listening to her band, he silently snubs her. Yet at this very moment of punk snubbing, the Rasta tour manager and bus driver Lawnboy (the reggae singer Barry Ford, from the appropriately named band Merger) recognizes Corinne from television and invites her band on the tour as another opening act.

This gesture initiates a kind of rock-music moral hierarchy, which stratifies reggae, punk, and heavy metal, in that order. And within the punk-music category itself, an intriguing tension emerges as the Stains' version of pre-riot-grrrl postpunk music vies for center stage with the classic male punk of the Looters. Throughout the film, Corinne inhabits Billy's punk identity more in/authentically than he; he is the real thing, but somehow according to the film, she is better at it, as a special kind of poseur. The Stains reinvent punk, with a gender difference. Slip-sync thus occurs in the film figuratively as a critical, feminist appropriation of punk music identity, most vividly, as we will see below, with the Stains' affectionate theft of their key song, "The Professionals."

Yet this crucial first encounter in the nightclub mobilizes another figurative sense of slip-sync as displacement and dislocation. When Billy takes to the stage in the beginning of the film, he shouts at the audience, "Where are we?" Especially coming from the film's most articulate punk character while he is onstage during a performance, this question—obviously figurative and critical, not literal—unfurls throughout the film as a slip-sync sense of space, or slip-space. Indeed, Billy more literally asks his agent this same question on the phone after their set. Further elaboration of this "Where are we?" theme is how *The Stains* dials into American independent cinema's road-movie formula.

The Stains thus might be best categorized as a rock concert-tour film, or what Canadian filmmaker Bruce MacDonald has called a "rock 'n' road" film. The nightclub scene in fact begins in the girls' bathroom, where Corinne, before seeing the Looters, gazes out the window at the concert tour bus in the parking lot, envisioning where she will soon be: on the road, on tour. During some of the later driving sequences, a reggae song plays nonsync, "I'm movin', I'm searchin'." After one member of the Metal Corpses overdoses, Tracy whines that she wants to go home, to which Corinne poignantly declaims, "You don't have a home." These classic details of the road-movie genre illustrate how *The Stains*—along with *Times Square* and *Smithereens* and *Liquid Sky*—emphasizes the traversal of space and the search for place as the literal and figurative means for the punk fan to enter the punk music scene or showbiz.

This trajectory can be understood as a broader articulation of the slip-sync performance idea, one in which punk alienation becomes coded as peripatetic displacement. The punk music scene that the characters move toward or away from or through reimagines slip-sync as slip-space. Neil Palmer touches upon this aspect of *The Stains* when he observes how the film responds to "the massive spreading out of punk from New York and Los Angeles throughout the US" by "relocating the transformative narrative of punk rock from cosmopolitan urban centres to the mid-west." He continues: "*The Fabulous Stains* narrates the clash of different cultures—local, provincial, national, as well as those borne of class and gender—and contextualises the subsequent alienation within punk rock" ("Disappearance and Re-emergence," 220). Thus, timing in punk music performance becomes less important than relocating within the punk music community—and most of these films vacillate between dystopian and utopian versions of this community.

✶ THE STAINS, PUNK FANDOM, AND ROCK HISTORY

Slip-sync in *The Stains*, as suggested earlier, articulates an ambivalent historicizing of punk rock and punk identity. In this and other punk narrative films of the time, this ambivalent historicizing typically appears on the surface as an animosity toward previous rock cultures, particularly early-1970s glam and, before that, late-1960s psychedelia. The ambivalence might be understood psychoanalytically: in carving out its own identity by denigrating past subcultures, punk engages in an Oedipal act of repression. To deny one's lineage, origins, or roots is to make a spectacle of such a denial, which becomes a way for the repressed to return. *Smithereens*, *Liquid Sky*, *Repo Man*, and *Sid and Nancy* each contain narrative variations on such historical repression—that is, scenes that mock the sixties. Such an attitude was widespread in the punk-music subculture as a whole. Yet the films exaggerate the repressive, and thus contradictory, ramifications of such an attitude, through a figurative, historically tinged take on slip-sync.

For example, after the Stains join the tour, three generations of rock rebels are thrown together inside Lawnboy's bus. Predictably, Billy physically assaults the lead singer of the Metal Corpses, Lou (Fee Waybill, lead singer of the protopunk band the Tubes), for going on about punk being a recycling of past rock forms. Waybill seems to be more or less playing himself, his exaggerated acting slipping between self-parody and authenticity (becoming, thus, another sample of slip-sync in/authenticity in the realm of rock-star casting and acting). Lou claims that he "was into leather in '64" as a Rocker—a nod perhaps to Winstone's role as a Rocker in *Quadrophenia*, but more likely to the Tubes as an early-1970s glam-rock precursor to punk (best crystallized by their hit "White Punks on Dope"). In any case, Billy sees Lou as a phony, pretentious parental figure, an intolerable affront to his authenticity. To break up the brawl, Lawnboy slams on the brakes, no doubt symbolic of reggae as a kind of transcendent musical genre able to negotiate these historical animosities.

Yet Billy himself provokes similar repulsion later from Corinne: full of hypocritical envy, he waxes nostalgic and parental, offering her advice.[4] Later, when the Stains start to become successful, he derides her as a sellout while watching Stains fans being interviewed on TV. Yet the fact that he is in bed with some anonymous female groupie illuminates the machismo underlying his righteous tirade. In another scene, he advises Corinne that she has "got to start eating," that he is not trying to "pull" her, and that he has "been around." But when he tries to light her cigarette, she is quicker with the light. Lighting her own cigarette becomes a loaded gesture in the context of her distinctly unimpressed demeanor toward him. She has to play properly and practice, he pontificates; but she points out that she did not ask for his advice.

The fact that this crucial intimate encounter around punk music is interlaced with erotic charge seems to cut both ways: pointing up his dubious and duplicitous interest, but also mitigating her resistance to his brand of punk patriarchy, since the scene transforms into a sex scene in which Diane Lane famously strips in the shower. Here is how it goes: he puts on a tape of his band as he begins to undress; Corinne clearly shoots him a subversive sideways glance, eyebrow raised. Explaining to her the authenticity of his song, he begins reciting the lyrics over the song as it plays, a gesture we can contextualize as a slip-sync moment of doubling. One voice as authenticity (spoken song

8.1. *She won't put out: Corinne (Diane Lane), flanked by her cousin and bandmate Jessica (Laura Dern), refusing to fuse with the tour manager or the audience at the Stains' first gig.*

lyrics) tries but does not quite sync up with the other (same, his) voice as simulated music performance. Delivered with venomous sarcasm, she asks him if he can write out the lyrics for her. When he proudly declaims that he believes what he writes, she goes into the bathroom and slams the door. His confession that he never learned to read is not only a bit unconvincing, but also a clear ploy to paint himself as a victim in need of healing. Despite such an insidious glorification of punk rock, the film continually deploys a feminist deconstruction of it. By exposing punk's own proclivity for indulging in nostalgia, the film slips punk out of sync with itself.

In thinking about the film as a punk musical, and in relation to the films previously discussed, I am struck by how Corinne so clearly and forcefully articulates a punk attitude precisely by not articulating it, but by embodying it. Kate, Amyl, and certainly McLaren all in different ways verbalize a kind of lofty punk social critique that is more related to putting on a show or theorizing about society. But here Corinne repeatedly makes impulsive but biting refusals of everyone's "story"—most especially Billy's—illustrating how she engages a pre-riot-grrrl critique of punk, from within. Not unlike the anger of *Times Square*'s Nicki (especially before the studio cuts to the film), Corrine's punk rage comes from her family and home situation; there is thus a certain ethnographic credibility to the film's portrayal of her punk identity and the punk music scene.

Moreover, Corinne and her band enact a DIY approach to music and life more potent than that of any other characters we have seen. Before their first nightclub gig as an opener on the tour, she refuses to wear the costume prescribed for her by Lawnboy. Instead, she creates her own bizarre look, which eventually generates the "skunk" fashion sensation among her fans (echoing *Times Square*'s "sleez bag" fans). Complementing and extending this showbiz-industry refusal, the Stains' status as true amateurs becomes a kind of authentic antispectacle, especially given their clumsy, nervous manner and the feedback from the microphone. Their song "Waste of Time" is raw, unpolished, and unprofessional, even relative to punk music: no drums, more like a half-baked demo of a song. Yet the lyric content and droning chord repetition clearly convey a punk-music critique of work and family. Underlining this roundabout punk authenticity, Billy nods his approval while listening from the bar.

Further lending punk authenticity to the Stains' debut, Corinne confronts her audience more forcefully than Kate—or the Sex Pistols, for that matter. The audience in turn seems repelled. Corinne stops the song and removes her cap, revealing her weird "skunk" hairdo and makeup. She then launches into a verbal frontal assault, chiding a young woman close to the stage. Next, Corinne removes her coat; more shocked gasps from the audience at her tights and underwear costume.[5] In a final punctuation of her mocking striptease mimicry, Corinne exclaims what will become her signature line, "I don't put out," and leaves the stage. We are not talking slip-sync performance in an aesthetic or musical sense here; but her interruption of her own performance does recall the tone of some of the slip-sync scenes previously discussed. This slip-sync sense of disjunction or interruption during performance typically negotiates anxiety around prerecorded music, the staging of music as a visual spectacle, or, as here, tension with the audience.

Perhaps the most compelling scene in this respect occurs when the Stains perform their rousing looted version of the Looters' "The Professionals" at an event called the "Westland Cultural Festival." Though they get second billing (the Metal Corpses having quit the tour), the huge audience is primarily made up of "skunks," young female Stains fans, in costume. Waiting to go on for the next set, Billy is clearly nervous about being superseded by being parodied; ex–Sex Pistol Steve Jones comments right away that she is doing the song better than Billy himself. Tying together several of the film's thematic strands, her appropriation, or poaching, of Billy's punk musical identity becomes a kind of slip-sync, especially when he watches and hears "himself" through her, but differently. The fans exacerbate this slip-sync effect by going wild over the song. And their mimicry of the Stains, in costume and attitude, conveys another slip-sync effect of the performance as the fans double, or poach, the group.

The character of news reporter and anchorwoman Alicia Meeker (Cynthia Sikes) also contributes to the film's distinctive articulation of punk-music fandom. She seems intended to embody the socially critical potential of mass media, functioning in a way as an unlikely sister figure to *Times Square*'s DJ LaGuardia. During her coverage of the event, she indeed sounds a bit like LaGuardia, describing how "here in nowhere-land, thousands learn that life is to be lived now." As this line suggests, both articulations of fandom—the Stains' revision of the Looters, and the skunks' imitation of the Stains—are coded as invigorating and inspiring.

It is thus important to appreciate how the Stains start as fans of punk, then transform into players. Fan identification becomes crucial to their artistic genesis but also to their public appeal and impact, something we have not seen thus far. *Breaking Glass*, for example, sketches Kate's fans with minimal strokes as dystopian ciphers of her loss of authentic punk identity. Yet the star-fan synergy in *The Stains* (a rather punk, noncorporate synergy) does not come at the cost of commercial pandering. Let us note that the Stains are the ones who shock, who become a Sex Pistols–like sensation; the main fan reaction to the Looters in the film comes early, in the form of Corinne's inspiration to DIH: do it herself. The "authentic" (or, in/authentic) punk band the Looters thus becomes a springboard for Corinne's revised punk vision. Indeed, throughout the film Corinne delivers numerous deliciously punk and feminist one-liners, sassy and irreverent (a testament to Dowd's script); Billy, in contrast, is just self-consciously "angry," often seeming to be posing as the Punk Rocker. Ironically, the way he periodically beats up on people ultimately casts him squarely within the realm of exploitative patriarchal showbiz. In an equally ironic reversal, the Looters open for the Stains at the height of their popularity.

However, *The Stains* clearly equivocates on this point by granting certain privileges to the Looters, which makes the film all the more intriguing. Perhaps again yielding to the potential profit to be made from star power, the film gives the Looters time and space for an entire song—all very dramatic and energetic and glitzy, shot with a dynamic montage of angles and camera moves. Comprising mostly young female "skunk" fans, the audience has been less than patient with the Looters, shouting them down throughout their song. Yet the film insists on putting both audiences—in and of the film—through the entire song.

It seems that because the Looters are supposedly the real thing, they get more diegetic time and space to show their stuff. In contrast, we never see the Stains do an entire song, except, significantly, during the closing music-video credit sequence, coded very much as not live. We might speculate that the musical genre elements in the film coalesce more around the "real" punk-rock band the Looters, whereas the indie and cult elements coalesce more around the Stains. In any case, such diegetic privileging of the Looters onstage also probably reflects the conflicting visions of Adler and Dowd: the preferences of the older, male director took precedence. Yet Dowd's feminism persists, since the film perpetually and dialectically inscribes the Looters as "authentic," only to deconstruct such in/authenticity through the Stains.

For the moment, though, the Looters hold center stage as authentic punk heroes, and Billy possesses the shouting voice of moral authority. After their song, by way of introducing the headliners, Billy castigates the entire "skunk" audience, eventually turning them against the Stains. His long-winded exposé on how they, the fans, have been sold out is noxiously heavy-handed. Thus, when the Stains do come onstage, they are greeted with mass antipathy. Barely into their first song, the audience stops them by hurling objects and insults.

As with their previous, nightclub gig, the film codes this music performance around fan-audience interactions. Here, instead of Corinne confronting her audience, she finds herself confronted by her fans. Both performances are built around spectacles of disruption (or disruptions of spectacle), highlighting the transgression of the performer-audience boundary, this sort of encroachment being, of course, a key tenet of punk-music ideology. Such disruption, or a sense of inchoate performance, likewise reconfigures the slip-sync gesture. The slippage from synchronization becomes more dramatic, a fissure not between lip-sync and sound track, or between voice and body, but between performer and audience. Such performance disruption or tension is not unlike the slip-sync articulations we have seen in *Blank Generation* (1978) and *Breaking Glass*.

✶ SLIP-SYNCING FROM GIRL GROUPS TO RIOT GRRRLS

And yet the Stains' "downfall" at the hands of this punk critique of mass culture becomes a way station, a precursor to their culminating phoenix-like rise, the latter a pretext for their own critique of punk's critique.

After Corinne's humiliating postdemise television interview with news anchorman Stu McGrath (John Lehne), she finds Billy waiting for her outside the television station. Reeking of affected remorse, he apologizes and invites her to join him. But it is clear to us and to Corinne that his plea is all about his possessing her; she says no thanks to his patriarchal rock-star romance.

At the very moment when he climbs into his band's tour bus—a familiar setup for a Hollywood-style last exchange of longing looks—a motorcycle riding by grabs Corinne's attention. Shown in tight close-up, she turns her head to see "skunks" on the bike—and suddenly, skunks everywhere. It is another improbable and illogical turn of events in which almost magically, as if in a kind of hallucination, she seems engulfed by her band's imprint and impact. Likewise, an enigmatic radio music track comes on, playing the Stains' songs.

Again in tight close-up, Corinne laughs; the camera freeze-frames this laugh, then dissolves to the final music-video sequence. Meanwhile, across this visual transition, Corinne's oddly disembodied voice-over is heard, as if in a first-person documentary: "I was like you, a nothing, but I didn't give up, and you shouldn't either. You made me what I am."

These loosely reflexive techniques overinvest the transition into the final music-video performance, a full-blown though idiosyncratic slip-sync sequence that both flaunts and mocks the Stains' mysterious fame and success. The music-video sequence that ends the film, apparently celebrating the advent of the band to pop-star status, is somewhat clumsy, inexplicable, and illogical, coming across as tacked-on.[6] On the one hand, this partakes of what Mark Crispin Miller describes as the excessively happy endings to many 1980s films, in which the merging of difference into unity becomes exacerbated by a "crowd-within-the-frame" applauding the characters as stars ("End of Story," 236–244). It also exemplifies Jeffrey Sconce's paracinema, in which excessively bad filmmaking draws attention to itself as being somehow accidentally provocative. In tandem with Dickinson's mismatch, Sconce's notion of paracinema seems especially suited to *The Stains*, *Times Square*, and other punk musicals, since their textual excesses (as exemplified in this concluding sequence of *The Stains*) designate a nexus where crappy production meets aberrant reception: "Paracinematic taste involves a reading strategy that renders the bad into the sublime, the deviant into the defamiliarized" ("'Trashing the Academy,'" 548).

And yet on a third hand, this concluding music-video sequence also seems to possess some self-mocking irony: is it celebrating the new "Fabulous" Stains (a montage of magazine covers now names the band as such) or parodying them? Musically speaking, this version of "The Professionals" is given a fully "professional" punk–New Wave arrangement and sound. Yet the playfully disparate montage and costume changes render such musical professionalism a bit unhinged or dissociated—that is, slip-synced. Though probably not by design, three quick close-ups of three different pairs of bright red lips lip-syncing to the song work effectively as a slip-sync allusion to those previously mentioned in *Rocky Horror* and *Times Square*. The sequence's overall erratic juxtaposition of multiple sets and locations, found footage, band members play-syncing, and fans lip-syncing is deployed for a patchwork history of the three-singer girl group. This dimension of historical collage presents a slippery shuffling together of different time periods and styles, which becomes more pronounced as the Stains slip-fully lip-sync across its impulsive textual and temporal jump cuts. In this way, the Fabulous Stains presumptuously insert themselves into this history.

Likewise, a compelling extension of slip-sync obtains around the edges of the production of the sequence: it was shot much later, after all principal

8.2. *The Stains become fabulous and famous: the music-video sequence concluding the film, rife with slip-sync and girl-group riffing . . .*

8.3. *. . . as playful jump cuts cut and paste their instruments, costumes, and settings throughout.*

shooting had wrapped, in a new time and place, thus rendering the sequence visibly, audibly, and tonally out of sync, or off-sync, with the body of the film. More slip-sync resonance is audible in how the sequence so remarkably envisions the postmodern aesthetic of MTV and, especially, Madonna. By historicizing themselves while also hearing and seeing the (yes, not no) future, the Stains here enact and embody a distinctly affirmative, potentially feminist version of punk–New Wave slip-sync.

Through its exuberant multiplicity of female identities, all grounded by the music, the slip-sync dimension of the sequence vividly illustrates Susan J. Douglas on the progressive prefeminism of early-1960s girl groups. She interprets girl groups like the Shirelles and the Supremes as part of a female rock discourse reacting to the first wave of dominant male rockers, as well as providing "an unprecedented opportunity to try on different, often conflicting, personas" (*Where the Girls Are*, 97). Especially in the context of Corinne's snub of Billy, the Stains' music-video remix of the Looters' song ends up laterally politicizing its original antimilitary message, which Billy had explained to her earlier, with their own ironic send-up of USO performances by the Andrew Sisters. The film's music-video climax thus revives and postmodernizes such girl-group fever, displacing the preeminence of punk musical identity by historicizing it. Somehow, the final freeze-frame of Corinne ecstatically thrashing around her long blonde hair, for and at the camera, intimates such a feminist mining of the past for a feminist postpunk future.

I think we must fully appreciate how this music-video segment comes right on the heels of her rejection of Billy's patriarchal offer, thus becoming a kind of pre-riot-grrrl antidote to the typical marginalized status awaiting a girl who would go off with him. Indeed, the slip-sync quality, related to the loose and playful montage, suggests a kind of reflexive and therefore distanced attitude toward the fame signified by the music video. It is highly mediatized and artificial; but it also points that out, which engenders a certain feminist credibility. In this respect, let us note how Billy of *The Stains* and Danny of *Breaking Glass* are more or less interchangeable in their attempt to keep the punk girl authentic while possessing her romantically. The significant difference is between Corinne and Kate. Instead of being pigeonholed between two ultimately dead-end choices (Danny's indie-sensibility romance or Bob Woods's corporate nightmare) as Kate is, *The Stains* allows Corinne not to have any of it.

Like *Times Square*, *The Stains* thus offers up an ambivalent, perhaps contradictory reflection on mass media and popular culture. The mass media glom onto Corinne and attempt to exploit her. But as we would expect and have already seen, she lashes back at almost every turn. Of particular interest, given the film's emphasis on gender roles and its critique of patriarchy, is again the character of anchorwoman Alicia Meeker.

As suggested earlier, her relationship with Corinne proves rather compelling. Meeker seems to function as a somewhat reluctant comrade for the lead skunk, one who inhabits the commercial realm of the news media. During one scene, Meeker challenges Corinne for saying that she does "not put out," yet dressing like a prostitute. Corinne explains that "I don't put out" has been misinterpreted. Not a comment on sexuality, she meant it rather in a broadly political sense: don't get had, don't get taken advantage of. Later, on the air with her right-hand anchorman, McGrath, Meeker defends Burns. With a superior smirk, McGrath states that he finds her "weird," but Meeker counters that she is "elegant"—then plugs the Stains' gig that night. In other scenes, Meeker continues to defend the Stains, on the air, against McGrath's sarcastic conservative prodding (another prophecy, this time of the "angry white male" pundit like Bill O'Reilly and Glenn Beck).

At times, Meeker articulates the Stains' message in blatantly feminist terms: they represent "resistance" to "life as women know it." It is rather telling that near the end of the film, McGrath interviews Burns alone; Meeker has been transferred to another assignment. This is a low point for Corinne (after her rejection onstage at the hands of Billy), and McGrath gloats in the spectacle of her humiliation. Meeker's absence negatively alludes to the negative patriarchal control of the news media. This renders the final triumph of the Stains a partial corrective to such sexist policy, almost filling the gap left behind by Meeker—a blow not only to Billy but to McGrath, a provocative conflation of male punk rocker and male news pundit.

For the most part, *The Stains* ridicules the agents and managers representing the corporate music industry; the latter make their play for the Stains, but ultimately can't control them. David Robell (David Clennon), the sleazy agent for the Looters, first tries to convince Corinne to dump the Looters after the Stains hit the big time; he then refuses to pay the Stains after they are booed off the stage. Like *Jubilee*'s Ginz, Robell snubs Corinne while he is on the phone selling his next act, two sisters, "the Smears"; like *Swindle*'s McLaren and the "sleez bag" vendors McLaren would have sponsored in *Times Square*, Robell makes a bundle selling "skunk" merchandise before their show.

But unlike what Kate or Amyl or Sid Vicious would be capable of, Corinne insists on forcibly taking her money from Robell, then donating it to Lawnboy for his unjustly imprisoned reggae partner in Jamaica. As in *Times Square*, the resistance Corinne embodies is effectively interlinked with the skunk fans. While the film simplifies them as a flock that imitates its idols, it also articulates fandom as meaningful agency, though not social critique. Corinne builds a kind of community that saves her in the end from both industry exploitation and the romantic interest of male managers and punks.

It is this fan community, perhaps inadequately expressed but sufficiently evoked, that the film's music-video slip-sync-performance finale seems most driven by. Put differently, if Corinne has been assimilated by the new corporate music business, it seems to have occurred on her own terms. The slip-sync dimension to the segment, for me, conveys this: a reassertion of her authenticity from within the new MTV culture as a relatively honest in/authenticity.

CHAPTER 9

NOW ENTERTAIN US

STARSTRUCK, SID AND NANCY,
TRUE STORIES

GARY OLDMAN DOING Sid Vicious doing Frank Sinatra doing Paul
Anka's "My Way"—this is the slip-sync scene par excellence, the one
that first inspired me to undertake this book. Perhaps no coincidence,
it is also the one that culminates the punk-musical cycle with a kind of swan-
song climax. As the most mainstream, most commercially successful, and in
many ways most fully realized entry in this punk-musical film cycle, *Sid and
Nancy* (1986) seems to appropriately close it down.

And yet while *Sid and Nancy* functions as an endpoint, it also signifies
a new beginning for punk film. Or at least a threshold across which punk
musicals traveled into a kind of remission before reemerging differently in the
mid-1990s.[1] Before turning to *Sid and Nancy* in more detail, I want to take a
brief detour through an odd film from Australia: Gillian Armstrong's second
feature, *Starstruck* (1982). Then, after discussing *Sid and Nancy* I will conclude
with some thoughts on an American film released the same year as *Sid and
Nancy*, *True Stories* by David Byrne and the Talking Heads. Along with *Sid
and Nancy*, both *Starstruck* and *True Stories* help complete this survey of the
punk slip-sync cycle by suggesting a new tonality, one defined by a smug, self-
satisfied irony, a transparent multiculturalism, and a pronounced reckoning
with television culture. Moreover, all three films stretch to the limits of the
terrain what "punk" might designate. This watering down occurs primarily
by integrating certain genre components: *Sid and Nancy* for its Hollywood-
biopic narrative structure and production values; *Starstruck* for its sanitized
New Wave musical format; and *True Stories* for its ethnographic parody of the
provincial southwestern United States.

TELEVISION STRIKES: *STARSTRUCK*

A truly quirky New Wave musical, *Starstruck* offers yet another angle on punk slip-sync, though one would be hard pressed to justify describing the film as punk. Even "New Wave" seems too hard-core for a film with such a heart-warming, light-hearted tone. At the same time, one cannot deny the punk–New Wave influence on the musical styles and fashions of *Starstruck*. More intriguing is the film's uncanny sense of self-parody, which owes much to the spirit of punk while at the same time satirizing it. *Starstruck* focuses on Jackie Mullins (Jo Kennedy), an aspiring New Wave singer who, like Kate in *Breaking Glass*, employs a technorobotic performance style. With her fourteen-year-old cousin as her "manager" and numerous cheesy New Wave dance numbers, the film recalls the early rock musical *The Girl Can't Help It* for its interweaving of camp, parody, and slightly embarrassing exuberance.

Linking with many previously discussed slip-sync scenes, that of *Starstruck* portrays some degree of resistance to the bottom-line machinations of the mass-culture industries. Here, the specific setting is a television studio, and television culture ultimately wins out. As we know, television has hovered closely around the punk slip-sync moment of performance: *Jubilee*'s punks listlessly watch their cohorts on Ginz's pop-music television show; *Smithereens*' Wren carries her television around as her prized possession; *Times Square*'s Pam and Nicki smash televisions as antispectacle; Corinne and her band in *The Stains* subvert television from the inside, whether they are on the news or in a music video. More generally, television seems to have always provided much fodder for punk style and histrionics: think back to the Sex Pistols' notorious appearance in 1976 on BBC's *Today*, Bill Grundy's television interview program. But here, with *Starstruck*, the slip-sync scene conveys a noxious assimilation of punk into television culture, erasing much of the tension marking the previous films' more confrontational encounters. As we will see in both *Sid and Nancy* and *True Stories*, television monitors, and their own respective versions of tele-visual camp, figure prominently in their slip-sync scenes.

Through an outrageous publicity stunt orchestrated by her cousin Angus (Ross O'Donovan), Jackie wins a chance to appear on a pop-music television showcase called *Wow*. But the producers will not let her do the song she wants to and will not let her band, the Wombats, perform with her; they force a sub-stitution of their own song and band. In contrast to Amyl putting on her own masquerade, or Corinne refusing the costume handed to her, here we observe Jackie being made over by makeup artists backstage into a more classical pop diva, her own garish postpunk look coming undone. Yet she does not seem to mind, cognizant of the showbiz opportunity knocking. Further underlining

9.1. *Jackie (Jo Kennedy) at her first big break in* Starstruck *(1982): a television spot in which in/authentic slip-ups trip her up.*

the in/authentic setting, we observe the television audience being directed to go wild with admiration—on cue.

Near the middle of the song, which has a pop-disco sound uncharacteristic of her, she gradually loses track of the vocal track. Probably not familiar enough with the program's song choice, Jackie becomes visibly confused and distracted by the arm signals directed at her by the camera technicians. Distressed and a little angry, she points back at the cameras, slipping out of sync. The song's refrain, "I believe in you," becomes especially ironic, since no one believes in her and she obviously does not believe in what she is doing. Like Amyl in *Jubilee*, she reacts negatively to the performance context's exceeding of her and manifests her own excess of resistance. As the song comes to a close, pubescent screaming girls rush the stage, goaded by television host Terry Lambert (John O'May). All join her for the final chorus, but she flees the stage, dramatically removing herself from the performance even as her voice faintly continues on the sound track, now buried beneath all the other voices. We should note that here there is no confrontation with the audience nor any interruption of the performance, as occurs for Corinne in *The Stains*. *Starstruck*'s approach to slip-sync, even compared to that in *Jubilee*, clearly privileges the mass-media context.

The mise-en-scène emphasizes the in/authentic prowess enjoyed by television culture as various fragmented images of her appear on television monitors. One of these is a television perched in the pub where she works, which is owned and operated by her family. Here, her rejected, "authentic" band pokes fun at her performance: its members knew right away what she came to realize during the song—that it was a sham and a sellout. This harks back to the scene in *Breaking Glass* in which Kate is shooting a music video, coded in the film's moral framework as an ultimate betrayal of her more authentic vision, which is associated with Danny.

However, as *Starstruck*'s slip-sync television scene continues backstage, we observe that Jackie is distraught, not over the invasive performance technology and entertainment industry that has transformed her, but over how "awful" she was. This moment of slip-sync drama, in which she blames herself, is unique; unique too is how Terry comforts her by inviting her to a party in his penthouse, where a rather goofy and bizarre musical number in his rooftop swimming pool simply washes away her slip-sync anxiety.

In the tradition of the classical musical, *Starstruck* goes on to resolve its slip-sync in/authenticity conflict through a harmonic integration that ultimately celebrates showbiz (Feuer, "Self-Reflexive Musical," 447–449). Indeed, the film concludes rather euphorically: Jackie and her Wombats are triumphant after sneaking in to a New Year's Eve rock-concert gala at the Sydney Opera House, where they win the top prize. This money will help save her family's pub from bankruptcy; watching on the pub's television, her family too breaks out into joyous song and dance; and Jackie is happily united with her boyfriend guitarist. Even virginal Angus finds a girl backstage to roll around with—the final shot of the film.

This is a classical narrative resolution that we have not thus far seen—though it was intimated through a more cynical or at least ambiguous lens at the close of *Times Square* and *The Stains*. One might read Jackie's success story in more feminist terms, as I read the narrative arcs of *Times Square* and *The Stains*. Yet I find myself reluctant to do so because *Starstruck* seems entirely uninterested in challenging the stereotypes Jackie fulfills; she seems bereft of the punk agency driving Corinne or Nicki. Indeed, Neil Rattigan warns against interpreting the "struggling female" focus of *Starstruck* as being compatible with Armstrong's previous, first feature, the feminist classic *My Brilliant Career* (1979) (*Images of Australia*, 282). Like our reading of *Breaking Glass*, his analysis of *Starstruck* notes the film's divided attention between performer Jackie and manager Angus, suggesting that "sex is strongly on the agenda of the film" (283). In any case—and perhaps supporting a view of the film as regressively feminist—the euphoric closure in *Starstruck* clearly signifies a disturbing merger of punk, television, and a neoclassical take on the musical genre. The film concludes with a kind of camp without the irony, recasting the tension of its earlier slip-sync scenes as a mere glitch on the way to all ending well.

Whether this tone is partially due to an Australian cultural inflection is difficult to speculate; but certainly the film's overall Australian take on the punk musical is full of personality.[2] Rattigan claims that though the film's "unrelieved sense of fun that runs to lunacy" is best appreciated alongside 1960s pop musicals like *A Hard Day's Night*, "*Starstruck* is one of the most Australian of recent films and simultaneously the most Australianized of borrowed genre formulas" (282–283). Jonathan Rayner sees *Starstruck* as a precursor to the Australian "kitsch comedy of the 1990s," though, like Rattigan, he champions the film as the first "Australianized" musical. He sees "the film's combination of parody of and homage to the brashness of the musical" as offering "a utopian vision for success of the Australian film" (*Australian Cinema*, 153–154).

Given the scant mention of punk or New Wave in these critical appraisals of *Starstruck*, I suggest seeing the film as revealing a general assimilation of punk into the mainstream as well as a certain internationalization of punk. *Starstruck* is thus significant for our cycle, moving punk across national and continental borders, translating punk into a classical musical but also into the national and cultural context of Australia. Rather than combining the musical genre elements with an independent or exploitation-trash sensibility, *Starstruck* pushes them forward, which, not surprisingly, links it with the earlier British films and, further back, classical Hollywood musicals (Rattigan, *Images of Australia*, 282). Its stagy musical numbers become all the more excessive by virtue of their tonal distance from punk. The film's Australian lens seems to involve a self-consciously camp sensibility, an over-the-top silliness and flashiness not entirely different from, but more tame than, the camp or cult excesses of *Rocky Horror*, *Rock 'n' Roll High School*, *Swindle*, and *Liquid Sky*.

✶ "A FABULOUS DISASTER": *SID AND NANCY*

The conservative shift that *Starstruck* signifies for the punk-musical cycle points us toward similar tendencies in *Sid and Nancy*, Alex Cox's big-budget international coproduction eulogizing Sid Vicious (Gary Oldman), Nancy Spungeon (Chloe Webb), and the Sex Pistols. After achieving substantial critical acclaim with his first feature, the Los Angeles cult-punk film *Repo Man* (mentioned in Chapter 6), Cox was hired by a major studio to direct this sweeping and polished punk film. Told in flashback just after Nancy's body is discovered, the film follows the mythical arc of Sid joining the Sex Pistols, his drug-addicted romance with Nancy, the disastrous American tour of 1978, Sid's short-lived fame as a solo artist, and the final days leading first to Nancy's death then to Sid's.

Without insisting on a direct link between the films, we should observe how *Starstruck*'s more passive and traditional female lead performer, its celebratory embrace of television, and its more classical narrative structure all become further exaggerated in *Sid and Nancy*. More earnest than *Starstruck*, *Sid and Nancy* also recenters the white male punk rocker in a more multicultural mise-en-scène and milieu. This becomes a key distinction for *Sid and Nancy* as the "big splash" culmination of the punk-musical cycle. Moreover, though the film persuasively reenacts the late-1970s punk scenes of London and New York, it also reflects struggles over gender and race in the mid-1980s' neoconservative cultural climate. To put it one way, the difference Oldman's Sid might embody in relation to the hard-bodied patriarchal heroes of blockbuster Hollywood gets negated, or at least blurred, by the demonized, domineering narrative presence of Webb's Nancy. That is, the film through Nancy insidiously reinscribes Sid, at least partially, alongside Rambo and Indiana Jones. His stage name, after all, is Vicious.

But let us first turn to the key slip-sync scene in *Sid and Nancy*, which, as described in Chapter 4, restages Sid's performance in a Paris nightclub for *The Great Rock 'n' Roll Swindle*. Typical of *Swindle*'s faux-documentary approach, the original "live" sequence features the real Sid Vicious pulling out a gun and "shooting" members of the upper-crust, sophisticated audience, thus undermining any sense of this being authentically "live." Cox and Oldman shift the scene from a nightclub to a television studio, embellishing their fictionalized version with numerous expressionistic details. The effect created is a postmodern hallucination capturing the dizzy, paradoxical heights of the most notorious punk rocker's popularity. Oldman performs Sid performing "My Way" as a doubly excessive parody of Sinatra's celebrated rendition. Oldman brings an intensified "method" authenticity to Vicious's baldly in/authentic and heretical version of Sinatra. Once again, we encounter the spiral of simulation and in/authenticity as one film version (in *Sid and Nancy*) re-presents a previous, artificially "live" production (in *Swindle*). Cox further emphasizes this theme of in/authenticity by structuring the revised performance around a rather exaggerated instance of slip-sync.

Donning his classic spiked hair, Doc Marten boots, black leather, and dog chain, Sid struts in shadow down a pristine, semifuturistic stairway toward the camera. As the lights click on, he begins the first verse of "My Way" in a goofy circus voice full of slurs and cracks, accompanied presumably by an off-screen smooth-jazz orchestra (though it is not clear whether the music is live or recorded). At verse two, a driving punk-rock sound kicks in; he pogos, flails, and snarls the rest of the song. We should note that the orchestra continues to accompany the punk-rock instruments, symbolic of a certain co-optation of punk. Along with the song choice, such orchestration intimates the link between punk and the 1950s, between punk and cheesy lounge and elevator music. As with most previous slip-sync scenes, there are no musicians visible

9.2. *The ultimate punk slip-sync gesture: Sid Vicious (Gary Oldman) stops lip-syncing to "My Way" to stare down, then gun down, his television studio audience.*

on stage, invoking a sound design that equivocates regarding sync and non-sync, a sound design that contradicts or problematizes the production design. Up to this point, Sid has appeared to be actually singing; it is rather convincing lip-sync (Gary Oldman sang all parts for the film).

Then, as the last verse begins, the slip-sync gesture occurs as the singer dis-engages from the sound track. Most vividly recalling Amyl in *Jubilee*, he strikes an angry pose at the key moment of dissociation. But unlike her, or Jackie in *Starstruck*, he does not seem even remotely perturbed by the slip-sync. In fact, more like Kate in *Breaking Glass*, he appears to have deliberately caused it, rendering "slip" perhaps not as accurate a prefix as "quit"(-sync). Kate slip-syncs as a kind of formalized, somewhat indirect affront to her audience of train passengers. Sid's slip-sync is more directly confrontational. He seems to suddenly recognize the audience members for what they are: contrived for television, mostly middle-aged upper-class theater-going types. He eventually pulls out a gun and starts firing on members of the crowd, which includes Nancy and McLaren (David Hayman). McLaren looks on, impassive behind dark sunglasses; Sid does not shoot him. But he does exchange an angry glare with Nancy, who seems to dare him with her look—so he shoots her, as the culmination of spectacular violence and rage. After "dying" in bloody slow motion, she wakes up, shakes it off, and joins him on stage for a kiss, just as the song ends. They march back up the steps together as the lights switch off and the orchestral denouement fades out.

The scene seems to perfectly embody all the contradictions within and surrounding punk. On the surface, Sid's slip-sync as gangster becomes a refusal, a destruction of the gaudy televisual artifice of the performance context. But this negation of television in turn (at the same moment) becomes recuperated through the artifice of the film medium's textual effects. That is, the film's visual and audio tracks collude with the television performance to rearticulate rebellion as commodity spectacle. The exaggerated blood splatter, the horrified gestures of audience members, and the slow motion all underline how this "spontaneous" outburst of anger and disengagement from performance is itself staged and mediatized. On the one hand, Sid enacts excessive punk rebellion, appearing to break out of the contrived performance. On the other hand, such spontaneous rage becomes "spontaneous rage," a contrived effect of the performance spectacle.

In contrast to similar occurrences in both *Jubilee* and *Breaking Glass*, here the double excess of slip-sync becomes truly absorbed into the overall performance mode: his dissociation, his excess as angry punk, seems itself part of the staged excess of the performance spectacle. Look carefully at the way he pulls the gun from its holster, which is neatly folded into the lapel of his tuxedo—or at the mystical reunion of the romantic couple on stage, "beyond death." These are Hollywood clichés of gangsters and lovers who never die as screen personas. Its violent rupture all a sham, the slip-sync does not challenge the performance but becomes a "challenge" that ultimately serves the performance.

Such quality derives partially from how the "My Way" sequence occurs inside a sound and music design that suspends narrative logic and linearity. First, the performance itself seems to transpire in a kind of narrative limbo, a dissonant netherworld; there is no clear narrative link into or out of the scene, intimating it as a kind of hallucination, not from any character's subjectivity, but of the film itself. The scene is framed on either end by conspicuous non-synchronous sound bridges, an eerie atonal sliding scale of notes (which Cox faithfully borrowed from *Swindle*). During the first bridge, we cut elliptically to the television stage from a somewhat unrelated restaurant scene; then, as the "My Way" sequence closes with the same sound bridge, we straight cut from a black frame to a new scene: a bird's-eye view of Sid and Nancy at home asleep. While Sid's performance is hardly subtle—and, of course, viewers in the know will recognize it from Temple's film—there is an ambiguous hallucinatory quality to the place and function of the sequence in the overall narrative. Did this really happen? Was part of it in Sid's mind? How did we get to this scene?

Like a music video but also like a classical musical number, "My Way" is set off, self-contained by the predominance of the music track, but not entirely explained or justified by the narrative structure. Especially in the absence of dialogue, the music overdetermines the narrative ambiguity of the scene, "framing," if you will, the visuals with an aural register. The scene thus becomes a compelling punk example of Rick Altman's notion of melodramatic or musical-performance sequences that are "too much"—an excess—for classical narrative: "Unmotivated events . . . overlong spectacles—these are the excesses in the classical narrative system that alert us to the existence of a competing logic, a second voice" (cited in Williams, "Film Bodies," 728). In our postclassical, postmodern context, such a "second voice" as excess is no longer second. Rather, a primary excess, one deriving from punk sensibility and subject matter, determines the slip-sync scene and the film cycle overall.

The televisual context of the slip-sync scene seems like a kind of inverse articulation of the film's broader concern with drug addiction. On this note I would comprehend a later scene transition under the shadow of the film's central slip-sync scene. Sid and Nancy are watching, on television, junkies waiting in line at a methadone clinic; the next shot frames the television image as a point-of-view shot; the third shot match-cuts precisely to a location shot of the same line—with Sid and Nancy waiting in it. This subtle hallucinatory technique of realizing a TV image, and of that image consuming Sid and Nancy, suggests an underlying correspondence between the mass media and drugs. As we saw in Chapter 5, *Breaking Glass* too suggested this correspondence when Kate's increased popularity and exposure through the mass media was clearly accompanied by her dependency, whether voluntary or forced, on drugs.[3] Drugged out in front of the television, Sid and Nancy become living effigies symbolizing society's contradictory addiction principle.[4]

But there is more. *Sid and Nancy*'s slip-sync scene perfectly anticipates Auslander's concept of liveness. From the start, it connotes both live and recorded; it exudes both realism and expressionism. But the "My Way" performance also effectively articulates the dialectical ramifications of Attali's key notion of noise, in which composing (nihilistic excess) struggles to break through repetition (commodified reproduction), and repetition in turn struggles to contain and package composing. Both concepts, liveness and noise, help unpack the density and complexity of the scene's various slip-sync levels.

As the song begins, we recognize it on a semantic level; we also recognize the orchestral-arrangement style, smooth jazz. But Sid's voice is an ugly excess, "noisy," out of sync—not literally here, but figuratively. From another angle, his histrionic blubbering and "dumbed down" vocal intonations express a certain punk authenticity: inhabiting and destroying conventional popular music from within. When the punk music instruments and rhythm begin, this conveys a second level of punk's slip-sync negation from within the song. Oldman's warped vocalizing becomes doubled, or embellished, by the instrumentation as he kicks and screams the song now, a more frontal attack on both it and the studio audience. Yet another, more compelling aspect of slip-sync occurs when he actually stops lip-syncing and stares down the audience, disengaging from his own performance while his "voice" continues on the music track. This gesture most dramatically conveys Auslander's liveness and my in/authenticity: Sid is a phony, yet he steps out of this phoniness to rebel against his own spectacle; but this rebellion in turn is coded as a phony spectacle. There is an ambiguous hyberbolic collision between his body's voice, which dissociates, and the voice of the televised, simulated spectacle, which is also his voice, this being the key slip-sync paradox. The final punk slip-sync gesture occurs when he pulls out a gun and starts shooting the audience. This spectacle of "death" anticipates the end of the film and the end of their lives. For "My Way," Nancy wears a bridal gown, as she will in the final scene "after" Sid dies, joining him in death; for "My Way," she perhaps invokes "bride of death" imagery associated with the horror genre and with gothic in general.

Indeed, this slip-sync scene not only serves as the narrative and thematic center for the film, but also elucidates the film's somewhat elusive genre inflections. *Sid and Nancy* does not on the surface appear to be a text that combines different genres. But in fact several genres seem to overlap within it. The film noir genre is evident in the "detective investigation" framing device as well as through Nancy's role as femme fatale on the scene of Sid's more innocent disorientation. According to the film, she lures him into a world of drugs and fame ostensibly antithetical to the "pure" punk subculture she contaminates. Likewise, the high melodrama of the rise-and-fall biopic traces the classical arc of Sid's earthy, amateur beginnings, through his stellar trip as the ultimate punk celebrity, then catastrophically down to earth and into his early grave: a tragic narrative of high flying and fast falling. This narrative formula is haunted by at least a third genre influence, the melodramatic woman's film.

Through this lens, the emotional excesses associated with Nancy, her nagging and hysterical pitches, become understood through her body, specifically her voice. The film makes an excessive aural spectacle of her voice as whining, annoying, grating, as if to ensure that she incurs none of the sympathy more typically accorded the lead female performer in a woman's melodrama. As a kind of inverted mirror of Sid's slip-sync in the limelight, her voice throughout is too much or out of sync with her body; her body produces a voice that goes too far, that invades and corrupts. Put differently, her voice problematizes Mary Ann Doane's notion of the "phantasmatic" bodily coherence that depends in cinema on a certain representation of the voice. In this respect, the film's portrayal of Nancy seems not unrelated to Linda Williams's concept of "body genres," in which the female body becomes excessively sensationalized in a state of erotic ecstasy (pornography), fear and terror (horror), or emotional suffering (woman's film). With a bit of a stretch, we might understand Nancy's vocal and corporeal excesses as a unique combination of all three genre takes on the excessive female figure ("Film Bodies," 728–730).

Yet another significant aspect of *Sid and Nancy*'s staging of slip-sync is its representation of gender and race. This reveals a problematic, ambivalent use of women and minorities as figures that contrast with, or at least frame, the white male punk-rock-star protagonist and his twisting into and out of sync. As we have seen throughout this book, the use of people of color as "critical others" constitutes a subtextual marker of the ideology informing slip-sync. What occurs in *Sid and Nancy* is a more insidious tension that begins with coding gender as female. By localizing a harsh and invasive femininity within Nancy's body and voice, the film renders punk's viral other as female. This gender hierarchy is then set up against race, a kind of peripheral battle for and through the main white male character. Given that this punk musical is the most mainstream and the most classical one of the period, and the one most deeply embedded (chronologically and ideologically) within the Reagan-Thatcher era, the shift back to the white male lead seems provocative, to say the least. Whether accurately based on the real Nancy or not, the film's character-ization of her resuscitates several traditional conventions of gender and race.

Interestingly, the excess and exhaustion associated with her presence is not just sexual, romantic, and familial, but also work-related, since she pushes him to "work hard for the money"—a betrayal of the codes of punk ennui and punk resistance to commodity culture. In this way, she represents a kind of big-business ethos run amok, an intriguingly punkified trope for the mid-1980s deregulation frenzy. Nancy suddenly seems like a feminized version of the punk-musical manager character, one more fully demonized than *Jubilee*'s Ginz or even McLaren himself. Let us note that unlike either of them, she gets severely punished for pushing the boys around in the world of punk showbiz. Her drugs too become a cipher for consumerism gone wild. She is not at all a Reagan-era hard body, but an excessively feminine hysterical body that may very well embody the backlash against feminism so prominent in public dis-course during the 1980s. Not unlike what *Fatal Attraction* (1989) did for the Glenn Close character a few years later, *Sid and Nancy* codes Nancy as pos-sessing too much masculine drive, a familiar alibi from film noir for wreaking violence on the femme fatale.

Put differently, Nancy embodies a liberated career woman of the 1980s, rejecting laziness, domesticity, and anything countercultural. For example, when Nancy brings pizza to the band's rehearsal as Johnny is being bandaged up, she reproves Sid for not learning his part of a new song. Likewise, she becomes incensed when Sid suggests she clean the kitchen at his hippie mother's home; defying Johnny's accusation, mentioned above, Nancy proceeds to mock her, trashing her hippie clothes, to Sid's dismay. In many other instances throughout the film, she pushes Sid, as his manager, to be a professional musician, to share drugs with her, to follow through on their suicide pact. Nancy flings herself at his erect knife, though this filmic version of events is reportedly one speculation among others (Savage, *England's Dreaming*, 507–508). These sequences establish Nancy as the American corrupting influence on the emerging British punk subculture, although according to Jon Savage, Sid was already into drugs when he met Nancy (427). Her active and independent role in the film ultimately becomes a menace, one that hastens Sid's doom.

The antidote for all things Nancy, according to the film, appears to be race, signified by black characters. In an essay published a few years before the release of *Sid and Nancy*, Robert Stam and Louise Spence suggest that often well-intended representations of race can be both progressive and regressive. *Sid and Nancy* seems guilty of displaying both the "positive images" and the "naïve integrationism" ("Racism and Representation," 883) they observe in "many anti-colonialist films," in which "a kind of textual uneven development makes the film politically progressive in some of its codes but regressive in others" (889). With a heavy hand, *Sid and Nancy* reifies African Americans as static ciphers of moral responsibility and authenticity.

Several minor but key black characters stand out in the film as beacons of ethical concern, opposed to the self-destructive drug and media excesses of Nancy and Sid. For example, band manager McLaren's assistant, a light-skinned black woman, tries to talk Sid out of using smack several times. Codified as possessing insider insight on such a matter, she seems to be positioned opposite Nancy, but undergoes virtually no character development. Another example is the black man administering at the methadone clinic. Confronted by the two white punks on dope, he lectures them moralistically about how he fought in Vietnam, but only so the CIA could funnel drugs into the United States; and about how the system "keeps them stupid" while they are hooked on dope. Finally, near the end of the film, a similar character, a black policeman, reproaches Sid for his comfortably tough time after he gets bailed out for Nancy's murder; he reminds Sid that he has no braces on his legs, implying that he has never really suffered.

At the close of the film, such progressive-regressive attitudes toward race and gender come together. After getting out on bail, the first thing Sid does is to devour a pizza, foreshadowing Nancy's "return" from the dead. Wandering in a wasted, postindustrial landscape, he encounters a group of young black "ghetto" kids dancing to some soul-disco on their boom box. Apparently, they recognize him (a bit far-fetched): they affectionately harass him not to be so stuck up, inviting him to dance with them, which he does, trying to imitate them.

Then a cab pulls up out of a sudden foggy gloom, and the psychedelic music returns, displacing the "authentic" disco. In other words, nondiegetic music from beyond the grave, coded as inauthentic, displaces the authentic diegetic music. Nancy is inside the cab, all dolled up in a white bridal gown, beckoning him coyly with her eyes to forsake the positive future signified by the black kids. He gets into the cab and goes off, kissing her and following her, as the credits reveal, to his own death. The black kids chase the car, both to egg him on and to try to catch up—perhaps to rescue him. The cross-racial and intermusical bond becomes a fleeting gimmick, a fork in Sid's road, a pretext for Sid's final bad move.

Whereas Nancy, drugs, and the mass media come to represent an excess that destroys Sid, blacks provide the contour of productive conduct. Localizing this value in blacks partakes of what Cameron Bailey analyzes in *Something Wild* (1988): using blacks as "repositories" of authenticity, as an antidote to urban white angst. "Marginal cultures in these films work as repositories of the real" and tend to be drained of their own culture, presented instead as "interesting ciphers" ("Nigger/Lover," 30). A more optimistic view would interpret *Sid and Nancy*'s "progressive racism" as a step in the right direction.

✱ NOT SO WILD LIFE: *TRUE STORIES*

Rife with postpunk irony and some slippery Orientalism, David Byrne's *True Stories* (1986) offers a very different yet complementary slip-sync approach from that of *Sid and Nancy* and *Starstruck*. As suggested earlier, all three films offer slip-sync portrayals that in distinct ways invoke a more multicultural or international flavor as well as a formal incorporation of, and reflection on, televisual aesthetics. In the spirit of *This Is Spinal Tap* (1984), *True Stories* (coproduced by *Spinal Tap*'s Karen Murphy) is a self-consciously modest, tongue-in-cheek mockumentary focusing on a "specialness" celebration in the small fictional town of Virgil, Texas.

But the film also functions as a promotional and artistic cinematic vehicle for the Talking Heads, one of the most important and innovative New Wave bands to emerge from the late-1970s New York punk scene. A couple of years before *True Stories*, the Talking Heads made a splash in film as the subject of Jonathan Demme's much-acclaimed concert documentary *Stop Making Sense* (1984). Yet their music always possessed a keen cinematic sensibility, perhaps dating from the invocation of Hitchcock's Norman Bates in their first single of 1977, "Psycho Killer." By the time the Heads get to 1986 and *True Stories*, "synergism is a definite factor" in the production and marketing of the film, with portions of the $5 million budget coming from Sire Records and Penguin Books (Denisoff and Romanowski, *Risky Business*, 590).

In *True Stories*, director Byrne serves as the first-person tour guide who ferries us through the lives of the quirky inhabitants of the town. The film's particular version of slip-sync performance corresponds with its understated satire of the town's naïve expectation of the economic benefits coming from the arrival a new local computer company, "Vericorp," apparently modeled on Texas Instruments.

After introducing us to the computer-chip plant where most of Virgil's new global villagers work, Byrne drives us out that evening to the local nightclub, its modest façade part of a pathetic strip mall. Here, various audience members, mostly characters we have already met, run up onstage in rotation, each lip-syncing a different verse of the Talking Heads' song "Wild Life," the single from the *True Stories* album released just before the film. Perhaps an accidental remake of the Sex Pistols' "audition" scene in *The Great Rock 'n' Roll Swindle*, this slip-sync scene mixes elements of karaoke culture, MTV's postmodern reflexivity, Warhol's fifteen minutes of fame (here, fifteen seconds), but also punk's DIY philosophy. In contrast to the "Anyone Can be a Sex Pistol" scene, in which each singer actually sings over the recorded musical track, here Byrne's original recorded voice remains, over which each "singer" lip-syncs a few lines. The performance is satirically coded as a live event.

The wall of TV monitors behind the band speaks volumes as a televisual performance mode overtakes the ostensible nightclub venue, the latter perhaps evoking faint memories of the late-1970s New York club scene the Talking Heads themselves participated in (famously documented in Poe-Kral's 1976 *Blank Generation*).[5] During the performance, the film cuts periodically to various close-ups of unrelated, obscure TV images, creating an effect of high-art video-meets-MTV that is appropriate to the Talking Heads' history and aura: former introspective art students turned self-effacing rock stars. Close-ups of each performer exaggerate how the lip-syncing slips as each "singer" mouths the words, sometimes a little off.

But there is also a sense of slip-sync in the conspicuous shift from one face to the next, each face inhabiting (or inhabited by) Byrne's distinctive voice. This, combined with the intercutting of the TV-monitor images, invokes the slip-sync sensibility, whereby "live" becomes liveness and in/authenticity reigns. Moreover, the rapid-fire star turn onstage for each audience member itself becomes doubled through their various impersonations of other stars: Elvis, Prince, Neil Young—even David Byrne himself. Most notable for us is the first impersonation, by Talking Heads keyboardist Jerry Harrison, of Billy

9.3. *Slip of the tongue-in-cheek: Talking Head Jerry Harrison doing Billy Idol (s)lip-syncing to the singing voice of Talking Head and* True Stories *director David Byrne.*

Idol. Like *Jubilee*'s Adam Ant, Idol was an original fan of the early London punk scene and supposedly attended the Sex Pistols' first gig in 1975, at St. Martin's School of Art. Also like Ant, he went on to become an early-1980s pop icon of punk gone New Wave. Having a Talking Head member "do" Billy Idol, decked out in caricatured punk regalia, is the scene's only direct, but perhaps overinvested, reference to punk.

Bearing even fewer visible traces of punk than *Starstruck*, *True Stories* is nevertheless postpunk, not so much by virtue of the Talking Heads' presence, but because of its cool, parodic embrace of pop culture. The film's slip-sync performance translates punk's DIY into a goofy audience participation, one that harbors a faintly condescending tone toward Middle America, and one that uncannily prefigures a show like *American Idol*. In this way, *True Stories* joins hands with *Starstruck* for their optimistic, mildly ironic mainstreaming of punk and New Wave. It is a little too easy to perceive the clever yet subtle mockery of these rural American yahoos. Less easy to perceive is a kind of affectionate embrace of them, integrating them, via television and "live" slip-sync, into the now-anachronistic punk-nightclub performance venue. An interesting slip-sync footnote to the sequence in this respect is that Byrne apparently envisioned releasing an album of the actors singing the film's songs, which were composed "with other voices in mind" (Denisoff and Romanowski, *Risky Business*, 596).

Such tonal ambivalence is in fact what gives the film its slinky multicultur-alism. On the one hand, people of color are speckled among the employees of the town, each racial other bringing his or her own brand of nativist ethnicity into creative expression through a pastiche of the American melting pot. How-ever, such representation of race is filtered through a condescending, almost patronizing tonal framework, one that idealizes the racial other as an exotic artifact. For example, the clever opening montage, on the "history" of Texas, deconstructs America's Manifest Destiny myth by exposing the racial conflicts and racism just beneath the surface of the expanding frontier. Yet the self-con-sciously eclectic and goofy found photographs, combined with the smirking voice-over, render such deconstruction a joke for those already enlightened. The extreme irony of the film in this respect becomes almost patriotic through the back door, coming full circle across its own ironic distance, absorbing its deadpan humor, and rearticulating it as straight—rather than "straight."[6]

★ PUNK SLIP-SYNC AND 1980S POLITICAL LIP SERVICE

Like *Starstruck* and *Sid and Nancy*, *True Stories* thus signals a certain closure of the punk-musical slip-sync cycle we have surveyed. These films, in distinct ways, went international or multicultural, but they also embraced a certain televisual aesthetic and sensibility that became intensified, across popular and marginal cultures, as the 1980s wore on. The original in/authenticity and dou-ble excess informing slip-sync as a tension perhaps became more acceptable, mere fun and games. This seems to be partly because of, among other factors, the increasing visibility and conventionality of playing with lip-sync, which became so prevalent on MTV, a more utopian and commercial format for the slip-sync gesture, one running parallel to our punk musicals. On this note, and by way of a conclusion, let us tentatively situate the historical and aesthetic slip-sync arc we have sketched firmly within or alongside the conservative cul-ture and postmodern politics embodied by Reagan and Thatcher.

For different, perhaps antithetical reasons, punk and this neoconservative discourse share some oddly collusive seams. For example, both ideologies deni-grated the 1960s counterculture; likewise, both celebrated a certain anarchy of consumption in the marketplace. There is also a way in which both the Rea-gan-Thatcher political machines and punk articulate an unnerving ambiva-lence around authenticity and inauthenticity, fiction and truth, spectacle and spontaneity, dissimulation and simulation. For example, Reagan's performance of authentic "commonsense" populist values within the context of an inau-thentic conservative propaganda machine (one driven by entirely unpopulist economic policies—thus "inauthentic") coincides more than chronologically with punk's interlocking of vehement rebellion and shameless media shamming. By focusing on a specific and consistent representational strategy that exaggerates in/authenticity, we have at least raised the possibility of thinking through the relationship between punk's nihilistic pastiche of popular culture, and the Reagan-Thatcher deregulation of market forces, not to mention their shrewd manipulation of misleading images.

After all, the realpolitik of slip-sync involves the operation during performance whereby a manufactured, commodified voice, an object of technological reproduction, displaces the actual voice and body of the performer. The double excess of slip-sync thus encapsulates a more general doubling that Linda Hutcheon identifies as key to postmodern art, culture, and politics. In a chapter titled "Political Double-Talk," she could be describing punk when she characterizes "postmodern challenges" as "paradoxically both inside and outside, compromised and critical," and "open to appropriation" (*Poetics of Postmodernism*, 205). Moreover, her pithy maxim "There is contradiction, but no dialectic in postmodernism" (209) helps bring Reagan and punk under the same umbrella. As Michael Rogin notes, Reagan too effected a kind of slip-sync within his presidential political identity by seamlessly incorporating his previous acting roles, thus embodying contradiction as doubleness: "He presents political events of his own making as if he were somehow not responsible for them" (*Ronald Reagan*, 8). Rogin situates such "easy slippage between movies and reality" within the postmodern shift from production to consumption, in which the opposition between "the authentic and the inauthentic" no longer makes sense (9).

Situating 1980s "popular conservatism" in direct relation to the "authentic inauthenticity" characterizing postmodern rock-music culture, Lawrence Grossberg sees both Reagan and Thatcher as paradoxical leaders of the new conservative political culture, each persona relying heavily on "common sense" and an "everyday" platform. Citing Stuart Hall's notion of Thatcherism as "authoritarian populism" (note the paradox), Grossberg describes Thatcherism's attempt to synchronize a "struggle to reshape the very terrain of common sense" and an "imaginary vision of British culture" (*We Gotta Get Out*, 245). On Reagan's inexplicable popularity, which was "never as great as it was often felt or represented," Grossberg notes, echoing Rogin: "If he acted in ways that contradicted his image or his public posture, his power remained intact. In fact, it was never clear what his image was for it was full of ideological and personal contradictions" (253–254). Certainly the phenomenal media blitz surrounding Reagan's death in 2004 reached a hysterical pitch, fueled by rampant antihistorical, hypermediated confusion around in/authenticity. Goaded on by the Bush administration, mainstream media accounts eulogizing "the great communicator" consistently deployed the trope of authenticity to characterize (and mythologize) the collective memory of perhaps the most shrewdly inauthentic president ever.

It is not my intention to conflate such "bad" postmodern politics with the postmodern negation that punk's self-conscious and reflexive in/authenticity promises. However, perhaps Sid Vicious doing "My Way" is not such a grotesque parody. Perhaps it contains an insidiously affectionate allusion to Frank Sinatra—who, of course, parallels Reagan's own political swing from left to right. Put differently, perhaps punk harbors an elusive nostalgia that looks back not to the parental counterculture of the 1960s, which it consistently derides, but to the grandparental, Eisenhower 1950s: the era of James Dean, the Beats, and the birth of rock and roll; but also of Sinatra's prime, the birth of television, and the Cold War ideology and military-industrial power nexus that would crucially shape Reagan's political persona (and that thrives today, resurrected for the in/authentic interventions of a new globalized American empire).

Indeed, the more multicultural narrative milieu of *Sid and Nancy*, within which the spectacle of Sid's weird punk hero's journey occurs, further intimates the broader neocon culture that absorbs black activism, for example, into a tolerated state of state-sponsored "multiculturalism." The film creates a kind of audience within the narrative, made up of people of color, who guide Sid from the sidelines of his epic "star-struck" rise and fall. By doing so, the film suggests a political shift from late-1970s race activism, in America but especially in Britain, which was intimately connected with the first punk movement, to the more tokenistic assimilation strategies that characterized the conservative mid-1980s. Anna Marie Smith, for example, has described in detail how the Thatcher program effectively recast "imperial racism" in "suitably 'tolerant' post-colonial terms," coding new, racist immigration policies as inclusive and as serving the interests of Britain's diverse citizenry (*New Right Discourse*, 56). Given director Cox's lucid and clever critique of Reaganism in *Repo Man*, it seems possible that *Sid and Nancy* is deliberately, or at least self-consciously, revising 1978 as 1985 so as to point up the surprising and disturbing trajectory from punk to neocon.

With David Byrne and Sid Vicious driving the punk-musical slip-sync narrative in 1986 through a cinematic landscape where people of color furnish dramatic shading, I think we would not be imagining neocon fingerprints on either Byrne's smirking, faux tour guide of Texas, or Sid's unabashed mugging for the camera. The poor black kids swarming Sid's final limo ride, or the Latino microchip assembly workers lighting up Byrne's ethnographic gaze, become a "multicultural" audience for the white male punk icons, lending a neocon ring to punk's audience participation. As we have seen, people of color have problematically been made to serve this purpose in *Breaking Glass, Swindle, The Stains*, and many of the other films. I think that because the majority of these films were led by female punk performers, this engendered a certain critical edge to their slip-sync motifs, especially in the context of race and gender. That the later films display a certain return to traditional gender roles favoring the male seems to be a sign of the times, one that also signifies a certain subtextual shadow regarding race that has always haunted punk.

Yes, Sid's performance of "My Way" is full of irony and mockery; but it also conjoins a Reaganesque individualist bravado and punk's anarchic DIY. While Derek Jarman's subversive punk mining of Elizabethan literary England is radically opposed to Margaret Thatcher's strong-arming of Elizabethan imperial England, there is at least a sliver of contact. The ludic reflexive play of *True Stories* coyly intimates a television culture run amok. "Anarchy in the UK," in some ways, is just what Thatcher inflicted on the British welfare state; "my way" returns through punk as a code phrase for privatization, deregulation, and rogue militarism. At best, the double excess of punk slip-sync thus offers a critical mirror, a double, for the conservative double-talk of postmodern political culture.

★ POSTSCRIPT

SLIP-STREAMING

I BEGAN THIS STUDY by invoking various contemporary scandals around live lip-sync, among them Milli Vanilli, Elton John's castigation of Madonna, and Ashlee Simpson's debacle on *Saturday Night Live*. I proposed that a critical look at the punk slip-sync film cycle would furnish an aesthetic and historical framework for considering such phenomena and, more importantly, the larger cultural stakes around authenticity, simulation, performance, and new electronic technologies. In the spirit of pressing punk's potential for critical negation within popular culture, let us slip from live lip-sync to the virtual universe of Internet blogs, YouTube, and MySpace. Can the "explosion" associated with punk's genesis become an equally radical "implosion" in the ubiquitous realm of cyberspace?

In a recent issue of the *Chronicle of Higher Education*, Bill Ivey and Steven Tepper explore the cultural impact of the Internet and of cheap and accessible digital technologies. Through an overall optimistic lens, they see a "revitalized folk culture" (Jenkins) in which art making is "participatory." Their "Pro-Am" (professional amateurs) revolution bears loud echoes of punk's DIY philosophy: "From rap musicians who got their start by making homemade tape recordings . . . to the hundreds of thousands of bloggers emerging as a shadow news-media corps, citizens are increasingly spending significant amounts of their leisure time engaged in serious, creative pursuits" ("Cultural Renaissance," 2). From a more cynical angle, the authors also note a "more ominous trend": "a growing monopolization of culture brought about by the convergence and consolidation of media and entertainment industries" (4). Our survey of slip-sync in the punk musical film cycle has unearthed an early, dynamic, and prophetic meditation on these very issues.

Indeed, let us recall (in case we forgot) the distinctly punk connotation of Apple's standard consumer-level music-production software: GarageBand. And then there is the global cable-and-satellite news station and Web site, Current TV. Created by Al Gore and dripping with hip youth chic of the postgrunge variety, the independent media outlet clearly owes a lot, including its Internet interface and its user-produced podcasts and V-CAMs (viewer-created ad messages), to punk's DIY. A certain sense of slip-sync obtained, for example, in its "Hack the Debate" broadcast during the 2008 presidential debates; e-mailed viewer comments slipped across the screen, instantaneously intervening in mainstream political theater, critically exceeding the latter with a scrolling script of dissenting, disembodied "voices," if you will.

But let our closing remarks turn instead to the YouTube phenomenon for a glimpse of one of the more telling contemporary sites of slip-sync. First, listen to Chris Barber, from his recent essay "Polemics: Punk Cinema—like Punk Rock—Is Anti-Genre," in which he could be voicing a YouTube marketing slogan: "Punk rock is egalitarian, encouraging you to engage in production—your creative expression, as well as consumption; now a blurred duality. No more professional artistic maestros or star performers to be worshipped. . . . Anyone can have a go! Amateurs, fans and spectators can make a noise too" (11). On the other hand, Alexandra Juhasz has recently slammed the brakes on any such rush to conflate YouTube with punk DIY: "Sincere, or even cynical, contributions to the corporate machine do not a DIY ethics make" ("Five Lessons of YouTube," 145). The "fifth lesson" learned from her pedagogical experiment with YouTube is more nuanced but more explicit: "YouTube may be DIY, but it just ain't punk. That is, unless you hack it" (149).

Beyond such potential links between punk and YouTube, one might likewise note the slip-sync technical quality that characterizes much video streaming on the Web. At least for the present, such streaming seems to often involve a delay or slippage in synchronization of sound and image. This audiovisual seam in the process probably will be cured as faster and more precise Internet transmission technology becomes available. Yet through it, we can observe a kind of ubiquitous and free-floating slip-sync sensibility permeating the current presentation of digital images on the Internet.

One of these, a music performance I came across while writing this book, is a flash video of the infamous (or rather, now famous) "fat Dutch man" singing and dancing to a song by Ozone, "Dragostea Din Tei." The nerdy bespectacled youth himself is not singing, but lip-syncing along with the recording. His charming chunkiness and unabashed sentimental enthusiasm for "doing" the song renders the overtly amusing slip-sync that concludes the video stream all the more interesting. He has so faithfully lip-synced along with the song, and has so fervently timed and choreographed his corny arm-pumping gestures and eyebrow arches (!), that when he does slip out of sync, scrambling to salvage his show, the slip-sync seems to belong—entirely. No tension; an amateur-cum-star moment of endearing deprofessionalism that is picture-perfect for our current digital-era reality-show frenzy (a frenzy that in turn depends on the star-cum-amateur). His slip-sync occurs within an overall Web stream that expresses and celebrates the Internet's pixelized ontology of quivering slippage.

A more recent example of popularized slip-sync via YouTube was the CNN/YouTube Democratic presidential-candidate debate, which aired nationally on Monday, July 23, 2007. "Average citizens"—so CNN assured us—sent in their questions for the candidates in the form of YouTube Web videos; those selected by CNN were projected for the candidates, "live," during the debate. Notably, some questions came in the form of musical performances. But what marked all of the YouTube videos was a distinct slip-sync presentation mode in which the audio track verbalizing the question seemed permanently disengaged from the visual track of the person speaking or singing. Part of the effect was a sense that the audio and visual tracks were trying to find each other in order to sync up. But one always seemed to be behind or ahead of the other in a constant state of slip-sync that, all too ironically, resembled Poe-Kral's foundational 1976 punk-nightclub documentary, *Blank Generation*.

Can we characterize the YouTube generation as offspring of the Blank Generation? The answer seems to be "yes"—very much in quotation marks. YouTube's slip-sync effect is traceable back to the punk-musical cycle and all its contentious wrangling with in/authenticity; but it is likewise taken for granted as part of the mainstream political culture's incorporation of new media technologies.

So I began to think about the name "YouTube," and punk. A kind of flip-side to "MySpace," "YouTube" invokes "you too," updating punk's DIY for the Internet generation (perhaps even banking on the "U2" association; the Irish supergroup's powerful music video indicting George W. Bush's nonresponse to Katrina, "The Saints Are Coming," was a number one on YouTube). Not "*your* tube," which suggests possession and control of the technology, and which would be more authentically punk; but rather, you *are* the tube, the tube is you.

Put differently, perhaps: Big Brother is watching you, but you *are* Big Brother—so it is okay. A supposedly liberating inversion of Orwell's panoptic nightmare, yet more covertly resonant with Huxley's brave and new feel-good world, YouTube comes to designate a kind of cyborg identity, a neologism rendering two nouns, two beings, into one: a forced and very intimate synchronization of difference, yet one that comes to us through the slip-sync sensibility.

YouTube: radically implosive DIY "audience participation," as witnessed on the debate, in which millions of television viewers watch a live "town hall" audience watching the candidates watching the YouTube videos. Moreover, the people inside the videos themselves "watch" (that is, pretend to be directly addressing) the candidates, while also watching themselves being broadcast, from home. And a distinct sense of slip-sync characterizes the whole post-modern transmission, itself haunted by a version of punk that is surprising and perplexing.

In other words, all this is a strange inheritance of the goofy, sanitized, tele-visual irony *Starstruck* and *True Stories* first articulated back in the mid-1980s. The slip-sync of the "fat Dutch man" and the CNN/YouTube televised political debate fully conveys the convergence of the Internet, television, film, music, and politics. The Internet's blurry inversions of amateurs and stars, its anything-and-everything-goes mode, the YouTube-MySpace free-for-all that hopefully is not also a free-fall: a glorious fulfillment or betrayal, or both, of punk.

★ NOTES

CHAPTER 1

1. Connor highlights the "ambivalent, mysterious, and interrogative nature" of ventriloquism by referring to cinema, the medium in which "the dependence of what you hear upon what you see" is strongest and most vivid (*Dumbstruck*, 21). In other words, sound (especially of voices) in classical narrative cinema needs to be anchored to images. Ventriloquism and punk slip-sync, along with other experimental film practices, challenge this hierarchy, presenting "sourceless, autonomous, or excessive sound" that is "experienced both as a lack and an excess; both as a mystery to be explained, and an intensity to be contained" (23). The first chapter of *Dumbstruck* serves as a fascinating supplement to our analysis of punk slip-sync. To take just one example: in Connor's opening remarks, before specifically addressing ventriloquism, he explicates the phenomenon whereby technological reproduction of the voice (by, for example, the tape recorder) yields the disturbing effect of not recognizing one's voice, "proof of the voice's split condition, as at once cleaving to and taking leave from myself" (7–8)—all of which, we will see, seems to be at work and at stake in punk slip-sync scenes. However, let me clarify at the outset that I am not going to push the ventriloquist paradigm in my discussion of the films. Rather, I invoke it here as a tangential critical lens that will hover usefully, I hope, around my readings.

2. Even as recently as November 2008, Terrence Rafferty's piece for the *New York Times* on an "extremely peculiar" Punk 'n' Pie film series in Brooklyn, reflects the way public discourse views punk as "defiantly resistant to definition": "The whole point, after all, was to produce something inexplicable, unassimilable and as difficult to ignore as a mouthful of rotting teeth."

3. "New punk" here seems to mean new independent digital cinema, in which the homegrown and outsider possibilities of digital film are idealistically subsumed

under the "punk" moniker. Rombes acknowledges that this punk influence is a "tendency" rather than a "coherent, unified school of film" (*New Punk Cinema*, 3–4). It might be a bit of a stretch to apply the term "punk" to the Dogme films, *The Blair Witch Project* (1999), *Run Lola Run* (1998), *Gummo* (1997), and *Time Code* (2000). The recent anthology *No Focus: Punk on Film* deals more specifically with punk films, covering a wide variety of films about punk, including most of those I discuss.

4. The verdict is still out regarding the implications for women in punk. For Mavis Bayton and her sociological study of women in rock, punk, dovetailing with second-wave feminism, "was responsible for the single largest surge of women into music-making in the UK" (*Frock Rock*, 63). Yet Sheila Whiteley concludes that punk's "feminisation of rock," boldly illustrated in the music of Patti Smith and Siouxsie Sioux, never really came to fruition, partially because MTV, which overtook punk, insists on traditional codes of female glamour (*Women and Popular Music*, 113–114).

CHAPTER 2

1. It is notable that in discussing how punk "raises the question of authenticity in ways it cannot fully close off," Hegarty finds the film *The Great Rock 'n' Roll Swindle* "more punk" than the Sex Pistols' landmark album *Never Mind the Bollocks* (Noise/ Music, 95–96).

2. Jonathan Sterne reminds us that the concept of in/authenticity I am putting forward here is not historically confined to the 1980s (though I mean it and use it to reflect certain cultural and aesthetic features that are 1980s-specific). In reference to a singer's first experience of performing on radio in the 1920s (which swung from "horror" to "tremendous gratification"), Sterne proposes "the artifice of authenticity," in which "the original requires as much artifice as the copy" and in which "authenticity does not disappear altogether" but becomes relocated in the listening experience (*Audible Past*, 241).

3. More than twenty years ago, Simon Frith anticipated our notion of in/authenticity and its particular resonance for punk when he called punk "more truthful" and authentic than most other rock music because it reacted against technology ("Art versus Technology," 266), yet he later argued that such technology often makes rock authenticity possible (269–277).

4. Here is Peter Wicke on these tensions within punk: "To some people punk rock was the direct musical expression of unemployed teenagers' political protest against a society that had turned them into superfluous outsiders, while to others it was a particularly cunning capitalist subterfuge to overcome the decline in the record market because of the recession" (*Rock Music*, 137). And, more recently, Stacy Thompson: "Punks want to change the world, and many believe that what most needs to be changed is capitalism. Consequently, punk both raises and attempts to work through two related problematics, one economic and one aesthetic: Can the commodity form be taken up and used against capitalism? Can all aesthetics be commodified?" (*Punk Productions*, 3).

5. These in fact are the precise terms by which Susan McClary, in her afterword to Attali's *Noise*, identifies punk with composing (156–157); see also Thompson, *Punk Productions*, 11–12.

6. A word about my terminology. Throughout this book, I use two sets of sound terms more or less interchangeably: sync and nonsync, diegetic and nondiegetic. The first term, sync or diegetic, refers to sound "inside" the fiction, which the characters can hear; the second term, nonsync or nondiegetic, refers to sound "outside" the fiction, which the characters cannot hear. The fairly commonplace interchangeability of these terms is perhaps best evidenced by two popular introductory film textbooks: Richard Barsam's *Looking at Movies*, which prefers diegetic and nondiegetic (281), and Louis Giannetti's *Understanding Movies*, which prefers synchronous and nonsynchronous (227–229). Indeed, flipping through any number of introductory film textbooks will reveal numerous variations in terminology regarding this distinction. As will be seen, I tend to use sync and nonsync (obviously shortened from synchronous and nonsynchronous), since these terms resonate more keenly with my key critical concept of slip-sync, but also they connote the idea of sound source more specifically than do diegetic and nondiegetic, which are perhaps more suggestive of narrative sound function. Apologies to readers if this causes confusion.

7. Thompson likens Godard's early aesthetic to punk rock ("Punk Cinema," 33); see also Dugdale, "French New Wave."

8. In a chapter titled "The New York School of Indies," Emmanuel Levy briefly describes the punk film scene—without ever using the term "punk"—out of which Jarmusch and others emerged, citing *Eraserhead* and *Liquid Sky* (*Cinema of Outsiders*, 184–185); in a chapter on feminist sensibility, he quickly discusses *Smithereens* (356–357), eager to move on to Seidelman's next film, *Desperately Seeking Susan*. Greg Merritt gives similarly scant attention to punk films, referring to the same New York underground "micro-budget" punk film scene out of which *Smithereens* emerged (*Celluloid Mavericks*, 303–308).

9. Conrich's discussion of the sing-along cult-musical phenomenon, originating of course in the remarkable reception story of *The Rocky Horror Picture Show*, may be an interesting audience-participation twist on slip-sync.

10. On John Waters and punk, see Dugdale, "French New Wave," 59–60, and Barber, "You Got Bad Taste," 178–184.

11. Indeed, the critical work on excess in film initiated by Barbara Klinger and Linda Williams helps further set the stage of these punk musicals, since it addresses the relationship between genre and excess. Both theorists explore excess as a crucial and traceable motif that confers a subversive edge to certain genres. Klinger shows how excess becomes a conventionalized difference in "progressive" genres like film noir, family melodrama, and exploitation. These genres challenge the classical paradigm with pessimistic, transgressive themes and "baroque" or excessive formal devices ("'Cinema/Ideology/Criticism,'" 80–86). Revisiting many of these same or related low-grade genres (pornography, horror, and the woman's weepie), Williams focuses

on the female body as the site of systemic excess, speculating on audience members' bodily reactions ("Film Bodies," 142–143). Such "excessive" audience response evokes cult-film theory (Telotte, "Beyond All Reason," 7–8), while the female body identified by both Williams and Gaylyn Studlar ("Midnight S/Excess," 139) as the crucial locus of excess further furnishes an incisive framework for considering the punk musicals, since most feature a lead female punk performer.

12. On these theoretical links between cult film, excess, and punk, we should note that many punk or punk-related films, including some of those under consideration here, are "officially" considered cult films. No surprise that punk films such as *Liquid Sky*, *Smithereens*, *The Great Rock 'n' Roll Swindle*, and *Repo Man* figure throughout *The Cult Film Experience*. Gregory Waller's study of midnight-movie attendance during the period of the punk-musical film cycle concludes by suggesting the need to explore the link between the midnight movie (including many punk-rock films) and "the new wave of independent American feature films from *Eraserhead* to *Repo Man* and *Stranger Than Paradise*" ("Midnight Movies," 184).

13. Hoberman and Rosenbaum discuss *Jubilee* primarily as a punk offshoot of *Rocky Horror* (*Midnight Movies*, 282).

14. Scott Henderson makes a similar point about musical excess in postpunk, riot-grrrl-era films like *10 Things I Hate About You* (1999) and *Tank Girl* (1995). Here, the "unexpectedness, elaborateness and the absurdity and excessiveness of the performance" create a "disruptive aesthetic associated with the music video" ("Youth, Excess," 152). With its predilection for female leads and its slip-sync performance gesture, the punk-musical cycle proves to be a crucial backstory to Henderson's reading of these films as "progressive texts in terms of their construction of femininity" (147).

15. Ella Shohat, for example, sees these experimental feminist films as critiquing both the masculinist tendencies of Third Cinema and the ethnocentric tendencies of Euro-American feminism. This critique of identity occurs often through subversive kinds of voice-over, which for Shohat express a nonessentialist "exile" of the body itself ("Post-Third-Worldist Culture," 51–78).

16. The only work I know of that touches upon this angle regarding these punk-music films is Jon Lewis's *The Road to Romance and Ruin*. He situates the films as youth-culture films, criticizing what he perceives as punk's contradictory, ultimately reactionary politics. I wish to push such an interpretation much further by shifting the emphasis to the genre question (musical and indie film), but also by digging deeper into the various subtextual dimensions of the films, more along the lines of Goshorn's excellent reading of *Repo Man* ("'A Bad Area'").

CHAPTER 3

1. We should note these conflicting views regarding Jarman's directorial signature, punk, and *Jubilee*: "*Jubilee* is the film in which Jarman found his voice and style" (O'Pray, *Dreams of England*, 99); the film "is the most atypical of all Jarman's

films" (Dillon, *Jarman and Lyric Film*, 75); "*Jubilee* helped delineate the shape—that of being primarily a filmmaker—into which Jarman's life was beginning to form" (Peake, *Derek Jarman*, 252).

2. Tony Peake notes that "the final irony—that as punk was gathering momentum, Margaret Thatcher was assuming leadership of the conservative party—was one which, when it hit home in the following decade, made absolute sense to Jarman. Just such a political progression was what he foresaw in *Jubilee*, the film he was about to make" (*Derek Jarman*, 244–245).

3. "The impetus for *Jubilee* was provided by Jordan," according to Tony Peake (*Derek Jarman*, 245), though some writers see the crux and inspiration of the film coming not from Jordan but from John Dee's character (Dillon, *Jarman and Lyric Film*, 76–78). Apparently, Jarman had a rough script about John Dee that he transformed into *Jubilee*; see also O'Pray, *Dreams of England*, 100.

4. Wymer's suggestion is that either World War II–era or Renaissance England might be such a "lost period of authentic national identity" (*Jarman*, 60); he goes on to analyze *Jubilee*'s critique of violence and new, in some cases neo-Nazi, nationalism within punk; see also Pencak, *Films of Derek Jarman*, 39–41.

5. "When Jarman filmed Adam and the Ants at the New Victoria Theatre, they had only been going for two months. The line between fact and fiction is precarious in much of the film, but no more so than in this character, for which Adam virtually played himself, giggling at his fellow-actors' lines and awkwardly mumbling, a vacuous focal point for the rest of the characters" (O'Pray, *Dreams of England*, 97).

6. Throughout *Lipstick Traces*, Greil Marcus "situates" punk directly in relation to the French Situationist International; see also Plant, *Most Radical Gesture*, 144–146.

7. Steven Dillon, reading this sequence through the trope of performance art, finds it one of the most "Jarmanesque" in the film because of its "poetry" (*Jarman and Lyric Film*, 79–81).

8. Teasing out the film's "prophetic" quality, Jarman himself paraphrases this oft-quoted line in his autobiography *Dancing Ledge* (Peake, *Derek Jarman*, 251).

9. Apparently Jarman intended to dedicate the film to William Blake (Peake, *Derek Jarman*, 246).

CHAPTER 4

1. McLaren eventually insisted that his name be taken off the film's production credits; he also tried unsuccessfully to have all footage of himself removed (Taylor, "Impresario," 26). For all the details of the lengthy legal battles around the production of the film, see Savage, *England's Dreaming*, 498–538.

2. Impresario, maestro, Svengali, magician: such aggrandizing monikers bespeckle the McLaren mythology and evoke the specter of ventriloquism theorized by Connor, in which "the experience of a voice without an obvious origin" often underlies the exercise of excessive political power and often presents itself as "an overload of sound,"

an apt phrase for our focus (*Dumbstruck*, 23–24). In the history of film, the "wizard" in *The Wizard of Oz* (1939) comes to mind. In *Swindle* and beyond, wizard McLaren is clearly visible, both literally, and in rather high profile, as well as—and perhaps more importantly—figuratively, constructing himself as both the "voice" of punk and its puppeteer, orchestrating its theatrical, raging screams and "chaos" like a ventriloquist. A good illustration of this from *Swindle* comes during the "1780 The Gordon Riots" sequence early in the film, in which "The London Mob Created Anarchy in the UK." Here, eerie life-size effigies—dummies, if you will—of each Sex Pistol member, radically ripped out of sync, are strung up over a bonfire by a riotous mob as McLaren's voice-over narrates "how to manufacture your group" in a demonic whisper.

3. Temple's more recent documentary *The Filth and the Fury* (2000), made twenty years after *Swindle*, aims to right this wrong, or at least to tip the balance more fairly, by offering the perspective of the band members, notably Johnny Rotten, who refused participation in *Swindle* and denounced it.

4. On the legal battle between Rotten and McLaren, see Donnelly, "Entertainment and Dystopia," 172.

5. See Feuer's discussion of *Pennies from Heaven* in *The Hollywood Musical*, 128–129.

6. We might link such absurdist playing around with the musical genre with the British tradition of subversive film farce and parody, illustrated by the likes of the *Carry On* and Monty Python films. An especially relevant though indirect precursor to *Swindle* is the farcical musical dimension of *The Ruling Class* (1972).

7. On punk and the carnivalesque, see Nehring, *Flowers in the Dustbin*, 318.

8. *Who Killed Bambi?* was the title of the original film project first conceived by McLaren and Rotten early in the band's career; see Donnelly, "Entertainment and Dystopia," 172.

9. See also Donnelly's reading of the distinct approaches to music in *Performance*, "*Performance* and the Composite Film Score."

10. See Cynthia Fuchs's discussion of such noir Orientalism inflecting *Taxi Driver* (1976), a film not irrelevant to punk, appearing simultaneously with punk and concretely influencing one of punk's leading avatars, Joe Strummer of the Clash ("'All the Animals,'" 34).

11. Though David James does not discuss *Swindle*, his argument linking punk and pornography through the "hardcore" trope seems borne out by the film (*Power Misses*, 221–225).

CHAPTER 5

1. For historical context and continuity regarding this ideology of sound fidelity, see Sterne's discussion of a similar ad from 1908 ("Audible Past," 215–217).

2. See Andrew Higson on the heritage film as an example of this combination ("Re-presenting the National Past," 110).

3. A companion scene occurs later, when the band remedies a power outage during one of its first big concert-hall gigs by continuing acoustic (candlelight supplementing the loss of electricity, supposedly because of a strike). The scene looks surprisingly prophetic of MTV's hugely successful *Unplugged* series, which began airing around ten years later, coded as antidote to the channel's inauthentic, hyperreal programming.

4. Steven Connor makes the link between Chion's acousmetre and "many forms of ventriloquism" as "a specific form of maladjustment of sound and vision in cinema" (*Dumbstruck*, 20), which we are specifying further as various instances of punk slip-sync.

5. Note that U.S. release versions of the film do not contain this ending. Instead, they end on a freeze-frame close-up of Kate in concert. While I do not dislike this truncated ending, I will discuss the UK version's complete ending.

6. Donnelly makes a similar point about *Swindle* starting with McLaren—Danny's counterpart and figurative brother ("Entertainment and Dystopia," 173).

7. In "Images for Sale," Elsaesser explores this political ambiguity in institutional and aesthetic terms.

8. See also Neil Nehring's incisive concluding remarks on the ambivalence around women and punk (*Flowers in the Dustbin*, 320–322).

CHAPTER 6

1. The title card in the Poe-Kral *Blank Generation* reads *The Blank Generation*, thus officially distinguishing its title from Lommel's film title. However, the Poe-Kral film apparently is referred to everywhere as *Blank Generation*, dropping the "The" and causing some confusion between it and the Lommel film. Stacy Thompson's *Punk Productions* and Barber and Sargeant's *No Focus: Punk on Film* both refer to the Poe-Kral film as *Blank Generation*, the latter book including an interview with Poe himself, who drops the "The." Moreover, none of the DVD packaging has the "The." So I follow the prevalent use value and refer to both films by the same title.

2. The sax we hear is played by John Lurie, a member of the New York punk-lounge band the Lounge Lizards; he appears later in the film as a different street musician and went on to star in Jarmusch's next few films.

3. Another important punk film from this period is Penelope Spheeris's documentary *The Decline of Western Civilization* (1981), which takes a direct ethnographic look at the early-1980s punk subculture in Los Angeles. Spheeris would go on to direct *Suburbia* (1983), an ultraviolent take on punks terrorized by suburban vigilantes.

4. A notable exception to this distinction between the British and American punk films regarding fan-oriented narratives is *Rude Boy* (Jack Hazan and David Mingay, 1980). This semidocumentary film follows a Clash fan who eventually becomes a roadie for the group. Featuring much concert and recording footage of the Clash, with fan Ray Gange playing himself, the film seems more a punk documentary than

a musical, though I concede this is a debatable distinction (see Thompson, *Punk Productions*, 164–168).

5. Mas'ud Zavarzadeh sees the "crude, narcissistic, and relentless pursuit of power" characterizing Wren and the punk scene in general as a way for the film to judge the punk subculture as fascistic in order to reassert a conservative moral center (*Seeing Films Politically*, 175).

6. On this crossover between punk and science fiction, see also *The Atomic Café* (1982) and *UFOria* (1985). We should also take heed of Stephen Duncombe's point that the precursors of punk fanzines were the science-fiction fanzines of the 1930s ("Let's All Be Alienated," 428).

7. According to Serge Denisoff and William Romanowski, *Repo Man*'s substantial profit margin and critical acclaim helped Cox garner enough cachet to get major financing from Universal for his next punk film, *Sid and Nancy*, discussed in this volume's Chapter 9 (*Risky Business*, 580–581). We should note that Cox established himself as a punk auteur during the 1980s with the gritty but intriguing flops *Straight to Hell* and *Walker* (both 1987), both strongly punk-inflected antiwesterns.

CHAPTER 7

1. According to the accounts given by Moyle and lead actress Robin Johnson on the DVD audio commentary, most of the film's flaws, its "mismatches," resulted from Stigwood's company taking over the project and insisting on adding songs from the film's double-album sound track. Exposition and backstory scenes, including those elaborating the gay relationship between the two lead girls, were dropped or reshot, resulting in gaping continuity holes. Moyle, a Canadian director, is most remembered for his later pop-music film *Pump Up the Volume* (1990).

2. On the DVD audio commentary, Moyle and Johnson never use the term "punk." Instead, Moyle often uses "downtown" to characterize those sequences and music in the film that "work" (to employ Dickinson's phrase). In particular, he notes Lou Reed's "Walk on the Wild Side"—an important prepunk song—as well as Patti Smith and the Cars, as crystallizations of this "downtown" tone. The director later in the commentary links this tone with the "quirky" film he was trying to make, which butted heads with the "big and glossy" movie Stigwood was trying to make. The result was a film with a "schizophrenic sound track," a film that aimed to please everyone but ended up pleasing no one.

3. Moyle cites both scenes as casualties of Stigwood's intervention. In any case, Denisoff and Romanowski describe the film's portrayal of Times Square as "sanitized," and the concert concluding the film as "pseudo-punk" (*Risky Business*, 254). On the other hand, Johnson and Moyle see the film's mise-en-scène as an authentic timepiece, an "archive" of a New York that no longer exists. According to Johnson, "Times Square looks like Disneyland now" (*Times Square*, DVD audio commentary).

4. See Laderman, *Driving Visions*, 109–112.

5. It is interesting to hear Moyle on the DVD audio commentary describe this sequence as "ambitious but flawed" for its immaturity, its "gleeful anarchy."

6. Apparently, rooftop concert scenes have become a bit of a cliché in rock musicals. Two good comparisons to the one at the close of *Times Square* are those concluding *Bandits* (1997), a little-known German feminist rock-and-roll road movie I discuss in *Driving Visions*, and Julie Taymor's *Across the Universe* (2006). Possibly *Times Square* was an influence on both films.

CHAPTER 8

1. Neil Palmer draws upon the twelve-minute documentary essential for fans of *The Stains*, Sarah Jacobson, and Sam Green's *Ladies and Gentlemen, the Fabulous Stains: Behind the Movie* (1999), produced for IFC's *Split Screen* program and available on Sam Green's DVD *The Rainbow Man/John 3:16* (2004).

2. Some of the film's slippery production and direction that apparently irked Dowd on the shoot is audible, by default, in director Adler's otherwise disposable audio commentary on the recent DVD release of the film. Adler confuses the Looters and the Metal Corpses in some of his comments, likewise misnaming some of the actors and their roles. Regarding one scene of "Black Randy and the Metro Squad" auditioning for the Looters' agent, Adler "cannot explain" the prominence of an Israeli flag. Adler, who rather conspicuously never mentions anything about Dowd or the script, does make the offhand but telling observation that this was the last film he directed. And Black Randy, by the way, was an anomalous but legendary figure of the Los Angeles punk scene of the early 1980s. He and his band the Metro Squad supposedly performed punk-soul music in a campy, burlesque manner.

3. Another slippage in the film's identity: throughout much of the film, the group is known as the Stains; yet near the end, and in the title, they are called the Fabulous Stains.

4. Both Stephen Duncombe ("Let's All Be Alienated," 438) and Suzanne Moore ("Is That All," 233) speculate on nostalgia, and the conformity to punk signified by nostalgia, at work in contemporary punk zine culture and in academic theorizing on punk. *The Stains* seems to articulate punk nostalgia years before it actually emerged in zine culture, academia, or films like *SLC Punk* (1998). On the DVD audio commentary for *The Stains*, Diane Lane and Laura Dern remark that punk was "passé" at the time of filming and that ex–Sex Pistol Steve Jones was rather parental toward them.

5. Neil Palmer reminds us that the "briefs-on-the-outside stage wear sported by Corinne Burns was pioneered by Ari Up of the Slits," an early London all-female punk band ("Disappearance and Re-emergence," 220).

6. On the DVD audio commentary, Adler concedes that this concluding sequence was a "second ending" for the film, shot quite a bit later, in Malibu, just after MTV was launched. The mock logo "MVNTV" seems like a heavy-handed nod to the original MTV logo.

CHAPTER 9

1. We could label these as second-generation, punk-nostalgia films, distinct from our early-1980s cycle because of their transnational character and their incorporation of experimental, documentary, or mockumentary modes. Prominent, important titles include *Hard Core Logo* (Bruce MacDonald, 1996, Canada), *Pretty Vacant* (Jim Mendiola, 1996, U.S.-Mexico), *SLC Punk* (James Merendino, 1998, U.S.), and *Afro-Punk* (James Spooner, 1999, U.S.). Indeed, this second generation has continued into a more recent third generation of punk films, some of them musicals along the lines we have traced, including several documentaries eulogizing the Ramones; Jim Mendiola's Latino punk mockdoc *Speeder Kills* (2003); Don Letts' *Punk: Attitude* (2005); *American Hardcore* (2006); Julien Temple's paean *Joe Strummer: The Future Is Now* (2007); *Control* (2007), a dark narrative film focusing on Ian Curtis of legendary postpunk band Joy Division; and *What We Do is Secret* (2008), a punk-music biopic of Darby Crash of the Germs.

2. *Dogs in Space* (1987) and *Romper Stomper* (1992) offer more somber and disturbing Australian punk film narratives.

3. Avital Ronell provides a striking theoretical framework for thinking through this interdependency (or, to use her phrase, "pharmaco-dependency") between the mass media and drugs. Drawing on Ernst Junger and Paul Virilio in positing drugs as "technology's intimate other," she proposes a generalized notion of drug addiction at the base of Western culture. *Sid and Nancy*, *Breaking Glass*, and other rock-music films like *Tommy* and *Pink Floyd The Wall* become reflexive samples of her "hallucinogenre," where "narcossism" becomes a "toxic drive" that both haunts and makes possible the celebrity identities featured in the narrative (*Crack Wars*, 7–9).

4. Ronell's theory is perhaps best illustrated by *Requiem for a Dream* (2000), which director Aronofsky apparently characterizes as punk (Thompson, *Punk Productions*, 159).

5. Denisoff and Romanowski underline this sense of the scene's parody of punk's past as part of the film's overall tonal ambivalence: "Like the group in the 1970s appearing at Gotham's punk Mecca, CBGB, in Brooks-Brothers button-downs, *True Stories*, at minimum, is a postmodern duality. It highlights the foibles and mores of Middle America while satirizing an alternative culture" (*Risky Business*, 594).

6. Denisoff and Romanowski survey the critical reception of *True Stories*, emphasizing the problems with its "neutrality" (*Risky Business*, 595–596), though they do not relate this quality to the film's race fetish.

✭ WORKS CITED

Altman, Rick. *The American Film Musical*. Bloomington: Indiana Univ. Press, 1987.
———, ed. *Sound Theory/Sound Practice*. London: Routledge, 1992.
Asensio, Susana. "The Nortec Edge." In *Rockin' Las Americas: The Global Politics of Rock in Latina/o America*, edited by Deborah Pacini Hernandez, Eric Zolov, and Hector Fernandez-L'Hoeste, 312–331. Pittsburgh: Univ. of Pittsburgh Press, 2004.
Attali, Jacques. *Noise: The Political Economy of Music*. Translated by Brian Massumi. Minneapolis: Univ. of Minnesota Press, 1985.
Auslander, Philip. *Liveness: Performance in a Mediatized Culture*. New York: Routledge, 1999.
Bailey, Cameron. "Nigger/Lover: The Thin Sheen of Race in *Something Wild*." *Screen* 29, no. 4 (1988): 28–40.
Barber, Chris. "No Future Now." In Barber and Sargeant, *No Focus*, 48–58.
———. "Polemics: Punk Cinema—like Punk Rock—Is Anti-Genre." In Barber and Sargeant, *No Focus*, 9–14.
———. "You Got Bad Taste." In Barber and Sargeant, *No Focus*, 168–184.
Barber, Chris, and Jack Sargeant, eds. *No Focus: Punk on Film*. London: Headpress, 2006.
Barsam, Richard. *Looking at Movies: An Introduction to Film*. 2nd ed. New York: Norton, 2007.
Bayton, Mavis. *Frock Rock: Women Performing Popular Music*. Oxford: Oxford Univ. Press, 1998.
Bergstrom, Janet. "Androids and Androgyny." *Camera Obscura* 15 (1986): 37–63.
Biskind, Peter. "The Last Crusade." In Miller, *Seeing through Movies*, 112–149.
Braudy, Leo, and Marshall Cohen, eds. *Film Theory and Criticism*, 6th ed. New York: Oxford Univ. Press, 2004.

Bruno, Guiliana. "Ramble City: Postmodernism and *Bladerunner.*" In Sharrett, *Crisis Cinema*, 237–249.

Butler, Judith. *Gender Trouble: Feminism and the Subversion of Identity.* New York and London: Routledge, 1999.

Certeau, Michel de. *The Practice of Everyday Life.* Translated by Steven Rendall. Berkeley and Los Angeles: Univ. of California Press, 1984.

Chion, Michel. *Audio-Vision: Sound on Screen.* Edited and translated by Claudia Gorbman. New York: Columbia Univ. Press, 1994.

———. *The Voice in Cinema.* Translated by Claudia Gorbman. New York: Columbia Univ. Press, 1999.

Cogan, Brian. *The Encyclopedia of Punk.* New York: Sterling, 2008.

Cohan, Steven. *Incongruous Entertainment: Camp, Cultural Value, and the MGM Musical.* Durham, N.C.: Duke Univ. Press, 2005.

Connor, Steven. *Dumbstruck: A Cultural History of Ventriloquism.* Oxford: Oxford Univ. Press, 2000.

———. *Postmodernist Culture.* 2nd ed. Oxford: Blackwell, 1997.

Conrich, Ian. "Musical Performance and the Cult Film Experience." In Conrich and Tincknell, *Film's Musical Moments*, 115–131.

Conrich, Ian, and Estella Tincknell, eds. *Film's Musical Moments.* Edinburgh: Edinburgh Univ. Press, 2006.

Corrigan, Timothy. "Film and the Culture of the Cult." In Telotte, *The Cult Film Experience*, 26–37.

Denby, David. Review of *Times Square*, directed by Allan Moyle. *New York Magazine*, November 3, 1980: 84.

Denisoff, R. Serge, and William D. Romanowski. *Risky Business: Rock in Film.* New Brunswick, N.J.: Transaction, 1991.

Dickinson, Kay. *Off Key: When Film and Music Won't Work Together.* Oxford: Oxford Univ. Press, 2008.

Dika, Vera. *Recycled Culture in Contemporary Art and Film: The Uses of Nostalgia.* New York: Cambridge Univ. Press, 2003.

Dillon, Steven. *Derek Jarman and Lyric Film: The Mirror and the Sea.* Austin: Univ. of Texas Press, 2004.

Doane, Mary Ann. "The Voice in the Cinema: The Articulation of Body and Space." In Braudy and Cohen, *Film Theory and Criticism*, 373–385.

Donnelly, Kevin J. "British Punk Films: Rebellion into Money, Nihilism into Innovation." *Journal of Popular British Cinema* 1, no. 1 (1998): 101–114.

———. "Entertainment and Dystopia: The Punk Anti-Musical." In *Musicals: Hollywood and Beyond*, edited by Bill Marshall and Robynn Stilwell, 171–179. Portland, Ore.: Intellect Books, 2000.

———. "*Performance* and the Composite Film Score." In *Film Music: Critical Approaches*, edited by K. J. Donnelly, 152–166. New York: Continuum, 2001.

Douglas, Susan J. *Where the Girls Are: Growing Up Female with the Mass Media*. New York: Times Books, 1994.

Dugdale, Timothy. "The French New Wave: New Again." In Rombes, *New Punk Cinema*, 56–71.

Duncombe, Stephen. "Let's All Be Alienated Together: Zines and the Making of Underground Community." In *Generations of Youth: Youth Cultures and History in Twentieth-Century America*, edited by Joe Austin and Michael Nevin Willard, 427–451. New York: New York Univ. Press, 1998.

Elsaesser, Thomas. "Images for Sale: The 'New' British Cinema." In Friedman, *Fires Were Started*, 52–69.

"Fat Dutch Man—Funny Guy Dancing Ozone's Dragostea Din Tei." www.michou-net.com/fatman (accessed February 23, 2009).

Ferncase, Richard. *Outsider Features: American Independent Films of the 1980s*. Westport, Conn.: Greenwood, 1996.

Feuer, Jane. *The Hollywood Musical*. 2nd ed. London: Macmillan, 1993.

———. "The Self-Reflexive Musical and the Myth of Entertainment." In Grant, *Film Genre Reader II*, 441–455.

Friedberg, Anne. "The End of Cinema: Multimedia and Technological Change." In Braudy and Cohen, *Film Theory and Criticism*, 914–926.

Friedman, Lester, ed. *Fires Were Started: British Cinema and Thatcherism*. Minneapolis: Univ. of Minnesota Press, 1993.

Frith, Simon. "Art versus Technology: The Strange Case of Popular Music." *Media, Culture, and Society* 8 (1986): 263–279.

Frith, Simon, Andrew Goodwin, and Lawrence Grossberg, eds. *Sound and Vision: The Music Video Reader*. New York: Routledge, 1993.

Frith, Simon, and Trevor Horne. *Art into Pop*. London: Routledge, 1987.

Fuchs, Cynthia J. "'All the Animals Come Out at Night': Vietnam Meets *Noir* in *Taxi Driver*." In *Inventing Vietnam: The War in Film and Television*, edited by Michael Anderegg, 33–55. Philadelphia: Temple Univ. Press, 1991.

Gaar, Gillian G. *She's a Rebel: The History of Women in Rock and Roll*. New York: Seal, 2002.

Garwood, Ian. "The Pop Song in Film." In *Close-Up 01*, edited by John Gibbs and Douglas Pye, 89–166. London: Wallflower, 2006.

Giannetti, Louis. *Understanding Movies*. 11th ed. Upper Saddle River, N.J.: Pearson Education, 2008.

Giles, Jane. "As Above, So Below: Thirty Years of Underground Cinema and Pop Music." In *Celluloid Jukebox: Popular Music and the Movies Since the 1950s*, edited by Jonathan Romney and Adrian Wootton, 44–51. London: British Film Institute, 1995.

Gilroy, Paul. *"There Ain't No Black in the Union Jack": The Cultural Politics of Race and Nation*. London: Hutchison, 1987.

Goodwin, Andrew. "Fatal Distractions: MTV Meets Postmodern Theory." In Frith, Goodwin, and Grossberg, *Sound and Vision*, 45–66.

Goshorn, A. Keith. "'A Bad Area': *Repo Man* and the Punk Anti-Aesthetic." In Sharrett, *Crisis Cinema*, 37–76.

Grant, Barry K. "The Classical Hollywood Musical and the 'Problem' of Rock and Roll." *Journal of Popular Film and Television* 13, no. 4 (1986): 195–205.

———, ed. *Film Genre Reader II*. Austin: Univ. of Texas Press, 1995.

———. "Rich and Strange: The Yuppie Horror Film." In *Contemporary Hollywood Cinema*, edited by Steve Neale and Murray Smith. New York: Routledge, 1998.

The Great Rock 'n' Roll Swindle (1980). DVD audio commentary by Julien Temple and Chris Salewicz. Sony BMG Music Entertainment, 2005.

Grossberg, Lawrence. "The Media Economy of Rock Culture: Cinema, Postmodernity, and Authenticity." In Frith, Goodwin, and Grossberg, *Sound and Vision*, 185–209.

———. *We Gotta Get Out of This Place: Popular Conservatism and Postmodern Culture*. London and New York: Routledge, 1992.

Halberstam, Judith. *In a Queer Time and Place: Transgender Bodies, Subcultural Lives*. New York: New York Univ. Press, 2005.

———. "Oh Bondage, Up Yours! Female Masculinity and the Tomboy." In *Sissies and Tomboys: Gender Nonconformity and Homosexual Childhood*, edited by Matthew Rottnek, 153–179. New York: New York Univ. Press, 1999.

Hamsher, Jane. "Blogging Is So Punk Rock." *Wired*, March 2006, 89.

Hark, Ina Rae. "Fear of Flying: Yuppie Critique and the Buddy Road Movie in the 1980s." In *The Road Movie Book*, edited by Steven Cohan and Ina Rae Hark, 204–229. New York: Routledge, 1997.

Hawkins, Joan. "Dark, Disturbing, Intelligent, Provocative, and Quirky: Avant-garde Cinema of the 1980s and 1990s." In Holmlund and Wyatt, *Contemporary American Independent Film*, 89–106.

Hebdige, Dick. *Subculture: The Meaning of Style*. London: Methuen, 1979.

Hegarty, Paul. *Noise/Music: A History*. New York: Continuum, 2007.

Henderson, Scott. "Youth, Excess, and the Musical Moment." In Conrich and Tincknell, *Film's Musical Moments*, 146–157.

Higson, Andrew. "Re-presenting the National Past: Nostalgia and Pastiche in the Heritage Film." In Friedman, *Fires Were Started*, 109–129.

Hoberman, J. Review of *Ladies and Gentlemen, the Fabulous Stains*, directed by Lou Adler. *Village Voice*, March 12, 1985, 46.

Hoberman, J., and Jonathan Rosenbaum. *Midnight Movies*. New York: Da Capo, 1983.

Holmlund, Chris, and Justin Wyatt, eds. *Contemporary American Independent Film*. London: Routledge, 2005.

Hutcheon, Linda. *A Poetics of Postmodernism: History, Theory, Fiction*. New York: Routledge, 1988.

Huxley, David. "'Ever Get the Feeling You've Been Cheated': Anarchy and Control in *The Great Rock 'n' Roll Swindle*." In Sabin, *Punk Rock*, 81–99.

Ivey, Bill, and Steven Tepper. "Cultural Renaissance or Cultural Divide?" *Chronicle of Higher Education* 52, no. 37 (2006): B6.

James, David E. *Power Misses: Essays Across (Un)Popular Culture*. London: Verso, 1996.

Jeffords, Susan. *Hard Bodies: Hollywood Masculinity in the Reagan Era*. New Brunswick, N.J.: Rutgers Univ. Press, 1994.

Jenkins, Henry. *Textual Poachers: Television Fans and Participatory Culture*. New York: Routledge, 1992.

Jost, Jon. "End of the Indies: Death of the Sayles Men." In Holmlund and Wyatt, *Contemporary American Independent Film*, 53–57.

Jubilee: A Film by Derek Jarman (1978). DVD. Whaley-Malin Productions, Criterion Collection, 2003.

Juhasz, Alexandra. "Learning the Five Lessons of YouTube: After Trying to Teach There, I Don't Believe the Hype." *Cinema Journal* 48, no. 2 (Winter 2009): 145–150.

Kawin, Bruce. "After Midnight." In Telotte, *The Cult Film Experience*, 18–25.

Keightley, Keir. "Manufacturing Authenticity: Imagining the Music Industry in Anglo-American Cinema, 1956–1962." In *Movie Music: The Film Reader*, edited by Kay Dickinson, 165–180. London: Routledge, 2003.

King, Geoff. *American Independent Cinema*. Bloomington: Indiana Univ. Press, 2005.

———. *New Hollywood Cinema: An Introduction*. New York: Columbia Univ. Press, 2002.

Klinger, Barbara. "'Cinema/Ideology/Criticism' Revisited: The Progressive Genre." In Grant, *Film Genre Reader II*, 74–90.

Knee, Adam. "*Liquid Sky*, *Repo Man*, and Genre." *Wide Angle* 8, nos. 3–4 (1986): 102–113.

Laderman, David. *Driving Visions: Exploring the Road Movie*. Austin: Univ. of Texas Press, 2002.

———. "(S)lip-Sync: Punk Rock Narrative Film and Postmodern Musical Performance." In *Lowering the Boom: Critical Studies in Film Sound*, edited by Jay Beck and Tony Grajeda, 269–288. Urbana and Chicago: Univ. of Illinois Press, 2008.

Ladies and Gentlemen, the Fabulous Stains (1981). DVD audio commentary by Lou Adler. Paramount Pictures, Rhino Entertainment, 2008.

———. DVD audio commentary by Diane Lane and Laura Dern. Paramount Pictures, Rhino Entertainment, 2008.

Lastra, James. "Reading, Writing, and Representing Sound." In Altman, *Sound Theory/Sound Practice*, 65–86.

Lawrence, Amy. *Echo and Narcissus: Women's Voices in Classical Hollywood Cinema*. Berkeley and Los Angeles: Univ. of California Press, 1991.

Leblanc, Lauraine. *Pretty in Punk: Girls' Gender Resistance in a Boys' Subculture.* New Brunswick, N.J.: Rutgers Univ. Press, 1999.

Levy, Emmanuel. *Cinema of Outsiders: The Rise of American Independent Film.* New York: New York Univ. Press, 1999.

Lewis, Jon. *The Road to Romance and Ruin: Teen Films and Youth Culture.* London: Routledge, 1992.

MacDonald, Scott. *The Garden in the Machine: A Field Guide to Independent Films about Place.* Berkeley and Los Angeles: Univ. of California Press, 2001.

Marchetti, Gina. "Documenting Punk: A Subcultural Investigation." *Film Reader* 5 (1982): 269–284.

Marcus, Greil. *Lipstick Traces: A Secret History of the Twentieth Century.* Cambridge, Mass.: Harvard Univ. Press, 1989.

McGillivray, David. "Twenty-five Years On: Julien Temple and *The Great Rock 'n' Roll Swindle.*" In Barber and Sargeant, *No Focus,* 15–26.

Merritt, Greg. *Celluloid Mavericks: The History of American Independent Film.* New York: Thunder's Mouth, 2000.

Miller, Mark Crispin. "End of Story." In Miller, *Seeing through Movies,* 186–246.

———, ed. *Seeing through Movies.* New York: Pantheon, 1990.

Moore, Suzanne. "Is That All There Is?" In Sabin, *Punk Rock,* 232–236.

MySpace.com. *Ladies and Gentlemen: The Fabulous Stains!* Home page. http://www.myspace.com/lagtfs.

Nadel, Alan. *Flatlining on the Field of Dreams.* New Brunswick, N.J.: Rutgers Univ. Press, 1997.

Nehring, Neil. *Flowers in the Dustbin: Culture, Anarchy, and Postwar England.* Ann Arbor: Univ. of Michigan Press, 1993.

———. *Popular Music, Gender, and Postmodernism: Anger Is an Energy.* London: Sage, 1997.

Nelson, Chris. "Lip-Synching Gets Real: The New Technology and Etiquette of Faking It." *New York Times,* February 1, 2004.

O'Brien, Lucy. "The Woman Punk Made Me." In Sabin, *Punk Rock,* 186–198.

O'Pray, Michael. *Derek Jarman: Dreams of England.* London: British Film Institute, 1996.

Olson, Jenni. *The Ultimate Guide to Lesbian and Gay Film and Video.* London: Serpent's Tail, 1996.

Orr, John. *Cinema and Modernity.* Cambridge: Polity, 1993.

Palmer, Neil. "The Disappearance and Re-emergence of *Ladies and Gentlemen, the Fabulous Stains.*" In Barber and Sargeant, *No Focus,* 218–224.

Peake, Tony. *Derek Jarman: A Biography.* Woodstock, N.Y.: Overlook, 1999.

Pencak, William. *The Films of Derek Jarman.* Jefferson, N.C.: McFarland, 2002.

Plant, Sadie. *The Most Radical Gesture: The Situationist International in a Postmodern Age.* New York: Routledge, 1992.

Porter, Martin. "Stereo TV: An Idea Whose Time Has (Almost) Come." *Rolling Stone*, September 17, 1981, 88.

Quart, Leonard. "The Religion of the Market." In Friedman, *Fires Were Started*, 15–34.

Rafferty, Terrence. "What're You Staring At?" *New York Times*, November 16, 2008.

Rattigan, Neil. *Images of Australia: 100 Films of the New Australian Cinema*. Dallas: Southern Methodist Univ. Press, 1991.

Rayner, Jonathan. *Contemporary Australian Cinema: An Introduction*. Manchester, UK: Manchester Univ. Press, 2000.

Reay, Pauline. *Music and Film: Soundtracks and Synergy*. London: Wallflower, 2004.

Rickey, Carrie. Review of *Times Square*, directed by Allan Moyle. *Village Voice*, October 15–21, 1980, 50.

Rock 'n' Roll High School (1979). DVD audio commentary by Allan Arkush, Michael Finnell, and Richard Whitley. New World Productions, Concorde–New Horizons, 2001.

Rogin, Michael. *Ronald Reagan, the Movie*. Berkeley and Los Angeles: Univ. of California Press, 1987.

Rombes, Nicholas. Introduction to Rombes, *New Punk Cinema*, 1–18.

———, ed. *New Punk Cinema*. Edinburgh: Edinburgh Univ. Press, 2005.

Ronell, Avital. *Crack Wars: Literature, Addiction, Mania*. Lincoln: Univ. of Nebraska Press, 1992.

Sabin, Roger, ed. *Punk Rock: So What?* New York: Routledge, 1999.

Sargeant, Jack. *Deathtripping: The Cinema of Transgression*. London: Creation Books, 1995.

———. "Downtown Upheaval: NYC 1975; An Interview with Amos Poe." In Barber and Sargeant, *No Focus*, 81–88.

———. Introduction to Barber and Sargeant, *No Focus*, 6–8.

Savage, Jon. *England's Dreaming: Anarchy, Sex Pistols, Punk Rock, and Beyond*. London: Macmillan, 2001.

Sconce, Jeffrey. "'Trashing' the Academy: Taste, Excess, and an Emerging Politics of Cinematic Style." In Braudy and Cohen, *Film Theory and Criticism*, 534–553.

Sharrett, Christoper, ed. *Crisis Cinema: The Apocalyptic Idea in Postmodern Narrative Film*. Washington, D.C.: Maisonneuve, 1993.

Shary, Timothy. *Generation Multiplex: The Image of Youth in Contemporary American Cinema*. Austin: Univ. of Texas Press, 2002.

Shohat, Ella. "Post-Third-Worldist Culture: Gender, Nation, and the Cinema." In *Rethinking Third Cinema*, edited by Anthony Guneratne and Wimal Dissanayake, 51–78. New York: Routledge, 2003.

Silverman, Kaja. *The Acoustic Mirror: The Female Voice in Psychoanalysis and Cinema*. Bloomington: Indiana Univ. Press, 1985.

Sjogren, Britta. *Into the Vortex: Female Voice and Paradox in Film*. Urbana and Chicago: Univ. of Illinois Press, 2006.

Smith, Anna Marie. *New Right Discourse on Race and Sexuality: Britain 1968–1990*. Cambridge: Cambridge Univ. Press, 1994.

Smith, Jacob. *Vocal Tracks: Performance and Sound Media*. Berkeley and Los Angeles: Univ. of California Press, 2008.

Smith, Jeff. *The Sounds of Commerce: Marketing Popular Film Music*. New York: Columbia Univ. Press, 1998.

Smith, Susan. *The Musical: Race, Gender, and Performance*. London: Wallflower, 2005.

Stam, Robert, and Louise Spence. "Colonialism, Racism, and Representation: An Introduction." In Braudy and Cohen, *Film Theory and Criticism*, 877–891.

Sterne, Jonathan. *The Audible Past: Cultural Origins of Sound Reproduction*. Durham, N.C.: Duke Univ. Press, 2003.

Sterritt, David. Review of *Times Square*, directed by Allan Moyle. *Christian Science Monitor*, December 18, 1980, 19.

Straw, Will. "Pop Music and Postmodernism in the 1980s." In Frith, Goodwin, and Grossberg, *Sound and Vision*, 3–21.

Studlar, Gaylyn. "Midnight S/Excess: Cult Configurations of 'Femininity' and the Perverse." In Telotte, *The Cult Film Experience*, 138–155.

Taylor, Paul. "The Impresario of Do-It-Yourself." In *Impresario: Malcolm McLaren and the British New Wave*, edited by Paul Taylor, 11–30. Cambridge, Mass.: MIT Press, 1988.

Telotte, J. P. "Beyond All Reason: The Nature of the Cult." In Telotte, *The Cult Film Experience*, 5–17.

———, ed. *The Cult Film Experience: Beyond All Reason*. Austin: Univ. of Texas Press, 1991.

———. "The New Hollywood Musical: From *Saturday Night Fever* to *Footloose*." In *Genre and Contemporary Hollywood*, edited by Steve Neale, 48–61. London: British Film Institute, 2002.

Thompson, Stacy. "Punk Cinema." In Rombes, *New Punk Cinema*, 21–38.

———. *Punk Productions: Unfinished Business*. Albany: State Univ. of New York Press, 2004.

Times Square (1980). DVD audio commentary by Allan Moyle and Robin Johnson. Starz/Anchor Bay, 2000.

Waller, Gregory. "Midnight Movies, 1980–1985: A Market Study." In Telotte, *The Cult Film Experience*, 168–186.

Weinstock, Jeffrey. *The Rocky Horror Picture Show*. London: Wallflower, 2007.

Whiteley, Sheila. *Women and Popular Music: Sexuality, Identity, and Subjectivity*. London: Routledge, 2000.

Whitley, Richard, and Russ Dvonch. "Essay by Screenwriters Richard Whitley and Russ Dvonch." In *Rock 'n' Roll High School* DVD Special Edition Booklet, 17–20. Concorde–New Horizons, 2001.

Wicke, Peter. *Rock Music: Culture, Aesthetics, and Sociology*. Translated by Rachel Fogg. New York: Cambridge Univ. Press, 1990.

Williams, Linda. "Film Bodies: Gender, Genre, and Excess." In Grant, *Film Genre Reader II*, 140–158.

Wollen, Peter. *Singin' in the Rain*. London: British Film Institute, 1992.

Wurtzler, Steve. "She Sang Live, but the Microphone Was Turned Off: The Live, the Recorded, and the *Subject* of Representation." In Altman, *Sound Theory/Sound Practice*, 87–103.

Wymer, Rowland. *Derek Jarman*. Manchester, UK: Manchester Univ. Press, 2005.

Zavarzadeh, Mas'ud. *Seeing Films Politically*. Albany: State Univ. of New York Press, 1991.

★ INDEX